Josephine C

308 Me

D0151967

Doing Business in
the New Latin America

Doing Business in the New Latin America

Keys to Profit in America's Next-Door Markets

Second Edition

Thomas H. Becker

 PRAEGER

AN IMPRINT OF ABC-CLIO, LLC
Santa Barbara, California • Denver, Colorado • Oxford, England

Library of Congress Cataloging-in-Publication Data

Becker, Thomas H.
    Doing business in the new Latin America : keys to profit in America's next-door markets / Thomas H. Becker. — 2nd ed.
        p. cm.
    Rev. ed. of: Doing business in the new Latin America : a guide to cultures, practices, and opportunities. 2005.
    Includes bibliographical references and index.
    ISBN 978-0-313-38381-6 (hbk. : alk. paper) — ISBN 978-0-313-38382-3 (ebook)
    1. Business enterprises—Latin America. 2. Corporations, American—Latin America. 3. Investments, American—Latin America. 4. Business etiquette—Latin America. 5. Corporate culture—Latin America. 6. Latin America—Commerce. 7. Latin America—Commercial policy. I. Title.
    HF3230.5.Z5B43   2011
    330.98—dc22   2010034859

ISBN: 978-0-313-38381-6
EISBN: 978-0-313-38382-3

15   14   13   12   11   1   2   3   4   5

This book is also available on the World Wide Web as an eBook.
Visit www.abc-clio.com for details.

Praeger
An Imprint of ABC-CLIO, LLC

ABC-CLIO, LLC
130 Cremona Drive, P.O. Box 1911
Santa Barbara, California 93116-1911

This book is printed on acid-free paper ∞

Manufactured in the United States of America

To
Diane, my finest companion and steadiest compass point in life's
astonishing excursions.
Colleen, Mary Ellen, and Tom, like the different republics of the Americas
in which each was born, you build the future not by repeating history, but
by reaching beyond history's grip.

Contents

Illustrations

Figures

Tables

Part I

PEOPLE, PLACES, AND POSSIBILITIES

Only a comparatively few U.S. executives have had extensive firsthand experience doing business in Latin America. Fewer still can point to an unbroken record of success in doing business in one or more of the 20 Spanish- and Portuguese-speaking countries with which the United States shares the Western Hemisphere. Yet, the epic changes now taking place in that vast region are creating unprecedented opportunities for U.S. companies. The economic and social transformations occurring in Latin America are tailormade to respond to the competencies at which U.S. small- and medium-size enterprises (SMEs) excel. When conditions are shifting rapidly, the SME's ability to turn on a dime gives it an edge in spotting, shooting at, and taking home moving targets of opportunity. It is that strength that has made the SME the powerful growth engine of the U.S. economy during the last three decades.[1] That same strength is now positioning the SME to become the pivotal point of business growth between the United States and Latin America during the foreseeable future.

This book describes business as it is practiced and lived in Latin America today. It is written especially for forward-looking SME executives who are prepared to apply to Latin America the success lessons they have learned in the North American market. They are well positioned to use their U.S. experience to cash in on business opportunities now surfacing in Latin American markets. Many of the market opportunities now emerging were formerly either nonexistent or closed to smaller players. Under today's new game rules, smaller domestic players are able to compete successfully in the international league. Whether they are exporters seeking new customers, distributors looking for new suppliers, owners of know-how wishing to license their technology, or manufacturers wanting to outsource to low-cost vendors, many smaller companies are learning that new and powerful forces are at work, reshaping the way business is done in the Western Hemisphere. These firms have recognized that, like life itself, economies do not stand still. As history always has shown, when economies are rapidly transforming, deep-seated forces open windows of opportunity that were formerly closed. To exploit those momentary windows of opportunity, SMEs need practical knowledge about how to break into the new Latin American marketplace, converting its potential profits into real cash flows. This book satisfies that need, explaining the widespread changes that are taking place and relating them to the special competencies of smaller U.S. firms.

The two chapters in Part I of this book explain what Latin America is and why it will pay for you to learn about its business potential. Chapter 1 introduces you to the lands of Latin America from a business perspective, sketching the varied panorama of its vast territory and providing a scouting patrol's account of the region's diverse nations. Chapter 2 describes the size and shape of Latin America's windows of economic opportunity and introduces a unique data set to aid company planners in appraising each national market.

Note

1. John Haltiwanger, Ron Jarmin, and Javier Miranda, "Business Formation and Dynamics By Business Age: Results from the New Business Dynamics Statistics," Center for Economic Studies, U.S. Census Bureau, 2008.

— Chapter 1 —

Where and What Is Latin America?

What is your mind's-eye image of Latin America?

The land of Chiquita Banana? Or Juán Valdez?

The legend of Simón Bolívar? Or Pancho Villa? Or Ché Guevara?

The aroma of a street vendor's tacos cooking on a wood stove?

Easy memories of noontime sand, sun, and Tecate beer, followed by a late-afternoon bullfight?

Marimba notes floating across a plaza on soft tropical evenings as children play and lovers kiss?

A *curandero* (traditional healer) chanting over an ailing child?

A tattered Indian praying in a ruin to an ancient sun-god?

A bull crocodile roaring its challenge to the Amazon night?

A lazily gliding condor framed against a snowcapped Andean peak?

Because Latin America is a world where magic is real, all of those images are as real as bedrock, and reading this book will not diminish their vibrancy. But as you turn the pages that follow, you will find another image unfolding, of Latin America as an emerging powerhouse in today's world economy, an evolving market frontier beyond which profitable business opportunities are coming to life.

This book is a chart for traveling along the sometimes twisting road that leads to that new frontier. It begins by describing some of the landmarks of that vast and diverse realm we call Latin America.

AMERICAS AND AMERICANS

Will the Real American Please Stand?

Many otherwise savvy marketers would be surprised to learn that the American marketplace contains about three times more consumers than are found in the United States. Their surprise, of course, stems from the mistaken assumption that the only one of the 35 countries of the Western Hemisphere qualified to be called America is the United States of America. Many residents of the United States appropriate for their own exclusive use the nationhood label "American." Although no harm is intended, the assumption underlying that self-description is understandably offensive to the half-billion souls residing in the other 34 nations of this hemisphere's two continents.

As residents of the United States of America, we have grown accustomed to the territorially covetous habit of calling ourselves "Americans." However, when we do so, we risk offending millions of Argentines, Brazilians, Colombians, Mexicans, and nationals of all the other countries who also reside in the Western Hemisphere. Perhaps the most common solution is to call ourselves *Norteamericanos* (North Americans) when in the company of Latin Americans. But this stakes out as our own exclusive national property a piece of real estate that is as territorially overstated as it is geographically erroneous. That huge error occurs because the geographic boundaries of the North American continent take in all of the Western Hemisphere lying north of the Panama-Colombia border. In addition to the United States, those "North American" boundaries would include all of Central America and the Caribbean, Mexico, and Canada.

If you wish to be even more precise and tactful, you may describe yourself as *Estadounidense* (literally, "Unitedstatesian"). Whichever term you choose, *Estadounidense* or *Norteamericano*, you will lower the risk of offending the justifiable nationalistic sensitivities of Latin Americans, a few of whom may still harbor dark suspicions that you or your firm serves as a conspiratorial tentacle of U.S. economic and cultural imperialism.

As a general rule, it is best to use the self-descriptions just mentioned to avoid being perceived as culturally myopic, geographically unsophisticated, or historically uninformed when dealing with Latin Americans. But, for the important purpose of enabling you to read these pages in a natural, smooth-flowing manner, this book violates that general rule. In the interest of convenience, "Anglo American" and "Anglo" are used interchangeably from this point forward as shorthand references to persons raised in the northern European cultural tradition of the United States.

Scope and Size

The territories of the New World that were colonized by Spain and Portugal are uniquely marked by what an anthropologist would call a "similar character structure."[1] Yet, in spite of unmistakable similarities in their historic and cultural connections, they constitute a geographic region of such diversity that it eludes easy labeling. The noun component of "Latin America" is accurate because it conveys the common location of those erstwhile colonies in the Americas. However, when the adjective "Latin" is used to designate only the Spanish- and Portuguese-speaking peoples of the Americas, it fails to acknowledge the presence of the hemisphere's francophone populations, peoples whose language was also derived from the Latin spoken by the Roman legions that once occupied Europe. Although the cultural richness possessed by France's present and former New World colonies cannot be denied, the dim growth prospects for such economies as Haiti and French Guiana explain their exclusion from a book written to identify promising business opportunities. Nor does the term "Latin America" represent either the cultural legacy of the tens of millions of indigenous peoples who inhabited the Americas ages before the arrival of their Iberian conquerors, or that of the masses of Africans who were introduced soon thereafter. Although the umbrella descriptors "Hispanic America" and "Ibero America" at least perfunctorily imply the cultural heritage of the African slaves held in preconquest Spain and Portugal, they ignore the influence of the Inca, Aztec, Maya, Chibcha, and scores of other pre-Columbian societies that have contributed so vitally to the region's culture.[2] Equally exclusionary is the term "Indo America," which leaves out both the Iberians and the Africans. And although the label "Indo-Afro-Ibero-America"[3] qualifies as a comprehensive descriptor, it does not slide easily off the tongue. Despite its many limitations, therefore, "Latin America" will be the default term used in this book to describe those Spanish- and Portuguese-speaking societies that share the Western Hemisphere with the United States. By derivation, "Latin" and "Latins" will be used as shorthand terms to describe peoples and persons of Latin American cultural origins.

Because it includes only the Spanish- and Portuguese-speaking territories of the Western Hemisphere, Latin America is not a contiguous geographic

Figure 1.1
Middle America

entity. It embraces Middle America, which includes Mexico, Central America (except Belize), and the Caribbean states of Cuba, the Dominican Republic, and Puerto Rico (see Figure 1.1); and South America, excluding Guyana, Suriname, and French Guiana (see Figure 1.2). Covering more than 8 million square miles, it has a land area almost three times that of the contiguous United States and a population that surpasses it by 75 percent.

A BIRD'S-EYE VIEW OF LATIN AMERICA

Poring over a decent atlas is a good first step toward understanding Latin America. The region's varied topography and climate underscore its immense diversity. Yet, a map cannot convey the ways in which geography has been intertwined with history to weave the tapestry of human behavior. To bring life to a flat map, let us adapt a venerable historian's device to our purpose: imagine you are an economic anthropologist, and you are observing Latin America as an air traveler.[4]

Mexico and Central America

Your 15,000-mile swing around the continents of North and South America begins over the scorched desert of the U.S.-Mexico borderland. It is

Figure 1.2
South America

a no-man's-land that uncounted thousands of refugees, fleeing from hopeless poverty farther south, have risked death crossing to find work in the fields, factories, kitchens, and construction sites of the United States. Their readiness to work makes it possible for innumerable smaller U.S. businesses not only to survive but also to provide good jobs for U.S. citizens.

Placing the unbroken ridgeline of the Western Sierra Madre on your left and the glittering Pacific beach sands on your right, you soar over a panorama of modern commerce ranging from automobile assembly plants, winter-vegetable farming, and tourism spas to marijuana farming, cocaine trafficking, and prostitution—all driven by the U.S. market. As you approach the 1.5-mile-high Valley of Mexico, your thoughts slip back to 1521. The modern skyscrapers of Mexico City fade away, and your mind's eye sees the gleaming temples of Tenochtitlán, the heart of the Aztec Empire. Seeing Cortés offer gifts to the Aztec chief, you imagine the Spanish *conquistador* barely able to conceal his glee as the interpreter conveys the welcome extended by Moctezuma: *"Mi casa es su casa"* ("My home is your home"). Of the two leaders, only Cortés can come close to imagining the extent to which that gracious greeting was to foreshadow the most massive transfer of wealth the world has ever known.

Continuing southward, you are struck by a curious change that has occurred in the world below you: altitude has replaced latitude as the primary determinant of climate. Whereas one travels north or south to experience climate change in temperate zones, in tropical latitudes one goes higher or lower to observe changes in climate-driven economic and cultural behavior. A half mile of vertical separation in the tropics can make more difference than thousands of miles of north-south distance in the ways that people dress, eat, build shelters, and earn their living. The economies and lifestyles of the highlands of Mexico, Central America, and South America have more in common with each other than between these peoples and their neighbors who inhabit the nearby lowland coastal plains or rain forests.

As you fly farther south, you observe more and more poverty. And as you watch, Mexico's southern states and Central America's republics are being linked under a revived initiative labeled Mesoamerica Project (previously known as the Puebla-Panama Plan).[5] Designed to counter the specter of hunger that forces workers in Central America to move north to find jobs in Mexico's overcrowded cities and in the United States, the Mesoamerica Project aims to move the jobs south to the workers, replacing the traditional northward migration of workers to the jobs. The multibillion-dollar project is designed to ignite the area's economic potential by linking and upgrading its fragmented and deficient highways, telecommunications, and energy systems into an integrated, competitively viable economic structure.[6] Although opposed by some nationalist and environmental groups, the project holds the promise of putting both food on the tables of jobless workers in the south and sales on the orderbooks of Asia-threatened companies in the north.

The flight over southern Mexico and Central America takes you along the *Ruta del Maya* (Route of the Maya), 1,400 miles dotted with ruins of more than 200 Mayan complexes, where, over 1,000 years, this extraordinary civilization mapped the heavens, developed writing, and devised the ancient world's most sophisticated system of mathematics. Along the way, you are introduced to the broad variety of its cities: shining, Indian-faced Guatemala City; business-friendly San Pedro Sula in the north, and bureaucratic Tegucigalpa in the south of Honduras; dynamic, democratic, and dollarized San Salvador; Managua, the economic victim of political paralysis; friendly San José with a healthy, diversified economy anchored by tourism and Intel's $800 million chip factory; and Panama, where European, Asian, and African blood mix to form a world-class financial, logistics, and tourism center.

South America

Central America's crowded puzzle-board of small neighbors contrasts with the vastness of South America, a landmass stretching 4,500 miles from north to south and 3,200 miles from east to west. Leaving the low-lying green ribbon of Panama behind, you pass over the Spanish Main of Cartagena, yesterday's gateway to colonial riches and today's popular and safe tourist destination in Colombia's long and bloody struggle to turn the tide against heavily armed, well-financed drug-traffickers and rebel forces. The steep-sloped Magdalena River valley cleaves its way inward and upward to the elbow of the Andean cordillera. Below you sprawls the plains of Bogotá, where this massive range turns south after running west from Venezuela and continues to the tip of Chile.

The 5,000-mile stretch of the Andes is an unbroken two- to four-mile-high barrier that, paralleling the Pacific Ocean, bars access to the broad remainder of the continent from its narrow coastal strip. With perpetual snow at the top and suffocating heat at the base, the Andean geography has historically promoted a pattern of local trade and cultural links within a succession of naturally bountiful microclimate valleys that permitted small populations to survive in relative isolation from one another. At the same time, its frigid north-south ridgeline and deep east-west cuts have blocked the wider economic ties that could have knitted the continent into a regionally integrated economic and political system of the kind that developed in the United States.

Just after crossing the equator, you pass over picture-perfect Quito. Nestled on a 9,300-foot plain between snowcapped Andes ranges, Ecuador's political capital enjoys three seasons on most days: spring mornings, summer afternoons, and fall evenings. Down below, on the coastal horizon, is steamy Guayaquil, ambitiously dubbed the "Pearl of the

Pacific." As Ecuador's bustling commercial capital, its port is ringed by a chain of freighters bringing in consumer and industrial goods and carrying off bananas, oil, frozen shrimp, sugar, coffee, and cacao.

Continuing southward into Peru, your gaze is drawn to mysterious and stunning Machu Picchu. Clinging to a cloudy peak high above the white waters of the Urubamba River, the concavely cut and seamlessly fitted multiton stones of the Lost City of the Incas give long-silent testimony to the sophisticated economic organization and technical prowess of the Inca civilization. Not far away, the Tiahuanaco civilization, precursors of the Inca, had built the largest city in the world in the 10th century. Its ruins guard the secret to the mystery of how they transported, without wheels, and fitted with hair-width precision, massive megaliths from quarries at least 25 miles away.

Dropping down the mountain ledge toward the Pacific, you notice a sharp transition in the coastal environment: Ecuador's drenched coastal zone has given way to Peru's bone-dry dunes and scorched sands that stretch from the coast to the Andes foothills. You have entered the Atacama Desert, 2,000 miles of a tinder-dry biosystem, squeezed between the mighty Andes and the Pacific. Almost nothing survives in these windblown tracts, broken only intermittently by oases where crops of long-staple cotton, sugarcane, alfalfa, dates, mangoes, rice, and asparagus thrive. The largest of these refuges is Lima and its port, Callao. Studded with magnificent parks and flower-lined avenues of posh colonial-era neighborhoods in its center, and ringed by wretchedly poor *pueblos jóvenes* (young towns), the City of Kings mirrors the social tension that plagues Latin America. Turning away from the Pacific coast, you cross the barren coastal desert and climb toward the towering Andes. The chain of white-capped jagged crests stretches as far as you can see, with little sign of human activity, save occasional packmule or llama trails that wind through icy, narrow passes at 14,000 to 16,000 feet. In this severe setting, your attention is captured by Lake Titicaca, through which the Peru-Bolivia border passes and, at 12,500 feet, is the world's highest navigable body of water. Almost within sight of urban La Paz, the scene on this lake is surreal: the high altitude makes colors appear deeper and more intense, like the colors of the body dress of the Uro and Aymará natives who inhabit the lake's floating reed islands—man-made structures that will make you feel you are walking on a mammoth water bed. It is of marketing interest to note that the black Bowler hats worn by virtually all Aymará women trace their origin to the 1880s, when an enterprising British hat salesman, anxious to dispose of a factory overrun, convinced indigenous leaders that the hats were the rage in Europe. As European fashion was considered the last word in civilized standards, the hats (and the ubiquitous billowy hoop skirts) became—and remain—the style norm for indigenous women in the Peruvian and Bolivian Andes.

Proceeding southward from the starkness of 13,000-foot La Paz, you soon find yourself over the long, narrow strip of northern Chile's section of the Atacama Desert. A wasteland today, this zone's huge deposits of bird guano brought nitrate wealth to Chile from the 1880s to 1920. As you approach Santiago in mid Chile, the scene below transforms from empty desert to fruited groves. Thanks to the protective wall of the Andes, these fertile vineyards were spared destruction by the *Filoxera* insect plague that devastated grape producers over the world during the late 1800s.[7] Since the late 1900s, enterprising Chileans have exported from those same vineyards to fill U.S. demand for high-quality table grapes during the off-season months for California growers. Life in the shadow of the Andes has been good for Chilean fruit growers. But it also has been kind to much of the Chilean populace. Indeed, Chileans (although typically modest) can justifiably boast of having one of the most forward-looking economic policies and management practices, as well as democratic political processes, in Latin America.

Turning east from Santiago, you cross the Andes and enter the rich grasslands of Argentina's vast pampas, finally arriving at Buenos Aires on the banks of the Río de la Plata. Its residents, who are seldom criticized for being too unassuming, may be right in claiming that the broad boulevards, tree-lined avenues, belle époque theaters, majestic mansions, upscale restaurants, sidewalk cafés, and late-night bookstores of their city make it the most cultured and cosmopolitan metropolis of the Americas.

Heading north from the birthplace of the soulful *tango*, you cross tiny Uruguay, created as a buffer between its two giant neighbors, Argentina and Brazil. Soon, you reach aggressive, fast-paced São Paulo, the Chicago of South America and the center of Brazil's industrial production. For a more casually paced experience, you fly on to Rio de Janeiro, hailed as "the world's happiest city" in a recent *Forbes* magazine survey.[8] The shining beaches of Ipanema and Copacabana, the massive granite blocks thrusting up abruptly from the heart of the city, the island-studded harbor, and the jagged backdrop of Mount Tijuca may make Rio the hemisphere's most stunning city.

After departing Rio, you seem to be flying endlessly over the Amazon basin. Nicknamed "the lungs of the world" for its ability to absorb much of the planet's carbon dioxide and to generate 20 percent of its oxygen, the Amazon basin covers the greater part of Brazil and reaches into

Bolivia, Peru, Ecuador, and Colombia. The Amazon River itself stretches farther than the distance between New York and London. Rising high in the Andes, it discharges into the Atlantic a volume of freshwater four times that of the Mississippi River and greater than that of any river in the world. For years it was hoped that agriculture would transform the water-wealthy Amazon rain forest into the breadbasket of the world. Regrettably, the basin's rains are so heavy that they leach its thin soils of soluble nutrients. Soil fertility is further inhibited by high temperatures, which restrain the growth of fungi and the formation of humus. An unmistakable sign of the Amazon's demise is the horizon-to-horizon smoke you see as the virgin forest is burned to clear its canopy, providing secondary growth for cattle to graze on, thus dooming the unprotected, leafless topsoil to be washed away by drenching rains. That topsoil, together with great trees and shrubs, can be seen as a muddy runoff extending some 200 miles into the Atlantic Ocean from the Amazon Delta. To promote nonagricultural job growth, Brazil offers generous tax incentives to attract industry to Manaus, 1,000 miles upstream from (and only 100 feet above) the river's mouth. Some smallish original-equipment manufacturers and second-tier suppliers to the country's 22 automobile producers have responded by building assembly and light production facilities.

As you fly over Venezuela's great *llanos* (plains), the Amazon basin falls behind you, and the land below begins to rise. Soon you rejoin the Andes at its most easterly spur, where the plateau upon which Caracas was built is located. Once agriculturally self-sufficient, Venezuela's economy became hostage to petroleum almost 60 years ago. While agriculture was allowed to languish, oil revenues were concentrated in the hands of the powerful for rebuilding the urban centers they inhabited. The result was an oil-dominated economy that held one of the world's records for unequal income distribution. Its effects endure today: Caracas's impressive—if not pretentious—downtown center and its wide, curving boulevards are ringed by squalid settlements of cardboard and tar-paper shacks. Over time, the social and economic misery that festered in these slums bred support for a populist political leader whose economic policies are arguably even more damaging than those of his kleptocratic predecessors. Venezuela suffers the highest level of inflation in Latin America. It has to import most of its food supplies (its black beans, the diet staple of the poor, are mostly grown in Colorado), as well as most of its continuously large demand for capital equipment, intermediate goods, and alarmingly large arms purchases. Save for oil and secondary petroleum products, it is not internationally competitive in any major industry.

The Caribbean

Leaving Venezuela at the port of La Guaira (a short journey down the mountain slope from Caracas), you follow the ring of the Lesser Antilles toward Puerto Rico. Topped by afternoon clouds, the northern slope of its mountainous interior opens to meet San Juán's crowded port. To wrest a share of the growing market for regional cargo transshipment, Puerto Rico is investing $750 million to expand the port of Ponce, on the south side of the island. The 50-foot channel that has been dredged will be the deepest in the Caribbean. It will give Ponce an advantage over Freeport, Bahamas, Kingston, Jamaica, and Panama, its leading competitors, in receiving the new deep-draft Panamax container ships (the largest that can currently traverse the Panama Canal), breaking down their cargo, and then reshipping it in smaller vessels to other Caribbean and U.S. ports.[9]

A 10-minute flight over waters covering the 2.5-mile-deep Mona Trench brings you to the eastern tip of the Dominican Republic's Samaná Peninsula. After another 20 minutes of flight, with the clear waters of the Caribbean lapping against palm-fringed, gleaming-white beaches below and the green mountains of the Cibao interior off the right wing, you arrive over colonial Santo Domingo, the first permanent European settlement in the New World. Although it shares two-thirds of the island of Hispaniola with Haiti, the half-as-numerous Dominican population has fared better, enjoying a per capita income more than seven times that of its neighbor.

Some 30 minutes after flying over the appalling spectacle of earthquake-hammered Port-au-Prince, the eastern shore of Cuba comes into view. If you choose to land at Habana's José Martí international airport, you may wonder what the U.S. trade embargo against Cuba really has accomplished, as a recent-model Ford F-250 pickup pulls up to position the passenger staircase for your plane. After becoming accustomed to the time-warp-like scenes of 1956 Chevrolet Bel Airs rolling past 16th-century colonial buildings, your reconnaissance of this anachronistic economy soon leads you to make a tentative conjecture: when relations between the United States and Cuba become normal, the entry of Cuba as a low-cost competitor will trigger large disruptions in today's patterns of international trade in tourism, winter fruit and vegetable production, and low-labor-cost assembly operations. To gear up for expanded trade in those sectors, of course, Cuba would require sizeable imports of capital goods, supplies, and services—for most of which, nearby U.S. vendors will be the preferred source.

Although you have put the Caribbean's balmy beaches behind you (and have survived the stern-faced U.S. Immigration officer's interrogation about your visit to Cuba), your tour is not complete. Your return to the United States occasions an opportunity to survey at close range the swiftest-growing of all Latin American markets.

The U.S. Republic of Latino

This segment does not profile one of the 20 country markets shown on a map of Latin America, delineated in its own color and lying somewhere south of the United States. Rather, it profiles a market that is so close at hand that, like the air you breathe, you tend to ignore it. In a few brief decades, this market has gone far beyond our doorstep, having become a permanent part of our national home. It can no longer be ignored. Not only has it become the most rapidly growing of all Latin markets, it is more easily accessible than any of them. You will not need a passport to visit customers in this nearby Latin market. They may be found in your own home, living next door, or working in the adjacent office. To make doing business with those customers even easier, you will not have to pay any import taxes when you deliver your product, accept any pesos when you take payment, or settle any business disputes outside a U.S. jurisdiction.

If you think Canada is a large market for U.S. products, you would certainly be correct. Indeed, Canada is the number one trading partner of the United States. But here is a curious fact: there are nearly three Latinos in the United States for every two Canadians in Canada.[10] If they were formed into a single separate nation, the 47 million Latinos residing in the United States[11] would constitute the second-largest Spanish-speaking population in the world and the third-largest economy in Latin America (placing behind only Brazil and Mexico). Latino growth has outstripped that of any other segment of the U.S. population, and in 2002 Latin Americans surpassed African Americans as the largest U.S. minority group.[12]

Indeed, U.S. history is no longer being written in black and white. The greatest multicultural show in history is now playing in the United States. Unlike the cast of black and white actors who starred in the ethnic drama of the previous century, the current performers are following a script written as a bridge for people to cross through cooperation, not as a great divide that keeps people separate through confrontation. As Generation

Ñ takes center stage and matures, its economic power, cultural vitality, and political clout are combining to shape U.S. lifestyles.

An early indicator of the potency with which Latin culture was to permeate U.S. daily life and markets came into view in the 1970s with the explosion of national chains of self-defined Mexican restaurants and fast-food restaurants. Just as U.S. consumers were quick to discover that Taco Bell was not a Mexican telephone company, so was their growing awareness of Latin cuisine soon to affect supermarket buying habits. As the U.S. consumer palate began to acquire a taste for south-of-the-border flavors, food- and beverage-shopping patterns shifted correspondingly. U.S. chili consumption doubled between 1980 and 2000, red peppers usage tripled in the same period, and between 1990 and 2000, imported beer, led by Mexican brands, doubled its U.S. market share.[13] By the year 2000, tequila consumption in the United States had surpassed that in Mexico.[14] In 1991, *salsa* sales had overtaken ketchup in U.S. supermarkets.[15] Food is a metaphor for culture. So whether it is a breakfast *burrito* and *chipotle* chicken wrap at McDonald's or a bag of *limón y chile* potato chips and a bottle of *horchata* in a supermarket cart, U.S. gastronomy is regularly being nurtured by Latin culture. Alert to the swift growth in Latino consumers, U.S. market leaders Procter & Gamble and Walmart have stepped up their efforts to tap this segment's retail purchasing power. P&G has created Ariel USA, a floral-scented version of its top-selling U.S. laundry brands, and packaged it in the 1.5-kg and 3-kg Spanish-language bags that Latinos are used to finding on the shelves of stores in their home countries. Walmart opened two new store formats in 2009 with inventory tailored to Latino shoppers: Supermercado de Wal-Mart and Mas Club discount warehouse.[16] Breaking through the Tortilla Curtain in the opposite direction was Mexico's Bimbo brand, which gained access to the U.S. market for tortilla, bread, and snacks after having invested almost $1 billion in acquiring U.S. companies between 1998 and 2002.[17] Using its success in the U.S. Hispanic-focused market as a springboard, Bimbo had become the world's largest baker by 2009,[18] and in 2010 it announced plans to expand its 18-country geographic reach.[19]

The influence of *Hispanidad* on U.S. lifestyles and markets extends well beyond ethnic cuisine. Between 1996 and 2006, the growth in Latino purchasing power was two and one-half times the corresponding U.S. rate. Recent forecasts show the purchasing power of Latinos, as a share of total U.S. purchasing power, increasing from 9.3 percent in 2009 to 12 percent in 2015, an amount representing as much as $1.3 trillion.[20] Whether fashionable or faddish, favorite attractions like Jennifer López, Emilio and

Gloria Estefan, Martin Sheen, Anthony Quinn, Antonio Banderas, Shakira, Selma Hayek, José Feliciano, *La Bamba,* and *La Macarena* attest to the growing impact of the Hispanic presence on U.S. popular culture and entertainment.

In sports, it is hard to overstate how truly "American" baseball has become. It is rare today to watch a baseball game without seeing champion pitchers and hitters hailing from the Dominican Republic, Mexico, Cuba, and other parts of the Americas. If your child plays soccer, and you did not, that generation gap testifies to the swift increase in popularity that Latin America's favorite sport has had in U.S. athletics.

Their social stereotype is another feature of the U.S. Hispanic presence that has undergone an image remake. No longer predominantly seen as lazy and slow-witted laborers, rebellious Cholos, Chicano low-riders, or violence-prone drug dealers, mainstream Hispanics (the term used by the U.S. Census Bureau to classify Latinos) are increasingly recognized as an entrepreneurial and upwardly mobile social force, conservative and more likely than blacks to own their own businesses and homes,[21] and less likely than blacks to be attached to the public sector or to collect social benefits.[22,23] Whereas they reflect the overall U.S. population in its propensity to buy concert, event, or movie tickets and DVDs, Latinos are more likely buyers of consumer electronic goods and home-delivered groceries.[24] Accounting for some 11 percent of the total U.S. online market, Latinos increased the amount of time they spent online by 6.9 percent in 2009 (almost five times the increase in time spent by the overall U.S. population).[25] Not only does the average Latino exceed the overall population in time spent online, but Latinos as a group are closing the gap in Internet usage rate. Between 2006 and 2008, Internet usage among adult Latinos grew by 10 percentage points (from 54 percent to 64 percent). The corresponding increase among whites was four percentage points (from 72 percent to 76 percent) and two percentage points among blacks (from 61 percent to 63 percent).[26] Best Buy reported in 2008 that visitors to its Spanish-language pages spent twice as much time on page as visitors to its English-language pages, probably because there were few alternatives that Spanish-speakers could turn to for product information.[27]

And, what about politics? Although a common campaign practice now, for the first time ever, during the 2000 U.S. presidential run, the candidate of each major party appealed to U.S. voters in both English and Spanish. By 2001, both Republican President Bush and congressional Democrats were recording their weekly radio addresses in English and Spanish. In 2009, another first was made when Judge Sonia Sotomayor was appointed to a seat on the Supreme Court of the United States, and by 2010, President Obama had named more Hispanics to prestigious government offices than any preceding president.[28] The rise of Hispanic importance on the U.S. political stage is likely to accelerate in the foreseeable future: whereas Hispanics constituted just 3.6 percent of the U.S. voting-age population in 1988, their voting strength had more than doubled, to 7.4 percent, in 2008, and is estimated to reach to as much as 25 percent in 2050.[29]

It is a fact of history that, for all of the 16th century and well into the 17th, Spanish was the only European voice heard in the lands that were to become the United States. Is it merely a curious echo of history that, five centuries later, the voice of the U.S. marketplace, entertainment industry, sports arena, and political realm is acquiring an unmistakable Spanish accent?

Given the wildly diverse ingredients of the cultural salad formed by minorities in the United States, it is a challenge for members of any ethnic group to sustain a vibrant sense of their national heritage. A deep sense of cultural identity explains why so many immigrants from Latin America and their descendants cling to tradition as a way of honoring their homelands and remembering their past. For a product to gain acceptance in the patchwork quilt of U.S. Latin markets, it is essential to create an emotional link with the homegrown customs specific to each national community. Some ethnic groups can be reached by tying in with their country's military traditions, such as Mexico's *Cinco de Mayo* celebration. However, the passion many immigrants once felt for national symbols has cooled as the separations imposed by geography and time take their toll. More commonly recognized, and more warmly received by those many immigrant families whose once-fervent emotional attachment to their homeland has cooled, are promotional appeals tied to the religious traditions and celebrations of each country, as noted later in Quick Notes: Country Visit.

A NAME, A PLACE, A SECRET, AND A PROMISE

There is no one-size-fits-all description of Latin America. Each country has its own striking idiosyncrasies. Nonetheless, there are strong threads of commonality woven throughout the length and breadth of the region. As connecting fibers of a single, coherent historical and cultural tapestry, those tightly intertwined strands hold Latin America together as a shared human experience. The chapters that follow emphasize key traits that lend a sizeable measure of uniformity to this astoundingly diverse region. As common denominators, these traits are essential knowledge for doing business anywhere in Latin America.

Latin America Close Up

Despite the region's several commonalities, as business takes you from one country to another, you will need more information about the peculiarities of specific locales. Although lacking the fine granularity of an encyclopedia, the country snapshots shown in the lists of this chapter and Chapter 2 display a wide-angle view of country particulars, without burdening you with details of places you may not visit. As you narrow your target-market focus, it will pay you to add flesh to the bare-bones information summarized in these lists. The descriptions in this chapter show at a glance features of leisure interest to business visitors; those in Chapter 2 contain information of business interest to business visitors. Arranged in a standardized format of seven categories, the Quick Notes: Country Visit are a first step to help you assess any of the region's 20 countries.

The country descriptions in the following Quick Notes listing are formatted to show:

1. **Country area (in square miles).**[30] Latin American countries vary enormously in size. Knowing that large countries tend to have more diverse and distinct submarkets can help you in scheduling an itinerary.

2. **Population.**[31] As one key indicator of market size, the number of potential consumers can point both to markets that are large enough to be of interest and to those that are small enough to be overlooked by large competitors.

3. **Literacy rate (male/female).**[32] Literacy rate (shown in percentages) is a rough proxy for the intensity of human capital available to perform skilled and semiskilled tasks, as well as the demand for education-intensive products and services. Gender differences in literacy rates can provide an estimate of the opportunities available for women, as they compete with men, in the labor force.

4. **Human Development Index (HDI).**[33] The HDI ranks countries (from 1 to 205, with 1 being most developed) on human well-being. It is a composite measure, taking into account life expectancy,

knowledge and education, and standard of living. Although created to inform economic development policy, some regard the HDI useful as a rough gauge of the extent to which a socially embedded U.S. visitor may feel at ease in a foreign society. The farther the host society's position from the United States, the less the sense of ease. The U.S. rank is 13.

5. **Climate.**[34,35] Knowing what weather to anticipate will help you pack for and schedule your visit.

6. **Holidays.**[36,37,38] Religious, national, and local holidays control the pace of business in Latin America and, hence, the availability of people you will want to meet. As most Latin American countries observe January 1 as New Year's Day, May 1 as Labor Day, October 12 as Columbus Day, December 8 as the Immaculate Conception, and December 25 as Christmas, these dates are not included in the country listings. Note: Be cautious about scheduling any meetings on the Monday preceding a Tuesday holiday or the Friday following a Thursday holiday. Latins often use those days as *puentes* (bridges) for a long weekend break. Be equally careful about scheduling meetings between mid December and mid January. Business engagements occupy an especially low priority during the Christmas period. Also, in the interest of realistic scheduling, remember that airline arrival times in Latin America tend to be early in the morning. This means that, although you can begin doing business early on your first day, you may feel good about not having scheduled an event for that evening, after having been without a good rest for the previous 24 hours or more.

7. **Quick Tips.**[39] Odds and ends are noted to tickle your curiosity or nurture your conversation as you go through the day.

QUICK NOTES: COUNTRY VISIT

ARGENTINA Sq mi: 1,073,514. **Pop:** 40,913,584. **Literacy rate:** 97.2 (97.2/ 97.2). **HDI:** 49. **Climate:** (Remember, seasons are reversed in South America.) Mostly temperate, arid in southeast, subantarctic in southwest, subtropical in northeast, hot in north. **Holidays:** May 25, Anniversary of Revolution (1825); June 8, Malvinas Islands Memorial; June 22, Flag Day; July 9, Independence Day; August 17, Anniversary of death of General San Martín. **Quick Tips:** (1) Argentines are justifiably proud of the *tango* (it originated in the bordellos of Buenos Aires in the late 19th century); their red wines (although not marketed heavily in the United States, they are of exceptional quality); and *parilladas*, grills serving massive portions of free-range beef (Argentines consume a world record of 132 pounds per capita of meat that is more flavorful and heart-healthy than U.S. grain-fed beef); and Jorge Luís Borges, prolific 20th-century writer whose works include *Ficciones*, a literary classic. (2) Both *La Recoleta*, Buenos Aires's chic shopping district, and its ornate, historically intriguing cemetery are worth a visit. (3) Avoid discussing Argentina's humiliating defeat in 1982 during the Falkland Islands War. If unavoidable, do not forget to refer to the islands as the Malvinas, their proper name in Argentina.

BOLIVIA Sq mi: 424,162. **Pop:** 9,775,246. **Literacy rate:** 86.7 (93.1/80.7). **HDI:** 113. **Climate:** Varying with altitude, can be humid and tropical in Santa Cruz to semi-arid in 13,000-foot La Paz, where it can freeze during the November–April rainy season. **Holidays:** La Paz Day; August 6, Independence Day (1825); September 24, Santa Cruz Day; November 1, All Saints Day. **Quick Tips:** (1) Bolivia has had 18 constitutions and more presidents than years of independence. (2) La Paz is the world's highest capital, and visitors should avoid *soroche* (altitude sickness) by arriving a day early to rest and acclimate, not using alcohol, and drinking *mate de coca* (coca-leaf tea, stimulating, but pharmacologically distinct from cocaine). (3) With conservative areas threatening to secede from the country, politics has been an especially polarizing issue among Bolivians since leftist Evo Morales, previously head of the coca-growers federation, was elected president in 2005. Regardless of the political leanings of your Bolivian associates, avoid discussing the topic. (4) Despite being highly mineralized (its now-depleted Potosí silver mines were once the richest in the world), Bolivia has long suffered high levels of poverty, a condition many attribute to its being landlocked: it lost its seaport on the Pacific to Chile during the 1879–1883 War of the Pacific, then lost its best river access to the Atlantic during the 1932–1935 Chaco War with Paraguay.

BRAZIL Sq mi: 3,287,594. **Pop:** 198,739,269. **Literacy rate:** 88.6 (88.8/88.4). **HDI:** 75. **Climate:** Mostly tropical, but temperate in south. **Holidays:** April 22, Discovery Day (1500); September 7, Independence Day (1822); November 15, Proclamation of the Republic. **Quick Tips:** (1) For years, Brazil has been the largest, most populous, and most industrialized country in Latin America, as well as the largest Portuguese-speaking country in the world. But by the time its nationally and internationally popular president, Luiz Inácio da Silva ("Lula"), departed the country's presidency in 2010, Brazil had also distinguished itself as a new and important force in the new world order.[40] (2) Fleeing just ahead of Napoleon's advancing armies, the royal family of Portugal took up residency in Brazil, thus establishing that country as an independent monarchy in 1822. Shortly thereafter, the United States became the first country to recognize Brazil's independence. (3) The rubber tree is indigenous to the Amazon rain forest. Until a British botanist bribed a Brazilian customs officer and smuggled its tightly controlled seeds to Southeast Asia in the 19th century, countless fortunes had been made from Brazil's monopoly of rubber production. Since that time, Brazilians have been touchy about the loss of their natural resources to foreigners. Notwithstanding their understandable sensitivity to the dark side of globalization, it should not be overlooked that Brazil's agricultural sector is underpinned by five imported plants: coffee (Ethiopia), oil palm (Africa), soybeans (China), sugarcane (Southeast Asia), and cacao (Ecuador and Colombia). (4) Cachaça, a potent sugarcane liquor used in the caipirinha cocktail, is the national drink of Brazil (by presidential decree). (5) As in Spanish-speaking Latin America, Brazilians commonly have two family surnames, the maternal surname and the paternal surname. In Spanish-speaking Latin America, the first of the two last names is the father's surname and is used as the form of address (Señor García Rodríguez, whose father is Señor Garcia and mother is Señora Rodríguez, would be greeted as Señor García). The order of surnames is reversed in Portuguese-speaking Brazil, so that Senhor Fernandes Amorim (whose mother is Senhora Fernandes and father is Senhor Amorim) is referred to as Senhor Amorim. (6) Be wary of crime in São Paulo and Rio, especially at night, and never venture into either city's *favelas* (shantytowns).

CHILE Sq mi: 291,930. **Pop:** 16,601,707. **Literacy rate:** 95.7 (95.8/95.6). **HDI:** 44. **Climate:** Temperate; Mediterranean in central region; cool and damp in south; Atacama Desert in north is one of world's driest regions. **Holidays:** May 21, Battle of Iquique; September 6, National Unity Day; September 18, Independence Day (1810). **Quick Tips:** (1) In Chile's rugged, temperate south, it is not unusual to hear residents speak German more often than Spanish. While there, wear sunblock, sunglasses, and a hat—the combination of altitude and proximity to the hole in the Antarctic ozone layer leaves your skin vulnerable to sun damage. (2) Crimes of violence are uncommon, corruption is infrequent, and

Chile's police (the Carabineros) are not notably prone to bribery. Even while waiting in lines, Chileans are peaceable, not pushing to get ahead, as is commonly experienced elsewhere in the region. (3) Isabel Allende (best-selling author), Gabriela Mistral (Nobel laureate), Saint Teresa de los Andes (a Chilean saint), and former president Michelle Bachelet (2006–2010) exemplify the relatively high status held by women in Chile. (4) If you have tattoos, try to cover them; Chileans may associate them with criminals.[41] (5) While you are sampling some of the world's finest wines, try *curanto*, a regional dish of shellfish, fish, beef, lamb, pork, potato, and local spices prepared as a stew. (6) You may be invited to take *once* ("eleven" in Spanish), a late-afternoon snack that features light foods such as cheeses, biscotti, and tea or coffee. Why would an event, occurring between four and eight o'clock, be called eleven? It is because *once* is code for *aguardiente*, a rumlike liquor that is often drunk at this time, and that word has eleven letters. Separated by distance and the Andes Mountains from much of the world, Chileans sense a tradition of isolation and can often be conversationally engaged in the subject of world travel.

COLOMBIA **Sq mi:** 439,734. **Pop:** 45,644,023. **Literacy rate:** 90.4 (90.7/ 90.1). **HDI:** 77. **Climate:** Tropical along coast and eastern plains; cooler in highlands. **Holidays:** July 20, Independence Day (1810); August 7, Battle of Boyacá; November 16, Independence of Cartagena. **Quick Tips:** (1) Media coverage of the recent past focused on the negative, creating an impression of endemic chaos and violence. In reality, the vast majority of terrorist crimes were committed against the poor in rural areas, not against foreigners or city dwellers. Although Colombia had reported the highest murder rate in the world in 2002,[42] that rate had fallen by more than half in 2009.[43] Moreover, cities like Bogotá have lower urban crime rates than many other world capitals. Reporters rarely write about the day-to-day lives of 45 million Colombian citizens going about their normal lives, untouched (except emotionally) by the misdeeds of some 10,000 malcontents. Although pockets of violence still exist, the country has become far more peaceful as the perverse influence of drugs on its economy and society has declined in recent years. Whereas cocaine accounted for 6.3 percent of Colombia's economy in 1987, it contributed less than one percent to the country's GDP in 2010.[44] Colombia's tourism record reflects the decline in drug-driven violence. As tourists are quick to respond to a risky environment, changes in tourism can be an indication of a country's reputation for violence. The rise of powerful, violent drug gangs spawned international headlines in the 1980s. As a result, international tourism shrank from more than 1 million annually in that period to 570,000 in 2002. After eight years under tough-minded President Álvaro Uribe, the Colombian government was estimating more than 4 million tourist visits to the country in 2010.[45] (2) Colombians enjoy engaging visitors in a discussion of the arts, perhaps about Gabriel García Márquez, Nobel Prize–winning author of works such as *One Hundred Years of Solitude* and *Love in the Time of Cholera.* (3) Panama was part of Colombia until 1903. In that year, the United States encouraged its independence, thus facilitating the building of the Panama Canal. U.S. involvement in Colombian affairs continues today as antinarcotics campaigns taken under *Plán Colombia* expand the scope of U.S. military and civilian operations there. Because local reaction to U.S. insertion in Colombian affairs may vary from love to hate, be cautious about discussing this topic. (4) Theft is common in Colombia, kidnapping less common but more disturbing. Burundaga (an indigenous plant form of scopolamine) is used by robbers and kidnappers to render a victim helpless. Colorless, odorless, and tasteless, it may be put into any food or drink. Be careful about ingesting or smoking anything offered by a "new friend." (5) Bogotá's *Museo de Oro* (Gold Museum) houses a spectacular collection of some 33,000 pre-Columbian gold relics. (6) Although Colombia is named for Christopher Columbus, the famed discoverer never set foot there.

COSTA RICA Sq mi: 19,730. **Pop:** 4,253,877. **Literacy rate:** 94.9 (94.7/ 95.1). **HDI:** 54. **Climate:** December to April is dry, May to November is rainy; San José has year-round spring. **Holidays:** September 15, Independence Day (1821); April 15, Battle of Rivas; April 11, Annexation of Guanacaste Province; July 25, Abolition of Armed Forces. **Quick Tips:** (1) Costa Rica is known as nature's vacation paradise, for its world-class ecotourism resources, democracy, pro-U.S. attitudes, political stability, and literacy. The peacefulness and literacy of the *Ticos* (affectionate nickname for Costa Ricans) are due in no small or coincidental part to the abolition of its standing army in 1949 and the consequent ability to support education with funds previously directed to its military. (2) Although you can walk to many appointments in downtown San José, finding where they are located can be confusing because landmarks (e.g., "30 *varas* east of the old fire station"), not street numbers, are used for addresses. (3) *Costa Rica* ("Rich Coast") was a misnomer. Not only did early Spanish settlers find no gold, but the coast was pestilent and the indigenous population could not be enslaved. As a result, colonies took root in the cool central highlands and the settlers worked their own small farms, an egalitarian practice that engendered the country's long tradition of democracy. (4) Colorful two-wheel oxcarts, a legacy of the colonial agricultural economy and an example of national folk art, are still seen in use on the roads and in the fields. Less functional, smaller versions of this conveyance are widely for sale and can be a unique souvenir, serving you at home as a distinctive coffee cart or bar. (5) An active tourism sector and a large colony of primarily U.S. and Canadian expatriates has made English widely understood, causing one U.S. retiree to describe Costa Rica as "Iowa with a Spanish accent." (6) *Ticos* tend to be formal, using conservative dress and looking down on profanity and other unprofessional behavior. Men do not often use the *abrazo* (back-slapping hug) common elsewhere in Latin America.[46]

CUBA Sq mi: 42,803. **Pop:** 11,451,652. **Literacy rate:** 99.8 (99.8/99.8). **HDI:** 51. **Climate:** Tropical, moderated by trade winds; dry season (November to April); rainy season (May to October); serious hurricanes can occur from June until December. **Holidays:** December 10, Independence Day from Spain (1898); May 20, Independence Day from U.S. control (1902); January 1, Independence Day from Batista control (1959); January 2, Victory of Armed Forces; July 25–27, Days of Rebellion; October 10, Anniversary of beginning of War of Independence from Spain (1868). **Quick Tips:** (1) Be aware that the U.S. government tightly restricts travel of U.S. citizens to Cuba, warning that, until at least early 2010,

> Cuba is a totalitarian police state which relies on repressive methods to maintain control. These methods include intense physical and electronic surveillance of both Cuban citizens and foreign visitors. Americans visiting Cuba should be aware that any encounter with a Cuban citizen could be subject to surreptitious scrutiny by the General Directorate for State Security (DGSE) of Cuba. Also, any interactions with average Cubans, regardless of how well intentioned, can subject that Cuban to harassment and/or detention, and other forms of repressive actions, by state security elements.[47]

Although large numbers of U.S. citizens disregard their government's travel restrictions and travel to Cuba, often through a third country such as Costa Rica, Dominican Republic, Panama, or Venezuela, you will be less likely to have your stress limits tested if you obtain the required license before you visit. The Office of Foreign Assets Control of the U.S. Department of Treasury (see http://www.treas.gov/offices/enforcement/ ofac/programs/cuba) provides strict guidelines for visiting Cuba. As of late 2010, they were not gracious about accepting apologies for infractions. (2) Cuba was officially an atheist state for most of the Castro era. In 1962, Castro shut down some 400 Catholic schools, charging they were seditious. But in 1992, the constitution was amended to make the state secular instead of atheist. Although Catholicism is the largest religion, Afro-Cuban spiritualism is widely practiced. (3) Never photograph any member of the armed forces or law enforcement or any guarded installation. Upon departure at the airport, be prepared to surrender your briefcase and luggage for a thorough inspection, taking care that they do not contain any documents of potential military significance or critical of the regime. (4) For a trip down memory lane to pre-Castro times, take a few moments to visit the choice Hotel Nacional. It preserves the photos and ambiance of the classic Hemingway and Hollywood high-life eras. Not far away is the *Plaza de Armas*, where you can relax, bask in the shade of the trees, people-watch, and marvel at the endless parade of 1950s-vintage cars that pass by. But avoid littering; it is illegal in Cuba. (5) Cubans gesture energetically and speak rapidly, emotionally, and loudly. Even with a good command of Spanish, it will take a while for your ear to become adjusted. (6) Since U.S.-affiliated credit cards, debit cards, bank checks, and traveler's checks will not be accepted, and since ATMs are few and far between, take cash (in clean, untorn bills) to cover your expenses. (7) Cubans are philosophical about their situation. A story heard recently on the island shows their ability to use humor as a foil to adversity: Visitor: "What is most difficult about life under communism?" Cuban: "The first one hundred years." Avoid talking politics with Cubans, whether of the Miami or Havana variety.

DOMINICAN REPUBLIC Sq mi: 18,792. **Pop:** 9,650,054. **Literacy rate:** 87.0 (86.8/87.2). **HDI:** 90. **Climate:** Tropical maritime; little seasonal variation in temperature, but variation in rainfall, with afternoon showers common in late spring and again in the fall; beware of hurricanes from June through November. **Holidays:** January 21, Feast of Our Lady of Altagracia; January 26, Duarte Day; February 27, Independence Day (1844); April 29, Dominican Labor Day (instead of May 1); July 16, Founding of Sociedad La Trinitaria; August 16 (celebrated on the closest Monday), Restoration of the Republic; September 24, Feast of Our Lady of Mercy; November 6 (celebrated on the closest Monday), Constitution Day.

Quick Tips: (1) The island of Hispaniola, of which Dominicans occupy the eastern two-thirds and Haitians the rest, was occupied by Taino Indians when Columbus established the first European settlement in the Americas in 1492. The combination of Spanish brutality and disease reduced the formerly thriving Taino population from 1 million to 500 in 50 years. To replace Taino labor on plantations and in the mines, the Spanish brought African slaves to the island. Today, the Dominican Republic is predominantly black with virtually no sign of its original indigenous inhabitants. (2) The capital, Santo Domingo, has been declared a UNESCO World Heritage site. The distinction is well deserved, as Santo Domingo can lay claim to some notable New World records: it is the oldest continuously inhabited European settlement; the discoverer Christopher Columbus, the conqueror Hernando Cortez, the explorer Vasco Núñez de Balboa, and the pirate Francis Drake are among history's luminaries who walked its oldest road, the cobblestone, pedestrian-only Calle de las Damas; its *Catedral de Santa María la Menor* is the hemisphere's oldest cathedral; the oldest fortification, the *Torre del Homenaje* (Tower of Homage), has defended the city under seven national flags; and the ruins of *San Nicolás de Bari* mark the oldest hospital. While you are visiting these historic record-breakers, take a break for yourself in the *Parque Colón* (Columbus Park). While you are having your shoes shined or entering notes in your journal, you can watch the colorful locals go about their day. For a more energetic break, take a stroll on the *Malecón*, the long sidewalk that fronts the palm-fringed Caribbean shoreline. And when you pass *El Vesuvio*, if you are hungry and if you are not on a tight budget, stop in for the best Italian food on the island. (3) If time permits and endless white-sand beaches on the shimmering Caribbean appeal to you, do not miss the chance to visit Puerto Plata and friendly, nearby smaller villages on the north coast.

ECUADOR Sq mi: 109,483. **Pop:** 14,573,101. **Literacy rate:** 91.0 (92.3/ 89.7). **HDI:** 80. **Climate:** Tropical along coast, becoming cooler inland at higher elevations; tropical in Amazonian jungle. Guayaquil and other coastal cities are hot and rainy between January and April. Quito and the cities of the *sierra* enjoy optimal climates: spring mornings, summer afternoons, and fall nights. **Holidays:** May 24, Battle of Pichincha (1822); July 24, Birthday of Simón Bolívar (1783); August 10, Independence Day of Quito (1809); October 9, Independence Day of Guayaquil (1820); November 3, Independence Day of Cuenca (1820); December 6, Founding of Quito (1534). **Quick Tips:** (1) Ecuador is one of Latin America's best travel bargains. If time is tight, its small size and immensely diverse landscape make it possible for you to enjoy dazzling Pacific beaches, high mountain glaciers, and steamy Amazon rain forest within a single two-day sojourn. You should set aside three to five days if you wish to schedule a proper visit to the Galapagos Islands, of Darwinian renown. (2) Old Town Quito preserves much of its early 16th-century colonial flavor, having been declared a World Cultural Heritage site by UNESCO. While there, you could try a local cuisine to refresh or repulse your colleagues at home by dining on either *cuy* (guinea pig, served completely intact with head, tail, eyes, paws, and fur) or *tronquito* (soup prepared from the penis of a bull, reputed to be a male enhancer).[48] (3) Do not casually initiate any discussion of Peru. The subject upsets many Ecuadoreans, as they lost almost half their territory after Peru invaded in 1941. Conflicts between the two neighbors have recurred regularly since, most recently in 1995. (4) Although Ecuador is the world's largest exporter of bananas and Latin America's fourth-largest oil exporter, a fringe collection of die-hard fortune hunters aspire to discover much greater riches: Atahualpa's Lost Horde. Their quest is fueled by persistent legends alluding to the gold and silver treasures that were hidden from the advancing *conquistadores* by Inca priests in the gloomy high-rain-forest region of the uncharted Llangañate region. (5) The *Panama hat* is a misnomer. These collector-quality hats are woven by hand in Montecristi, and they can be acquired in Ecuador less expensively than in Panama.

EL SALVADOR Sq mi: 8,124. **Pop:** 7,185,218. **Literacy rate:** 80.2 (82.8/77.7). **HDI:** 106. **Climate:** Tropical; rainy season (May to October); dry season (November to April); tropical on coast; temperate in uplands. **Holidays:** First Sunday and Monday in August, Feast of San Salvador; September 15, Independence Day (1821); October 11, *Día de la Raza* (Day of the Race); November 5, First Call for Independence. **Quick Tips:** (1) Animosities and easily available arms still remain from the decade-long brutal civil war in which over 70,000 perished and almost 1 million were forced to flee Central America's smallest and most densely populated country. As many Salvadorians are armed and may be easily provoked, you should never speak loudly or show anger. In this society, with one of the highest homicide rates in the world, it is a good rule to display a calm demeanor and a soft voice. (2) The Neopentecostal religion has attracted many businesspeople, who believe that wealth is evidence of God's favor and that the poor are paying the penalty for their weak faith.

Avoid arguing with these people. (3) The *pupusa* ("poo-poo-sah"—don't be put off by the pronunciation) is the national snack, if not the national passion. Vaguely reminiscent of tamales, *pupusas* are sold from ever-present street stands and neighborhood *pupuserías*, prepared at home with secret recipes passed proudly from mother to daughter over generations, and are the theme of songs and poems. Showing an interest in the institution of the *pupusa* will endear you to Salvadoreans.

GUATEMALA Sq mi: 42,042. **Pop:** 13,276,517. **Literacy rate:** 69.1 (75.4/ 63.3). **HDI:** 122. **Climate:** Tropical; hot and humid in lowlands, cooler in highlands. Guatemala City lows average 55°F; highs, 77°F. **Holidays:** April 9, Holy Thursday; April 10, Good Friday; June 30, Army Day; July 1, Bank Worker's Day; September 15, Independence Day (1821); October 20, Anniversary of 1944 Revolution. **Quick Tips:** (1) A visit to Antigua will repay your effort. It was founded in 1543 after Guatemala's first capital was leveled by an earthquake, and was itself destroyed by the same fate in 1773, after which Guatemala City became the capital. Preserved remnants of its colonial quaintness make Antigua a favorite of vacationers and Spanish-language students. (2) Latin American and U.S. leftists still recall the 1954 CIA-backed toppling of the popularly elected Árbenz regime as evidence of ongoing U.S. meddling in Latin America. The United States also comes under criticism for not having been more vigorous in opposing the brutal 1960–1996 civil war in which entire indigenous villages were massacred by the military. (3) As in El Salvador, memories of long periods of brutal civil violence remain much alive in Guatemala and are off-limits to foreigners as conversational topics. Also off-limits is military clothing in any form. It is illegal to bring it in or wear it in the country. (4) Be cautious about being especially attentive toward or taking pictures of children, particularly in rural areas. Acting on real or rumored threats of foreigners kidnapping children and selling their body parts, locals have attacked and killed outsiders they consider suspicious.

HONDURAS Sq mi: 43,267. **Pop:** 7,792,854. **Literacy rate:** 80.0 (79.8/ 80.2). **HDI:** 112. **Climate:** Tegucigalpa, the political capital (popularly referred to as *Tegús*), is notably cooler than San Pedro Sula, the commercial capital. April is the warmest month in Tegucigalpa, with average highs of 86°F; January and February, average low temperatures of 57°F; rainfall is heaviest in May and June, December to April is dry. **Holidays:** Holy Thursday, April 9; Good Friday, April 10; April 12, Easter; April 14, Pan

American Day; September 15, Independence Day (1821); October 3, Francisco Morazán Day; October 21, Armed Forces Day. **Quick Tips:** (1) Hondurans are nicknamed *Catrachos* by their Central American neighbors. (2) Honduras was the archetype of the "Banana Republic" until well into the 20th century because U.S. agribusiness firms controlled the country's economic and political life from their plantations along the north coast. Nonetheless, Hondurans are pro-U.S. (3) Every few years, between May and December, the country is hit by a category 3–5 hurricane. These storms can have disastrous effects, killing thousands and destroying whatever is in their path. Although Tegucigalpa is less affected, if you are visiting San Pedro Sula or the north coast, you should heed warnings of approaching hurricanes. (4) Honduras has a high incidence of tuberculosis. Get your inoculation series before traveling.

MEXICO Sq mi: 758,445. **Pop:** 111,211,789. **Literacy rate:** 91.0 (92.4/ 89.6). **HDI:** 53. **Climate:** Mexico City, Guadalajara, and Puebla have springlike temperatures, with highs averaging 80–85°F in April, lows of 43–48°F in January and February. Mexico City's pollution can irritate allergy sufferers and wearers of contact lenses. **Holidays:** February 5, Constitution Day; March 21, Birthday of Benito Juárez; May 5 (called *Cinco de Mayo* in Spanish), Battle of Puebla; September 16, Independence Day; November 2, All Souls' Day (commonly called *Día de Los Difuntos*—Day of the Dead); November 20, Anniversary of the Revolution; December 12, Our Lady of Guadalupe Day. **Quick Tips:** (1) Residents refer to Mexico City, the country's largest city and capital, simply as "Mexico." It is known for its hurried pace (by Latin American standards), and its sometimes discourteous residents are known as *Chilangos* in the rest of the country. With more affection, residents of Mexico's second-largest city, Guadalajara, are known as *Tapatios*. (2) Mexico has the largest Spanish-speaking population in the world and is Latin America's second-most populous country. The country has become heavily urban, as many flee hopeless unemployment in the rural southern areas to find work in its major cities and across the U.S. border. Mexico City is not only the world's most populous city but also among its most polluted and crime-ridden cities. Beware using taxis at night not associated with a hotel or designated taxi site. "Express kidnappings," in which taxi passengers are held and forced to repeatedly withdraw funds at ATMs until their account balance is exhausted, are not uncommon. (3) Although the country is reported to suffer the world's sixth-highest overall murder rate,[49] the greatest security threat to foreign visitors is concentrated in northern border cities (especially Ciudad Juárez, Nuevo Laredo, Mata-moros, and Nogales), Monterrey, Michoacán, and Durango.[50] These are locations in which violent conflict among powerful drug cartels, and between them and Mexican law enforcement, is most intense. (4) As Latin America's number one destination for international travelers, Mexico offers a vast and diverse range of tourism attractions. As only your budget and imagination limit the variety of historical, culinary, and sightseeing spectacles you can experience, plan your visit carefully. (5) *The Labyrinth of Solitude*, by Nobel Prize winner Octavio Paz, offers a wealth of insights into the character of Mexico and how it differs from that of the United States.

NICARAGUA Sq mi: 59,998. **Pop:** 5,891,199. **Literacy rate:** 67.5 (67.2/67.8). **HDI:** 124. **Climate:** Warm, tropical climate; rainy season is May to October. **Holidays:** July 20, Liberation Day; August 10, Managua Day; September 14, Battle of San Jacinto; September 15, Independence Day; December 7, Feast of *La Purísima* and celebration of *la gritería*. **Quick Tips:** (1) From the time of their establishment in the early 16th century, León and Granada were Nicaragua's major urban centers. Their bitter political and commercial rivalry caused Managua to be created midway between them to defuse the conflict. (2) Beginning in 1855, with the invasion of a group of U.S. mercenaries led by William Walker, Nicaragua has had a long history of interference from the United States. Daniel Ortega, the current president and former leader of the 1980s insurgency, shares the opinion of many Nicaraguans that the United States is an imperial power and that socialism is the only path for the country.[51] Tellingly, *compañero* (comrade) is a common form of address. (3) Nicaraguans maintain they have the world's highest proportion of poets, a claim surely made more plausible by the fact that Rubén Darío, one of Latin America's most revered poets, was born, died, and is buried there. (4) Many descendants of pirates inhabit the remote Atlantic coast and speak a curious form of English that may not be easily understood. (5) As the national obsession, baseball is a safe topic of conversation. (6) A popular "Whodunit?" topic revolves around the mystery of who paid for a large mosque constructed in a Managua residential neighborhood in 2009. Could it be a gift from the Iranian government to the anti-U.S. president Ortega?[52]

PANAMA Sq mi: 29,120. **Pop:** 3,360,474. **Literacy rate:** 91.9 (92.5/91.2). **HDI:** 60. **Climate:** Temperatures in the 70s and 80s year-round; rainy season is May through December. **Holidays:** Last week in February,

Carnival; August 15, Founding of Old Panama; October 11, Revolution Day; November 1, Day of the National Anthem; November 3, Independence from Colombia Day; November 4, Flag Day; November 10, Day of First Cry for Independence; November 28, Independence from Spain Day. **Quick Tip:** (1) Panamanians are no strangers to U.S. ways: With U.S. backing, the country seceded from Colombia in 1903. In 1904, construction began on the Panama Canal on a strip of land ceded to U.S. control. The canal was completed in 1914, and its control was returned to Panama in 1999. Also, in 1904 the U.S. dollar was adopted as the official currency. The Balboa is the official currency today. As it is kept at parity with the U.S. dollar, the economy is effectively dollarized. (2) English is a common second language. (3) Although overall poverty fell from 37 to 29 percent and extreme poverty fell from 19 to 12 percent between 2001 and 2007, Panama suffers Latin America's second-most unequal distribution of income. (4) Perhaps more than anywhere in Latin America, Panama is obsessed by boxing, producing world champions like Roberto Durán. (5) Panama City, often simply referred to as Panama, is a magnet for international investors that see its banking and taxation laws as a safe haven and its real estate as a booming sector.

PARAGUAY Sq mi: 157,047. **Pop:** 6,995,655. **Literacy rate:** 94.0 (94.9/ 93.0). **HDI:** 101. **Climate:** (South American) summers are hot, with January and February highs around 95°F, falling to the low 70s during July and August; there are no prominent dry or wet seasons, but significant rainfall in the east, transitioning to semi-arid in the west. **Holidays:** February 3, San Blás Day; March 1, Heroes Day; May 14–15, Independence Days; June 12, End of Chaco war; August 15, Founding of Asunción; August 25, Constitution Day; September 29, Victory of Battle of Boquerón; December 8, Virgin of Caacupé. **Quick Tips:** (1) A society in no hurry to catch up with the rest of the world, but of charming contrasts, Paraguay contains solitary German-speaking colonies, proud and independent Guaraní Indians, a military reminiscent of the Napoleonic era, and a sense of isolation from the modern mainstream. (2) As some 95 percent of the population is mestizo (of mixed European and Guaraní heritage), Paraguay has the most homogeneous society in Latin America. It is also unusual in having two official languages, Spanish and Guaraní, the latter being understood by 95 percent of the population (virtually all businesspersons you contact will speak fluent Spanish). (3) Unwisely, Paraguay fought the War of the Triple Alliance against Argentina, Brazil, and Uruguay between 1864 and 1870, losing half its population and almost half its territory in the conflict. Another injudicious war was waged against Bolivia between 1932 and 1935, resulting in the loss of 35,000 lives as well as natural gas and petroleum resources, these becoming Bolivia's most important source of exports today. As neither conflict is a source of national pride, avoid their mention in conversation. (4) The Tri-Border Area (especially the essentially lawless Ciudad del Este), where Paraguay, Argentina, and Brazil converge, has been a well-known center for money laundering, counterfeiting, drug smuggling, and terrorist fund-raising.[53,54,55] Travelers returning from Paraguay may be questioned from law enforcement authorities regarding the places and purpose of their visit.

PERU Sq mi: 496,222. **Pop:** 29,546,963. **Literacy rate:** 92.9 (96.4/89.4). **HDI:** 78. **Climate:** The country varies from tropical rain forest in the east to dry desert in the west, and temperate to frigid in the Andes. Lima's January–March temperatures can reach into the mid 90s, falling to the mid 40s in June–September; although rain is scarce, the *garúa* (light drizzle) is a frequent and uncomfortable feature of Lima (the capital) and the coastal climate. **Holidays:** May 29, Saints Peter and Paul Day; July 28 and 29, Independence Days; August 30, St. Rose of Lima; October 12, Battle of Angamos; November 1, All Saints Day; December 8, Immaculate Conception Day. **Quick Tips:** (1) Peru's rich Spanish and indigenous heritage shape its social, artistic, and cultural faces. Do not miss any opportunity to visit its wealth of museums, Inca and pre-Inca ruins, and colonial towns (the spectacular ruins of Machu Picchu should be high on your sightseeing wish list). (2) Through migration from the highland countryside to the coastal cities, a more homogeneous national culture is coming into being. But the historical socioeconomic divide between the relatively prosperous mestizo-dominated coast and the impoverished Amerindian culture of the Andes Mountains is still very much in evidence. (3) Travelers to the Apurimac and Ene river valley should exercise caution. The once-dormant Shining Path narcoterrorists have reemerged in this region, and the military made acquiring counterinsurgency equipment its first budget priority for 2010.[56]

PUERTO RICO Sq mi: 5,324. **Pop:** 3,971,020. **Literacy rate:** 94.1 (93.9/ 94.4). **HDI:** (not ranked, likely similar to U.S. no. 13). **Climate:** Much like in the Dominican Republic, the coastal area is comfortable and warm throughout the year; hurricanes threaten during June through November. **Holidays:** January 12, Birthday of Eugenio María de Hostos; January 19, Martin Luther King Day; February 14, Valentine's Day; third Monday in

February, Presidents' Day; March 22, Emancipation of Slaves; April 20, Birthday of José de Diego; July 4, U.S. Independence Day; July 20, Birthday of Luís Muñoz Rivera; July 25, Commonwealth (of Puerto Rico) Day; October 12, Columbus Day; November 19, Discovery of Puerto Rico. **Quick Tips:** (1) Like Cuba, Puerto Rico's status changed from being a Spanish colony to being a self-governing U.S. possession as a result of the 1898 Spanish-American War. Unlike Cuba, Puerto Ricans were extended most of the benefits of U.S. citizenship in 1917 (some exceptions: Puerto Ricans pay no U.S. income taxes and they have no voting representation in the U.S. Congress). (2) Puerto Rico legitimately qualifies to be included in this listing because of the many cultural, linguistic, economic, social, and historical similarities it shares with other Latin American societies. (3) Afro-Cuban, Spanish, and U.S. influences blend easily to create a colorful culture in which few racial conflicts exist. Proud of their unique heritage, Puerto Ricans often identify themselves as *Boricuas*, a term the ancient Taíno Indian inhabitants used to identify the island. (4) Visit Old San Juan during the day for its historical sites, during the night for its partying sites.

URUGUAY Sq mi: 68,036. **Pop:** 3,494,382. **Literacy rate:** 98.0 (97.6/ 98.4). **HDI:** 50. **Climate:** Winter (May–August) temperatures rarely reach freezing, Montevideo summer (November–February) temperatures can soar into the 90s. **Holidays:** April 19, Landing of the 33 Patriots; May 18, Battle of Las Piedras; June 19, Birthday of General Artigas; July 18, Constitution Day. **Quick Tips:** (1) Traditionally one of the region's most statist economies and socialist societies, highly literate, middle-class, and egalitarian Uruguay is evolving toward a free-market and capitalist orientation. (2) A commonly held suspicion of business may be traced to both a history of sluggish economic growth and a popular abhorrence of a cruelly repressive military junta that was probusiness. Eduardo Galeano, a prominent Uruguayan author, in referring to this brutal regime, says that "people were imprisoned so that prices could be free."[57] (3) Like the United States, Western Europe, and Japan, it is also becoming an elderly society because of its low birthrate, high life expectancy, and high rate of emigration of younger people. (4) Never very numerous, the native population of Uruguay was displaced or killed during the early years of the colonial era. As a result, today's population is predominately European, primarily of Spanish and Italian origin. (5) José "Pepe" Mujica, a former leftist rebel who spent 14 years in military prisons, won a runoff presidential election in November 2009. Mujica is a vegetarian who grows leeks in his backyard, leads a simple life, and is reported to say that "what is important in life is to work as little as possible so as to enjoy it more."[58] As Mujica's term unfolds, it will be engaging to observe how the homespun, outspoken manner of this leftist-turned-moderate will play against a backdrop of frequently more pretentious Latin political personalities. (6) Enjoy an authentic gaucho experience on one of Uruguay's estancias de turismo. These popular tourist attractions are family-owned-and-run dude ranches.

VENEZUELA Sq mi: 352,143. **Pop:** 26,814,843. **Literacy rate:** 93.0 (93.3/ 92.7). **HDI:** 58. **Climate:** Average temperatures in Caracas are in the low 70s, rainy season is June to October, Maracaibo averages in mid 80s with frequent rain. **Holidays:** April 19, Beginning of Independence Movement; June 24, Battle of Carabobo; July 5, Independence Day; July 24, Birthday of Simón Bolívar; August 3, Flag Day; September 4, Civil Servants' Day; October 12, Indigenous Resistance Day. **Quick Tips:** (1) Easygoing Venezuelans are both geographically and culturally the most Caribbean society of South America. (2) A long history of unequal income and weakly managed, corrupt government has made Venezuela a tinderbox for social unrest and violence (it reports the world's fourth-highest murder rate[59]). (3) To prepare for what he believes to be a U.S.-provoked invasion of his country by neighboring Colombia, Venezuelan strongman President Hugo Chávez has imported billions of dollars of weaponry from Russia.[60] (4) Chávez is such a polarizing figure that most of population may arguably be split into two passionate factions: the *Chavistas*, who support the president, and the *anti-Chavistas*, who refuse to accept him. Whatever your views on Chávez, keep them to yourself. You may not know the true loyalties of your conversational partner. Indeed, persistent rumor suggests that an inner circle of wealthy businessmen have profited from concealed links to Chávez.[61] Play it safe, and avoid being baited into voicing an opinion that could attract the unwelcome attention of the authorities. Unsurprisingly, another taboo topic is the strained relationship between the Venezuelan and U.S. governments. (5) Enjoy the panorama of Caracas from Cota Mil highway, and, if you are looking for local handicrafts and art, visit El Hatillo, an easily accessible, picturesque, colonial-era village.

SEPARATING FACT FROM FICTION

Facts are stubborn, but mistaken opinions can be even more tenacious. This uneven reality may explain why Dr. William Mayo, founder of the famous clinic, prayed: "Lord, deliver me from the man who never makes a mistake, and also from the man who makes the same mistake twice."[62] Before turning to the chapters ahead, we should clarify some of the anxieties that, directly or indirectly, almost invariably color any discussion of doing business in Latin America. Some of these anxieties are very real, whereas others are a product of confirmatory bias—the tendency to believe only information that confirms prior opinions. As a responsible author should be an honest broker to his readers, I will try to clarify the biases that my own experience and research bring to this book and that form the perceptual backdrop behind its lines.

Anxiety No. 1: Politics and corruption trump good management in doing business in Latin America.

Perception: Not long ago this anxiety would have rested on solid footing. Prior to the 1990s, executives in Latin America spent an inordinate amount of time, energy, and (frequently off-the-books) cash maneuvering within the political system. The combination of stifling bureaucracy, corrupt officials, and state-owned enterprises that monopolized key areas of the economy made it essential to focus daily management attention on complying with, circumventing, undermining, or swaying an unworkable structure of regulations, laws, and enforcement procedures. The demands of surviving in a political jungle left few managerial reserves available for production concerns. And because it was a seller's market, customer-centered marketing was an alien concept. Indeed, the primary functions of marketing departments involved little more than taking orders from credit-qualified customer accounts, then dealing with the ensuing headaches of product availability and delivery.

As the protected economies of Latin America's import-substitution era gave way to more open, consumer-driven economies in the 1990s, the prerequisite for business survival shifted from having political power to having market power. For example, top-notch management and information technology turned Cementos Mexicanos into a model of productivity for the industry by allowing it to manage almost all of its internal operations online. It reduced the size of its fleet of delivery trucks by using satellite systems to dispatch them to job sites, its buyers placed orders and tracked deliveries on the Net, and its managers had real-time information on inventories, finances, and sales. Beginning from a modest base in 1985, professional management had driven it to become the world's most profitable and third-largest cement producer by 2000.[63,64]

Anxiety No. 2: Globalization makes the poor poorer.

Perception: Globalization produces losers as well as winners. Among the winners are the world's poorest. As globalization has advanced in recent decades, global poverty rates have retreated. At the same time, however, inequalities in income, within and between countries, have risen.[65] This latter reality has spawned much of the sentiment against globalization. Yet, by subordinating deliverance from poverty to parity in poverty, does the antiglobalization movement build a better world?

Nicholas Stern, former vice president and chief economist of the World Bank, summarizes the effect of globalization on the poor:

> Some anxieties about globalization are well-founded, but reversing globalization would come at an intolerably high price, destroying prospects of prosperity for many millions of poor people. We do not agree with those who would retreat into a world of nationalism and protectionism. That way leads to deeper poverty and it is fundamentally hostile to the well-being of people in developing countries. Instead, we must make globalization work for the poor people of the world.[66]

Anxiety No. 3: Free trade has exported U.S. jobs and weakened U.S. manufacturing.

Perception: Many see free trade as a downward spiral, flushing jobs away to low-wage foreign countries and draining the U.S. standard of living. Research on the issue shows a different outcome, one that gives evidence of higher living standards in countries that practice free trade.[67,68,69] How can hard opinions be so at odds with hard facts? The Theory of Comparative Advantage could resolve that question, but its repeated explanation can be as tedious as a clam's night out.

More compelling are the changes in U.S. employment that occurred when the North American Free Trade Agreement (NAFTA) went into force in 1994. U.S. employment increased over the period of 1993–2007 from 110.8 million people to 137.6 million people. The average unemployment rate was 7.1 percent during the pre-NAFTA period of 1980–1993, compared to 5.1 percent in the post-NAFTA period of 1994–2007.[70]

During the pre-NAFTA period of 1982–1993, U.S. industrial production, of which manufacturing represents 78 percent, registered a growth of 28 percent. The corresponding increase for the post-NAFTA period of 1993–2005 was 49 percent.[71] Moreover, only 10 percent of the manufactured-goods trade deficit of the United States can be attributed to NAFTA.

In the manufacturing sector, NAFTA accounted for 43 percent of U.S. manufacturing export growth and only 28 percent of import growth.[72] These results underscore why, in a survey of U.S. manufacturing executives, 57 percent reported that NAFTA would make them more competitive in global markets in 2012. Only 11 percent believed that NAFTA would make them less competitive.[73]

Retaliation against protectionism prolonged what had been a likely recoverable recession into the world's Great Depression of the 1930s. Are we now watching this movie again? In early 2009, Mexico imposed $2.4 billion in punitive tariffs on U.S. paper, produce, and other goods. Mexico's action was taken in retaliation for the U.S.'s cancellation of a pilot program to allow Mexican trucks access to U.S. markets. Although the U.S. action violated its 1993 NAFTA agreement with Mexico, the U.S. Teamsters union, acting to protect its members' jobs from competing Mexican truckers, has blocked its implementation. According to the U.S. Chamber of Commerce and the National Association of Manufacturers, Mexico's retaliatory tariffs have cost the United States more than 25,000 lost jobs and $2.6 billion in lost exports.[74,75] One year later, in 2010 and during the same week that the White House launched an initiative to double U.S. exports within five years, Brazil announced some $830 million of penalties against U.S. exporters, a tariff hike that would cost U.S. exporters about $1 billion annually in sacrificed sales, as well as scrub jobs for an unknown number of U.S. workers.[76] Brazil's move was approved by the World Trade Organization (WTO) and was taken in retaliation for "years of anti-competitive subsidies paid to U.S. cotton growers."[77] Also in 2010, the European Union and Japan were considering a WTO-supported right to retaliate against protectionist antidumping policies the United States was imposing against their exports. If they exercised their right, more than $500 million of U.S. exports and an unknown number of U.S. jobs could be affected.[78] As politically influential groups are allowed to bend the rules to protect their own interests, bottom lines get smaller, unemployment lines get larger, and U.S. free-trade leadership gets a black eye.

It is naive to deny that the road to globalization can be brutal to those who cannot maintain its competitive pace, and menacing to those whose privileged position depends on protecting the status quo. But it is even more myopic to believe that the key to a strong economy is to protect the unprotectable by paying high wages for low skills, or premium prices for inferior products. The historical record and today's reality confirm commonsense logic in showing that a strong economy rests on maintaining a trained, productive, and well-paid workforce. Any other alternative dooms companies to financial failure, workers to falling incomes, and consumers to low living standards.

<u>Anxiety No. 4</u>: Free trade is destroying Latin America's environment.

<u>Perception</u>: Almost all businesses tend to degrade the environment. That stark fact is evident wherever industry is found. In places like Cubatão, Brazil's center of chemical production, the air is as thick as soup. Yet, it is notable that the worst polluters are Brazilian, not multinational, plants. As in smog-choked Mexico City or along the string of environmental-eyesore *maquiladora* (assembly facility) communities that dot the Mexican side of the U.S. border, much of the blame can be laid at the door of poor local planning, lax government policy, and economic need.

Banning international trade will not decontaminate the planet or stop global warming. Quite the contrary: if every country produced all and only the products it consumed, waste would be rife. International trade exists because of production efficiencies that are synonymous with conservation. But the environment's greatest enemy is poverty. People everywhere want to live in a healthier environment. Trade affords them the means to do so by raising their incomes. It remains a mystery why, in the words of a prominent Latin American, "[free-trade] protestors have come together to save the people of developing countries from development."[79] Moreover, multinational firms—the motors of international trade—tend to be environmentally cleaner than local firms because (a) their production technologies are designed for and attuned to global standards, and (b) the developed-country consumers of their products are more likely to penalize environmental abusers.

Although some, especially unconstrained local, industries continue to despoil Latin America's environment, globalization's counterforces are at work to slow the process. Indeed, trade and environmental goals often reinforce each other. Developed-country standards on pesticide residues, for example, are causing more and more "developing-country farmers . . . to respond by converting to organic production methods."[80] Breaking the myth that government is held hostage by powerful industries, Brazil is monitoring 15,000 Amazon cattle ranches by satellite to stop their expansion and further damage to the rain forest.[81] Nestlé is an example of how global business can advance environmental well-being, having been described by former president Ricardo Lagos of Chile as "a model of corporate social responsibility."[82] The company's purchasing guidelines "give preference to integrated farming methods that preserve soil, water, air, energy and genetic diversity, and minimize waste."[83] Nestlé's environmentally oriented production improvements reduced wastewater generation by 45 percent, water consumption by 26 percent, and greenhouse gases by 16 percent for each ton of product produced between 2001 and 2004.[84] Enel plans to invest more than 4 billion euros in Latin America between 2009 and 2014, thus enabling it to "avoid the emission of over 4 million tons of CO_2 a year" by developing renewable energy resources and building new plants.[85] Ecuador's San Carlos sugar mill entered an international joint venture over 40 years ago to utilize its bagasse, a residue from processing sugarcane, as the fibrous raw material for paper pulp, thus preserving trees that would otherwise have to be cut for pulp.[86] San Carlos continued its quest for eco-friendly projects, spending more than $1 million in 2008 on sustainability projects, such as reforestation, lubricant recycling, and a closed-loop system that enabled it to reduce water usage by 315 cubic meters per hour. San Carlos spent more than $1.5 million on environmental projects in 2009.[87]

Anxiety No. 5: If the United States does not accelerate construction of the wall along its southern border, our country will be inundated by illegal Mexican immigrants.

Perception: At the time of this writing, Mexican drug-traffickers are catapulting marijuana bales over border fences, a migrant-friendly Arizona borderland rancher is believed by many to have been murdered by a Mexican drug-cartel assassin,[88] and national concern is prompting the White House to consider deploying military forces to secure its southern border. It is a time when heated emotion can prevail over cooler reasoning, and when acting without forethought to quell an immediate threat could trigger more widespread damage in the near future. The key is to recognize that illegal migrants come in various shades of lawlessness.

For over a century, Mexican workers have followed a pattern of circularity, crossing the border as migrants to work hard, live peaceably, earn a few dollars, then return home. That pattern was fueled by the demand for low-cost labor from countless U.S. businesses in the agricultural, construction, manufacturing, and hospitality sectors. Since 2000, the border wall and tightened controls have made migrants reluctant to go home, fearing that they will not be able to return in the next season to work in the United States. As a result, the wall may have kept more Mexicans in than out, converting what had been migrant workers into immigrant settlers. The effect of disrupting the traditional pattern of migrant circularity is clearly seen in the numbers: from 1920 to 1970, the Mexican population in the United States numbered less than 1 million. That population has now swelled to about 12 million.

Many argue that it would be more beneficial for the United States to restore the pattern of circularity by creating a temporary-worker program. Such programs existed in the past. If reinstated and accompanied by incentives and punishments to ensure that Mexicans return home after working legally in the United States, they could sharply reduce the risk of terrorists, drug runners, or other undesirables slipping across U.S. borders.[89]

HOW THIS BOOK WILL HELP YOU

You have finished your first-level reconnaissance of Latin America. You are now prepared to learn how to do business profitably in its markets. The newly created markets of Latin America's rapidly unfolding 21st-century frontier are wide open for business. History tells us that whenever fresh economic frontiers are opening, those who are most able to stay ahead of the pack, and gain control of the competitive high ground, are those who will be best positioned to spot and seize the top prospects from among the explosion of new business opportunities. Use the five chapters that follow to help you stay ahead of the pack by applying their key lessons for finding profits in the new Latin America:

Chapter 2: learn where to find the top sales opportunities for your small- or medium-size business.

Chapters 3 and 4: learn the historic and cultural reasons underlying why and how your Latin American customers do business differently.

Chapter 5: learn how to negotiate with and sell to these customers.

Chapter 6: learn how to keep the good deal you have made from falling apart.

Notes

1. Frank Tannenbaum, *Ten Keys to Latin America* (New York: Alfred A. Knopf, 1964), 5.

2. For an engaging discussion of pre-European Western Hemisphere societies, see Charles C. Mann, *1491* (New York: Vintage Books, 2006).

3. Hubert Herring, *A History of Latin America from the Beginnings to the Present* (New York: Alfred A. Knopf, 1968), 3.

4. Ibid., 3.

5. "Mesoamerica Advance," *Inter-American Development Bank Features and Web Stories*, July 29, 2009, http://www.iadb.org/news/detail.cfm?id=5534 (accessed August 10, 2009).

6. "BID da recursos al Corredor del Pacífico," *Excelsior* (Mexico City), January 11, 2010, Dinero 14.

7. Harvey O. Beltrán, "El Aroma del Buen Vino Chileno," *American Airlines Nexos*, April/June 2000, 16.

8. Zack O'Malley Greenburg, "The World's Happiest Cities," *Forbes*, September 2, 2009, 32, http://www.forbes.com/2009/09/02/worlds-happiest-cities-lifestyle-cities.html (accessed December 9, 2009).

9. Richard Westlund, "Port of the Americas: A New Transshipment Hub Underway in Puerto Rico," *Latin Trade*, May/June 2009, 47.

10. Author's calculation from data shown in "Population Estimate," Statistics Canada, 2009, http://www.statcan.gc.ca/start-debut-eng.html (accessed August 12, 2009).

11. "B03002 Hispanic or Latino Origin by Race," *2007 American Community Survey* (United States Census Bureau, 2007), http://factfinder.census.gov/servlet/DTTable?_bm=y&-ds_name=ACS_2007_1YR_G00_&-CONTEXT=dt&-mt_name=ACS_2007_1YR_G2000_B03002&-redoLog=true&-geo_id=01000US&-format=&-_lang=en&-SubjectID=15233308 (accessed August 12, 2009).

12. Lynette Clemetson, "Hispanics Now Largest Minority, Census Shows," *New York Times*, January 22, 2003, 4.

13. Doreen Hemlock, "Savoring Success," *Sun-Sentinel* (Fort Lauderdale), April 2, 2002, 14–15.

14. "Viva Margarita," *American Way*, September 1, 2001, 17.

15. Barbara D. Phillips, "TV: The Latino Wave Hits the Small Screen," *Wall Street Journal*, June 26, 2000, 44.

16. Jonathan Birchall, "P&G Sales Drive Targets Hispanics," December 28, 2009. http://www.ft.com/cms/s/0/ddda80fc-f350-11de-a888-00144feab49a.html (accessed December 28, 2009).

17. Geri Smith, "Can Bimbo Cook in the U.S.?" *BusinessWeek Online*, March 2002, http://www.businessweek.com/@@*ctwolUQmG4luxYA/magazine/content/02=09/b3772148.htm. (accessed June 28, 2004).

18. Ramiro Alonso, "Bimbo Abre la Chequera," *El Universal.com.mx*, December 11, 2009, http://www.eluniversal.com.mx/finanzas/68094.html (accessed December 28, 2009).

19. Ramiro Alonso, "La Reinversión, el Principal Filón de la Empresa del Osito," *El Universal* (Mexico City), January 11, 2010, B7.

20. "Hispanic Purchasing Power: Projections to 2015," *HispanicBusiness.com*, https://secure.hbinc.com/product/view.asp?id=222 (accessed August 12, 2009).

21. "Through Boom and Bust: Minorities, Immigrants and Home Owner-ship," Pew Hispanic Center, May 12, 2009, http://pewhispanic.org/reports/report.php?ReportID=109 (accessed August 12, 2009).

22. "Latino Power at the Polls," *The Economist*, December 8, 2000, 30–31.

23. "Yo Te Quiero Mucho," *The Economist*, September 30, 2000, 30–33.

24. Juán Carlos Pérez, "Study: US Hispanics' Net Use Grows," IDG News Service/Latin American Bureau, January 27, 2003.

25. "U.S. Hispanic Internet Audience Growth Outpaces Total U.S. Online Population by 50 Percent," ComScore, April 16, 2009, http://comscore.com/Press_Events/Press_Releases/2009/4/U.S._Hispanic_Internet_Audience_Growth/%28language%29/eng-US (accessed August 13, 2009).

26. "Latinos Online 2006–2008: Narrowing the Gap," Pew Hispanic Center, December 22, 2009.

27. Armando Roggio, "Ecommerce Know-How: Marketing to the Hispanic Community," *Practical Ecommerce*, August 10, 2009, http://www.practicalecommerce.com/articles/1226-Ecommerce-Know-How-Marketing-to-the-Hispanic-Community (accessed August 12, 2009).

28. "Obama Is Appointing Hispanics at Record Pace," *Wall Street Journal*, December 22, 2009, A12.

29. Amy Casey and Susan Davis, "Politics Show in Spanish Set to Debut," *Wall Street Journal*, April 15, 2010, A6.

30. *The World Factbook 2010*, U.S. Central Intelligence Agency, 2009 (conversion to square miles by author).

31. Ibid.

32. Ibid.

33. "Human Development Report 2009-HDI Rankings," United Nations Development Program, 2009, http://hdr.undp.org/en/statistics/ (accessed January 21, 2010).

34. *Country Background Notes* (2006, 2007, 2008, 2009) (International Trade Administration, Washington, DC: U.S. Department of Commerce).

35. *The World Factbook 2010*.

36. *Country Commercial Guides* (2008, 2009) (Washington, DC: U.S. Department of State).

37. *Country Background Notes* (2006, 2007, 2008, 2009).

38. "Corporate Travel Guide to Latin America," *Latin Finance*, 2004, 22–27.

39. Author's experience and other sources (as noted).

40. Javier Santiso, "Brasil y el Nuevo orden mundial," *América Economía*, August 7, 2010, http://www.americaeconomia.com/revista/el-apetito-global-de-las-empresas-brasilenas (accessed August 10, 2010).

41. Isabel Allende, *My Invented Country: A Memoir* (New York: Harper Collins, 2003), 185.

42. "Murders (per capita) (most recent) by Country," Nationmaster.com, 2003, http://www.nationmaster.com/graph/cri_mur_percap-crime-murders-per -capita (accessed December 28, 2009).

43. "Not Yet the Promised Land," *The Economist*, January 2, 2010, 29–30.

44. Matthew Bristow, "Drugs Fade in the Colombian Economy," *Wall Street Journal*, April 3, 2010, A7.

45. Elizabeth Dickinson, "Memo to Iraq, from Colombia," *Foreign Policy*, February 2009, http://www.foreignpolicy.com/story/cms.php?story_id=4715&page=0 (accessed December 20, 2009).

46. Terri Morrison and Wayne A. Conaway, *Kiss, Bow, or Shake Hands: Latin America* (Avon, MA: Adams Media, 2007), 86.

47. U.S. Department of State, 2009, http://travel.state.gov/travel/cis_pa_tw/ cis/cis_1097.html (accessed December 21, 2009).

48. Kevin Michael Diran, *How to Say It: Doing Business in Latin America* (New York: Prentice Hall, 2009), 168.

49. "Murders (per capita)."

50. "Travel Alert," U.S. Department of State, 2009, http://travel.state.gov/ travel/cis_pa_tw/pa/pa_4491.html, (accessed December 28, 2009).

51. "Background Note: Nicaragua," U.S. Department of State, August 2009.

52. Steve Stecklow, "A New Mosque in Nicaragua Fires Up the Rumor Mill," *Wall Street Journal*, November 9, 2009, 1.

53. "International Narcotics Control Strategy Report," U.S. Embassy— Asunción, February 27, 2009.

54. "Country Reports on Terrorism (Paraguay)." U.S. Embassy—Asunción, April 30, 2009.

55. Anthony Faiola, "U.S. Terrorist Search Reaches Paraguay; Black Market Border Hub Called Key Finance Center for Middle East Extremists," *Washington Post*, October 13, 2001, http://www.encyclopedia.com/doc/1P2-4763 Castañeda 4 Castañeda 1.html (accessed December 29, 2009).

56. "Peru: Defense Minister Says Anti-insurgency Equipment Is First Priority," 2009, http://mx.mc383.mail.yahoo.com/mc/welcome?.gx=1&.tm=1262200 397&.rand=emhk829ju2jc5#_pg=showMessage;_ylc=X3oDMTBuNDFhNDczBF 9TAzM5ODMyNTAyNwRhYwNtcmtVcmVk&pSize=100&sMid=2&fid=Inbox&mId =1_790944_ABN9v9EAAR6GSzueiglVYVhKK3A&sort=date&order=down&start Mid=0&.rand=44630509&filterBy=&m=1_794620_ABh9v9EAABmwSzu49Ahuw CAjCpw%2C1_792110_ABd9v9EAAXSdSzumVAy%2BAAtKM1o%2C1_790944 _ABN9v9EAAR6GSzueiglVYVhKK3A%2C1_786518_ABd9v9EAANaaSzuUqgS86z

YXfqo%2C1_782111_ABR9v9EAAHJwSzuDBQACyUFfwEY%   79024_ABJ9v9EA
ACDlSzt0%2FwEspmeIKZg&mcrumb=0OYM25UoW1.&cmd=msg.markunread
&unreadMid=1_792110_ABd9v9EAAXSdSzumVAy%2BAAtKM1o&hash=71d2a
37e87779dd15d3c7204a8ab1e85&.jasrand=3248986 (accessed December 30. 2009).

57. Cited in: Kate Millet, *The Politics of Cruelty* (New York: W.W. Norton, 1994), 309.

58. Candace Piette, "Uruguay Election Offers Sharp Contrast," BBC World News, October 24, 2009.

59. "Murders (per capita)."

60. "Chavez Prepares Venezuela for 'U.S.-Provoked' War," *PressTV,* December 8, 2009, http://www.presstv.ir/detail.aspx?id=113150&sectionid=351020704 (accessed December 31, 2009).

61. Will Grant, "Venezuela Minister Resigns over Bank Scandal," BBC News, Venezuela, December 7, 2009, http://news.bbc.co.uk/2/hi/americas/8399268.stm (accessed December 30, 2009).

62. Louis E. Boone, *Quotable Business* (New York: Random House, 1992), 239.

63. Doreen Hemlock, "Surging Mexican Cement Giant Goes High-tech," *Sun-Sentinel,* December 18, 2000, 6.

64. David Hoyt and Hau L. Lee, "End-to-End Transformation in the Cemex Supply Chain," in *Building Supply Chain Excellence in Emerging Economies,* ed. Hau L. Lee and Chung-Yee Lee (New York: Springer), 2007, 345–369.

65. Ann Harrison, "Globalization and Poverty," National Bureau of Economic Research, Working Paper No. 12347, July 2006.

66. "Globalization, Growth and Poverty: Building an Inclusive World Economy," World Bank, May 2001, http://go.worldbank.org/1MQ7Q4FHH0 (accessed December 28, 2009).

67. Ibid.

68. Gary Burtless et al., "Globaphobia: Confronting Fears about Open Trade" (Washington, DC: Brookings Institution, 1998).

69. David Dollar and Aart Kraay, "Spreading the Wealth," *Foreign Affairs,* January/February 2002, 120–133.

70. "NAFTA Facts," Office of the U.S. Trade Representative, Washington, DC, March 2008.

71. Gary C. Hufbauer and Jeffrey J. Scott, "NAFTA Revisited: Achievements and Challenges" (Washington, DC: Institute for International Economics, 2005), 80, 97.

72. Frank Vargo, "It All Started with NAFTA" (Washington, DC: National Association of Manufacturers, April 23, 2009).

73. "Made in North America," Deloitte Research, based on a survey conducted by Canadian Manufacturers & Exporters, Deloitte Touche Tohmatsu

member firms in Canada, Mexico, and the United States, the National Association of Manufacturers and the Manufacturing Institute, 2008, 3.

74. Gary Fields, "Trade Dispute Divides U.S. Workers," *Wall Street Journal*, April 6, 2010, A5.

75. Meezna Thiruvengadam and Henry J. Pulizzi, "Mexico Tops List of Trade Issues Facing White House," *Wall Street Journal*, March 10, 2010, A4.

76. "World Tariff Wars," *Wall Street Journal*, April 9, 2010, A18.

77. "Trade Sanctions Issued on Range of U.S. Goods," *Wall Street Journal*, March 9, 2010, A14.

78. "World Tariff Wars," *Wall Street Journal*, April 9, 2010, A18.

79. Ernesto Zedillo [President of Mexico, 1994–2000], in a speech at Quinnipiac University, April 29, 2003.

80. Richard Steenbick and Dale Andrew, "Trade and Environment: Striking a Balance," *OECD Observer*, No. 233 (August 2002), http://www.oecdobserver.org/news/Trade_and_environment:_Striking_a_balance (accessed December 8, 2009).

81. *Global Development Briefing*, December 9, 2009, http://mx.mc383.mail.yahoo.com/mc/welcome?.gx=1&.tm=1260728926&.rand=3s5okaru0tsog#_pg=showMessage;_ylc=X3oDMTBuanIzZWtlBF9TAzM5ODMyNTAyNwRhYwNkZWxNc2dz&mid=1_6994_233347_ABh9v9EAAWfuSyNSigxcrizDIWg&fid=%2540B%2540Bulk&sort=date&order=down&startMid=0&filterBy=&.rand=614015046&hash=ca50b80571445653e29669f82698edfd&.jsrand=9878430 (accessed December 13, 2009).

82. *The Nestlé Concept of Corporate Social Responsibility as Implemented in Latin America* (Vevey, Switzerland: Nestlé, S.A., 2006), 33.

83. Ibid., 16.

84. Ibid., 40.

85. *Enel Latin America 2009*, http://www.enel-latinamerica.com/environment.htm (accessed December 14, 2009).

86. Author worked in Ecuador on this project from 1968 to 1970.

87. Elisa Sicouret, "Los Esfuerzos Ambientales y el Empresariado Ecuatoriano," *América Economía*, December 21, 2009, http://mba.americaeconomia.com/articulos/reportajes/los-esfuerzos-ambientales-del-empresariado-ecuatoriano (accessed December 23, 2009).

88. Randal C. Archibold, "Ranchers Alarmed by Killing," *New York Times*, April 5, 2010, A9, A11.

89. For a lucid review of the Mexican immigrant issue in the United States, see Jorge G. Castañeda, *Ex Mex: From Migrants to Immigrants* (New York: The New Press, 2007).

Chapter 2

Latin America Means Business

For some 50 years, I have had the benefit of doing business and working with, training, and having as friends a large and varied assemblage of executives who understand Latin America. Although the majority of these executives were Latin Americans, a few were Anglo Americans, and a handful were nationals of countries located outside the Americas. Over the years, I was privileged to learn from this multinational assortment of business veterans how they had earned their spurs in the rough-and-tumble business arenas of Latin America. The similarities I observed among their diverse and lively accounts of triumph and defeat began to take on recognizable and predictable patterns. These patterns form the bedrock upon which rest the foundations for success and failure that appear on these pages. Without weakening the muscle behind those executives' real-life lessons, I have organized the body of their experiences around a skeleton formed by my own years of doing business in and research on the region.

The guidelines resulting from that amalgam of practical experience and academic research are what make this book different. It contains concepts that clients and colleagues have put into practice to increase profits, decrease hassles, and reduce risks related to their Latin American dealings. I shall be delighted to learn from you, the reader, how this book has helped to sharpen your own competitive edge. I invite you to send me your comments via e-mail to: DrBeckerIs@yahoo.com.

The typical business scenario of the first 25 years of my own experience in Latin America was markedly different from that which I have been pleased to see gaining ground during the last 25 years. Although the past never dies in Latin America, a different future is unfolding there as this era's less corrupt, more democratic leadership unchains the region's economic potential by reducing transportation, communication, and tariff rates and by promoting access to world-class know-how. This process is revolutionizing the way business is being done in the 800-million-consumers megamarket of the Americas, as the fear of being left behind trumps the fear of change.

You will not find in this book one single key to doing business in Latin America. Success is tied to the whole key set. The keys that will unlock profits for the medium-size exporter of consumer goods are not the same ones that will open doors for the firm aiming to set up master franchises for industrial security systems. And the U.S. distributor of specialty furnishings will require yet another set of keys to find a reliable Latin supplier of custom chairs and tables fashioned by hand from tropical hardwoods. Nonetheless, among the many keys described in this book, there is a set that can open the doors you will need to make doing business in the new Latin America a productive and satisfying venture. The strongest foundation on which to ground that venture is an understanding of (a) the region's business possibilities and (b) the ways in which smaller businesses can exploit them.

FEEDING THE DRAGON

When exporters scan the globe for promising market targets, they may use GDP (gross domestic product) share to indicate how a particular economy is performing in relation to all the rest. Like market share, GDP share is a shorthand measure to gauge if an economy is gaining, falling behind, or just holding its own in the world. Figure 2.1 tracks the total economic output (measured by GDP) of Asia and Latin America as percentages of the total economic output of the world.[1]

We see Latin America gaining share in the 1970s. This was a period when international bankers were tripping over themselves to make loans to Latin America, as the mounting prices of the region's raw materials, combined with entry into the cash economy of rural migrants moving to urban centers, propelled its GDP skyward. The commodity bubble burst in 1981, ushering in Latin America's Lost Decade as plunging commodity prices, exacerbated by the competitive consequences of decades of protectionist policies, choked economic output. For seven years after the Lost Decade, Latin America gained GDP share, as the region's economies cashed in on newly adopted open-market reform policies, often labeled

Figure 2.1
Latin America and Asia: Share of World Economy

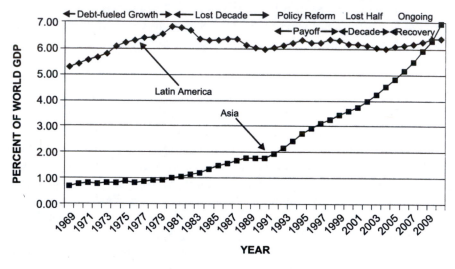

neoliberalism. But, while the Lost Half-Decade of 1998–2003 advanced, Latin America's GDP share steadily fell, due greatly to weakness in Argentina and Venezuela. Thanks to healthy foreign exchange reserves, sensible currency policies, contained inflation, and strong banks, the region's economy resumed its sturdy growth until the global financial crisis of 2009. Even in that year, Latin America's 2.5 percent economic contraction was mild relative to the sharp declines experienced in the developed world. For 2010 the World Bank estimated a GDP increase of 3.0 percent for the region, followed by 3.5 percent for 2011.[2] However, those growth estimates for the entire region mask some sharp differences within the region. Most at variance with the Bank's projections for the overall region are the statist economies of Argentina, Bolivia, Ecuador, Nicaragua, and Venezuela. The Bank estimated that, on average, those more closed economies will see their GDPs rise by only 1.58 percent and 2.34 percent, respectively, in 2010 and 2011.[3]

During the Lost Half-Decade, together with the alarmingly rapid closure of the gap between the GDP shares of Asia and Latin America, fear grew in Latin America that its economy was a slow-moving train wreck, being overtaken by Asia's bullet-train economies. Indeed, Latin America seemed to be caught in its traditional trap: it would sell its plentiful natural resources,

Asia (primarily China) would buy them, transform them into higher priced finished goods, and sell them back. The process favored Asia's higher value-added and more labor-intensive manufacturers, creating more wealth and jobs there. Simultaneously, Latin America's manufacturing sector became even less globally competitive as the region's currencies, strengthened by the boom in the natural resources sector, drove the international prices of its finished goods higher. Companies shut their factory doors, and those that could moved their production to Asia.

Since the end of the Lost Half-Decade, however, that fear has receded,[4] and much of the region's currently brighter spirits may be attributed to two delayed effects. First, many (primarily U.S.) firms, having abandoned outsourcing to Latin America during the 1990s and flocked to lower cost Asia for assembly and manufacturing, were rediscovering Latin America. Rising Asian labor and international shipping rates, costly inventory-stocking needs, slow turnaround times, and complications arising from time zone differences, was making some of the former Asian "off-shor-ing" return to Latin America as "near-shoring" in the later 2000s.[5,6,7,8] Second, while Asia's—primarily China's—insatiable appetite for oil, min-erals, and food was driving Latin America's commodity prices to record levels, Asia was simultaneously opening its checkbook wide to boost Latin America's industrial and infrastructure capacity to produce and export more of those goods.[9–13]

Is there not good reason to believe that China's newly prominent role in Latin America foretells an even brighter future in the Americas? After all, China's seemingly bottomless appetite for natural resources has been a decisive factor in driving up demand and prices for many of the raw materials that have helped Latin American exporters to prosper in recent years. Moreover, China's massive loans to stimulate production and export of raw materials have aided many Latin American econo-mies, especially those of energy-rich producers such as Brazil, Vene-zuela, Ecuador, Bolivia, and Peru. But what if the East wind were to still? By 2010, concern was mounting that China's record-setting rates of economic growth could not be sustained. If China were to experience an economic slowdown, Latin America could be among the first to suf-fer its consequences, as commodity revenues fall, new loan flows dry up, and old debt has to be serviced. Such a scenario argues for the region to break more rapidly from the stranglehold that raw materials have placed on its economic development. Free trade is an important step toward developing a more prosperous, diversified, and value-adding economy.

SIZE MATTERS

At least it does when countries compete in global markets. It is the reason why smaller countries join together to form market juggernauts like the European Union. By integrating their own markets with those of neighbors, smaller countries can collectively acquire the economic power and political clout needed to prosper and have influence in global affairs. In the process of gaining sway externally, members of free-trade agreements (FTAs) also gain strength internally. This happens as domestic companies, freed from domestic-only operations, can access the advantages of scale and scope available in the global marketplace. Of course, this competitive magic can only rub off on U.S. companies when the United States signs FTAs. Recognizing this, President Obama has stated, "If America sits on the sidelines while other nations sign trade deals, we will lose the chance to create jobs on our shores."[14] Others have recognized the importance to their economy's health of being globally competitive, and they are ahead of the United States in signing FTAs. For example, whereas the European Union has signed FTAs with 40 countries, the United States has struck trade deals with only 17 economies.[15] When the European Union, China, Canada, Japan, or others beat the United States to the punch in signing smart FTAs, U.S. companies are locked out of sweet market deals. A case in point is the Canada-Colombia trade pact. Since 2008, it has eliminated for Canadian exporters Colombia's average tariff of 12 percent on nonagricultural products, a cost burden that U.S. competitors must bear.[16] Also since 2008, the United States has been trying to pass a similar agreement with Colombia, but it has been blocked by the U.S. Congress. Since most Colombian products already enter the United States duty-free and the new agreement would simply open Colombia's door to duty-free U.S. exports, it is not easy to understand why the U.S. Congress would block such an agreement. Some argue that Congress is stalling because the AFL-CIO opposes the deal.[17] Evidence that signing FTAs is disproportionately important for U.S. exporters is the fact that, although countries with which the United States has struck FTAs control only 7.5 percent of world GDP (excluding the United States), those same countries account for 42.6 percent of U.S. exports.[18] Although a multiplicity of FTAs exist in Latin America, those that are likely to be of greatest consequence to most U.S. exporters are NAFTA, MERCOSUR, and CAFTA-DR.

NAFTA

Entering into effect in 1994, by 2002 the North American Free Trade Agreement had almost tripled U.S.-Mexico trade, had made both countries more competitive internationally,[19] and had propelled Mexico's economy into a world-class manufacturing and assembly powerhouse. By 2008, more than $1 billion of duty-free exports and imports were crossing the Mexico-U.S. border every single day. Still, NAFTA sparked controversies in both countries,[20] spawning countless myths in the process. But some of the more widespread myths are contradicted by facts that are too plain to be misunderstood:

Myth No. 1: NAFTA has cost the United States jobs.
  Fact: U.S. employment rose from 110.8 million people in 1993 to 137.6 million in 2007, an increase of 24 percent. The average unemployment rate was 5.1 percent during the post-NAFTA period 1994–2007, compared to 7.1 percent during the pre-NAFTA period 1980–1993.[21]

Myth No. 2: NAFTA has hurt the U.S. manufacturing base.
  Fact: U.S. manufacturing output rose by 58 percent between 1993 and 2006, as compared to 42 percent between 1980 and 1993.[22]

Myth No. 3: NAFTA has suppressed U.S. wages.
  Fact: U.S. business sector real (i.e., adjusted for inflation) hourly compensation rose by 1.5 percent each year between 1993 and 2007, for a total of 23.6 percent over the full period. During 1979–1993, the annual rate of real hourly compensation rose by 0.7 percent each year, or 11 percent over the full 14-year period.[23]

Myth No. 4: NAFTA has reduced wages in Mexico.
  Fact: Mexican wages grew steadily after the 1994 peso crisis, reached precrisis levels in 1997, and have increased each year since. Several studies conclude that Mexican industries that export or that are in regions with a higher concentration of foreign investment and trade also have higher wages.[24]

Myth No. 5: NAFTA has done nothing to improve the environment.
  Fact: NAFTA created two binational institutions that certify and finance environmental infrastructure projects to provide a clean and healthy environment for residents along the U.S.-Mexico border. To date, they have provided nearly $1 billion for 135 environmental infrastructure projects with a total estimated cost of $2.89 billion and allocated $55.1 million in assistance and grants for over 450 other border environmental projects. The Mexican government has also made

substantial new investments in environmental protection, increasing the federal budget for the environmental sector by 81 percent between 2003 and 2008.[25]

Myth No. 6:   NAFTA has made Mexico's poor farmers poorer.

Fact: Based on three independent studies, the World Bank concludes that "the decline of Mexican corn prices was a long term trend that preceded NAFTA, and . . . government producer-price subsidies actually kept such prices above what would have been the case under NAFTA without domestic price subsidies."[26]

MERCOSUR

After NAFTA, the largest integrated market in the Western Hemisphere (250 million consumers) is MERCOSUR (Common Market of the South, called MERCOSUL in Portuguese). Argentina, Brazil, Paraguay, and Uruguay established MERCOSUR in 1991. Chile, Bolivia, Peru, and Ecuador became nonvoting associate members in subsequent years. Pending ratification by Paraguay's Congress, Venezuela may gain full membership in 2010.[27] MERCOSUR has suffered from internal strains in recent years. In addition to routine spats, its members cannot agree on the guiding purpose of the organization. Should it exist, as Brazil advocates, solely to promote regional trade, or should it act to pursue political ends, as Venezuela proposes? This issue, and others regarding membership, underlie the creation of Unión de Naciones Suramericanas (UNASUR, Union of South American Nations), a new regional organization that could replace MERCOSUR.[28]

MERCOSUR is a customs union that, unlike NAFTA, requires its members to charge commonly agreed-upon tariffs to outsiders. Those tariffs can be high, making some see MERCOSUR as a mechanism to perpetuate the protectionism that sheltered Latin American economies from international competition until the 1980s. Larger firms can circumvent MERCOSUR's import duties by investing behind its tariff wall to set up local manufacturing (instead of exporting to supply its markets from the United States). Few small- and medium-size enterprises (SMEs) have deep enough pockets to follow that strategy. Hence, if high duties shut them out of the market for export sales, U.S. SMEs must use licensing, franchising, or contract manufacturing to tap into MERCOSUR revenues.

CAFTA-DR

The United States signed the Dominican Republic-Central America-United States Free Trade Agreement (CAFTA-DR) with five Central American countries (Costa Rica, El Salvador, Guatemala, Honduras, and Nicaragua) and the Dominican Republic in 2004. It is the first FTA between the United States and a group of smaller developing economies. Central America and the Dominican Republic represent the third-largest U.S. export market in Latin America (behind Mexico and Brazil), having imported $26.3 billion of U.S. products in 2008.[29] Although all U.S. exporters stand to benefit from the significant tariff cuts required under the CAFTA-DR, the agreement may be particularly friendly to SMEs. In 2005, SMEs sold 46 percent of the value of U.S. merchandise exports to the Dominican Republic and Central America, considerably more than the 29 percent share of merchandise that U.S. SMEs exported to the world in that year. More than 16,300 of the firms that exported to the CAFTA-DR region in 2005 were SMEs, accounting for almost 90 percent of all U.S. firms that exported to its member countries.[30]

FTAA—A Memorial

Proposed by the United States in 1994 as an extension of NAFTA, the Free Trade Area of the Americas was to unite all of the North American, Central American, South American, and Caribbean (except for Cuba) economies into a single massive trading bloc. Disagreement over the Doha Round of world trade talks, lack of cooperation between the United States and Brazil, protectionism, the exclusion of Cuba, and reluctance to support a U.S.-backed initiative have stalled progress on the FTAA. Having been in a deepening coma since 2005, the FTAA appeared by 2010 to have been cut off from most of its remaining life-support systems.

Fortress America?

The growth of intraregional trade within Asia, Europe, and the Americas during the 1990s gave rise to speculation in the 2000s that the world was moving toward a triad of powerful, self-contained economic fortresses. Early in the 2010s, amid high unemployment and economic uncertainty, the United States itself seemed to be moving toward protectionism. The "Buy America" provisions in the president's fiscal stimulus package; Congress's stalling on approving the long-awaited FTAs with Colombia, Panama, and South Korea; and its NAFTA-violating refusal to allow Mexican trucks on U.S. roads are disturbing signs. Why disturbing? These signs are disturbing because they are beggar-thy-neighbor acts that damage us in two ways: first, the "neighbors" are likely to retaliate, and second, our standard of living will fall as we cut ourselves off from the proven benefits of free trade and open markets. Already, in retaliation for the United States reneging on access to its roads, Mexico has raised tariffs on $2.4 billion of U.S. exports, destroying tens of thousands of U.S. jobs.[31] Protectionism is an especially virulent form of populism that can only harm U.S. exporters. If you find yourself watching *Creeping Toward Fortress America*, be forewarned—this movie will not have a happy ending.

LATIN AMERICA'S WELCOME MAT IS OUT FOR SMALLER BUSINESSES

Charles Darwin taught the world that it was not the strongest or the most intelligent species that survived, but the ones most adaptable to change. What Darwin knew about species applies equally to business. There are periods in history when great changes occur, and adapting to those changes controls whether a business survives or becomes extinct. Latin America is in one of those periods. The changes occurring in the region are tipping the scales of survival in favor of swift-to-adapt SMEs. As the central force driving those changes is globalization, trade-oriented SMEs are naturally well positioned to profit from them. To appreciate how SMEs in both of the Americas can benefit from globalization, consider how globalization is reshaping Latin America's social order and integrating its markets.

The Social Order: Why Democracy Matters to SMEs

The last two decades have been a defining period for Latin America. A crucial line was crossed between 1977, when only four Latin American countries had democratic governments, and 1990, when only Cuba was a dictatorship.[32] Although many ills of the past have not yet been laid to rest, the transition to democracy was reforming the old social order: dictatorships and crony capitalism were being discarded, and political and economic self-determination were being set as cornerstones of the new social order. Having hard-wired self-determination into their mindset, Latin Americans are now looking to the democratic principle of freedom as a beacon to reform political practice and inform economic policy. The ascendancy of political and economic freedom parallels the adoption of the entrepreneurship gospel, the central tenet of winning SMEs. The process of taking a giant step away from rule by the few and toward rule by the many has altered the old requirements for success in Latin American markets, and it tips the scales in favor of the entrepreneurial strengths in which SMEs routinely excel. As a result, smaller U.S. and Latin firms are better positioned to compete today than at any time in the past. Table 2.1 summarizes how the forces of newly expanded political and economic freedoms benefit SMEs.

Best Beats Big in the Information Age

Theory informs us that the main reason large companies exist is to lower their transaction costs. By doing business on a large scale when they buy and sell, large firms can capture economies of scale that small-fry buyers and sellers cannot achieve. But as technology, deregulation, and the Internet reduced transaction costs, the optimal profitable size for firms was similarly reduced. When David-size SMEs can buy and sell as cheaply as Fortune 500 Goliaths, size is no longer an insurmountable barrier to doing business across borders.

Size no longer is king where the complacent customers in the protected, brand-limited consumer markets of Latin America's past are being replaced by the value-aware, demanding shoppers of today's open, Internet-age markets. Customer focus and rapid-paced change are the defining conditions of 21st-century markets. They also define the market environment in which smaller firms' competitive advantages in customer service and innovation can be decisive.

Today's Internet allows smaller sellers to reach global audiences once reserved for large multinationals. But you must adapt your existing Web site. In addition to the obvious need to translate text into Spanish and/or Portuguese, you may have to adjust the visual appearance of your site, such as photos, logos, and graphics, to conform to the local culture. Adapting content is critical: compliance with local regulations, prices, terms of payment, and specifications must be consistent with the business practices, currency, laws, time zone, language, cultures, and infrastructures of the countries in which you intend to do business. Finally, being able to respond quickly with online technical assistance in the customer's language will go far to alleviate Latins' fears of dealing across international borders.[33]

Table 2.1
Democracy's Dividends to SMEs

These Trends toward *Political* Freedom . . .	. . . Make Smaller Businesses More Competitive by . . .
From rule by men to rule by law	Minimizing economic or political clout as a factor in settling disputes
From shadowy to transparent decision making	Reducing the uncertainty of the business environment
Less tolerance for corruption	Eliminating the necessity to pay bribes to win business
Greater availability of information	Creating affordable access to marketing and production data
The state: from planner and creator of growth to facilitator of growth	Creating access to SME-friendly infrastructure and services and to opportunities to compete fairly
Less government patronage	Enabling them to deal with rational bureaucracy (e.g., *ventanilla única*)

These Trends toward *Economic* Freedom . . .	. . . Make Smaller Businesses More Competitive by . . .
Power shift from producer to consumer	Allowing them to apply their customer service advantage
Lower international communication cost	Giving them knowledge of international markets, customers, and technology
Lower international transportation cost	Lowering the cost of access to international markets and inputs
Lower international tariffs	Enabling them to quote lower export prices
Lower domestic tariffs	Lowering the cost of imported inputs
Greater availability of small credits	Enabling them to finance working capital needs with debt
Easing foreign investment rules	Enabling them to finance investment capital needs with equity
Stable exchange rates	Lowering the cost and risk of doing business internationally

Outsourcing

Recent research evidences that international outsourcing can be a competitively powerful tool to help SMEs level the playing field with large multinational firms. Thanks to advances in communication and information technologies, many SMEs have taken their first venture into international markets through sourcing, rather than through exporting. By allowing SMEs to focus on their core competitive strengths, international outsourcing of noncore functions (e.g., installation and servicing, engineering and design, final assembly, back-office processing, and specialty manufacturing) has enabled firms to win customers that would otherwise be too costly or managerially demanding to serve.[34]

The SME-Customer Connection

As buyers of both consumer and industrial products, Latin Americans have become demanding and informed customers. This new buyer mentality is tailor-made for the customer-focused approach and nimble response to market shifts that are hallmarks of SMEs. Future stories about business successes within Latin America, and between it and the United States, are likely to feature SMEs launching new customer-centered ventures. The production-oriented firms that have dominated Latin American business for centuries have found it difficult to adapt as the pendulum of market power began to swing toward the consumer in the 1990s. For example, food giants Molinos Río de la Plata (Argentina—$1.4 billion sales) and Santista Alimentos (Brazil—$2 billion sales) suffered costly consequences for being slow to adapt to consumer marketing. Molinos's net profit margins were only 43 percent of Latin America's food industry average, while Santista's capitalized market value was less than half its book value.[35] Firms that fail to adapt to the new customer-dictated business rules are learning the hard way that if they continue to live in the past, they themselves will be history.

NARROWING THE SEARCH FOR BUSINESS OPPORTUNITY

We will tighten the focus of our SME-exporter telescope at this juncture, and scan Latin America's market horizon for promising sales targets.

Lose the Ouija Board

In business—as in sports, comedy, and romance—timing is everything. The Latin American window of opportunity has been opening wider to exporters during the last two decades. In the 2010s it is wide open for U.S. SMEs that adhere to a four-step procedure:

1. Understand the underlying forces that are propelling new business opportunities in Latin America.
2. Use this book to help you estimate whether your company's strengths in people skills, product offering, finances, and organizational culture are in competitive alignment with those forces.
3. Scan to find promising market and product matches for that alignment. Use the Quick Notes in Chapter 1 and in this chapter to screen for good personal and business fits.
4. Use Chapters 3 to 6 to prepare your approach, negotiate and close the deal, fill the order, and sustain the cash flow.

Can You Help Latin America Do an Infrastructure Makeover?

It Does Not Have a Pretty Face

Many U.S. executives would be appalled to see how run-down and inadequate the roads, ports, telephones, electricity and water systems, schools, hospitals, and other services are in Latin America. Yet, it is precisely the decrepit condition of the region's infrastructure that is now creating major business opportunities for exporters. As the forces of globalization force Latin American economies to compete in world markets, a colossal obstacle to success is the inability of run-down infrastructures to support modern production and distribution. Indeed, a large unanswered question is how Latin America has been able to sustain even moderate economic growth rates for most of the last 50 years with an infrastructure that has not even evolved with population growth, much less with the race to compete in a globalized economy. That race begins as a sprint to catch up and continues as a marathon to keep up. Along the way it creates business opportunities that would inspire any company's awe. The World Bank estimates that annual Latin American spending on infrastructure is less than two percent of its GDP, but spending would have to rise to four to six percent just to catch up to countries that once trailed it, such as South Korea and China. Adding in maintenance expense, developing an infrastructure that could be competitively sustainable would require annual expenditures of five to seven percent of GDP.[36]

Although the total cost of an inadequate infrastructure eludes precise measurement, the immediate effect on business of just one cost, an obsolescent logistics component (physical movement of goods at supply, production, storage, and distribution stages), is readily visible. A factory whose product has lower logistics costs than its rival in another country can source inputs and deliver its product over greater distances, thus enjoying a cost advantage in international markets. As unit cost advantage increases with the volume of units produced, and as Latin America can boast only a few firms large enough to enjoy substantial economies of scale, its smaller companies are handicapped by a cost disadvantage when they compete in global markets against Asia's huge multinationals.

Latin America Is Punching below Its Weight

Transportation accounts for 10 to 20 percent of the cost of imported products in most of Latin America, and, whereas transportation cost has generally fallen in the rest of the world, it has generally climbed in Latin America.[37] In addition to the high logistics costs of imports, Latin American companies suffer from the high costs of creep-speed supply chains. To put a fine point on the competitive disadvantage created by a substandard logistics system, consider the case of El Salvador. The average Salvadorian exporter suffers a delay of 43 days to make an overseas shipment, whereas a German exporter can ship merchandise out of the country in only 6 days.[38] Having its inventory held up over seven times longer in port and terminal handling, customs and inspection, and export and prearrival documentation, the Salvadorian exporter must tie up a proportionately greater amount of working capital. Adding to the competitive burden of a seven-times disadvantage in the amount of working capital required is the Salvadorian exporter's cost of that capital, perhaps paying interest rates two or three times greater than the German. As a result, the Salvadorian exporter may be competitively handicapped by financial costs that are 15 to 20 times larger than those of the German. But do not let direct-cost considerations obscure the perhaps greater competitive disadvantage the Salvadorian exporter faces on the revenue side as it begs an overseas sales prospect to wait over six weeks for delivery, perhaps four or five weeks longer than a rival bidder can promise.

Brazil provides a macroeconomic perspective on Latin America's desperate demand for infrastructure improvements. Brazil registered a 2008 GDP of $2 trillion. Given that transportation accounts for 12.63 percent of GDP, hauling goods amounts to about $252 billion. If Brazil were to enjoy transportation costs proportionate to those of the United States of 8.19 percent,[39] the savings of $89 billion would enable Brazil to more than double the amount it spends annually on education.[40]

The Salvadorian and Brazilian examples help explain research results showing that, as a country's transportation cost doubles, its trade falls by 80 percent, and that each additional day of delay in shipping a product out of a country reduces trade by at least one percent.[41]

Research done by RREEF Alternative Investments, a Deutsche Bank subsidiary, suggests that Latin America may require $900 billion in infrastructure investments by 2011.[42]

Whether it is perishable agricultural goods, bulk commodities, or time-critical consumer goods, Latin America's ability to be competitive against the Asian threat in world markets rests on better, faster, or cheaper delivery times. Such standards are not an option; they are a competitive mandate, and they signal selling opportunities for U.S. suppliers. Examples of the location, type, and size of several infrastructure projects that were active or on the planning boards in 2010 are shown in Table 2.2.[43]

Latin American Business Opportunities—One Country at a Time

Tu escoges la cuchara con que te vas a dar de comer. "You choose the spoon with which you are going to feed yourself." This venerable adage alludes to the importance of making the right choices in life. It especially applies to business, and to you now as you try to implement step #3 (from "Lose The Ouija Board," above). Use the information in this section as a first step to scan Latin America for promising trade or investment possibilities. The data have been collected from several sources (estimated by the author when sources are in conflict) and compressed into a standardized format to enable the reader to easily compare countries on 10 key business concerns. A word of caution before relying impulsively on Quick Notes: facts and fish are two items that are better used when fresh. Update the references mentioned to keep your country business facts fresh.

Table 2.2

Infrastructure Goliaths: Major Projects Launched in 2009 or 2010, By
Investment Estimates

	Project Name	Country	Sector	Investment (US$ Billion)
1	New refinery train[a]	Mexico	Hydrocarbon	7.464
2	Río Madeira Hydroelectric[b]	Brazil	Energy	6.200
3	Widening of Panama Canal[c]	Panama	Transportation	5.250
4	"Los Andes" railroad project[d]	Argentina-Chile	Transportation	4.800
5	"HidroAysén" hydroelectric power stations[a]	Chile	Energy	3.200
6	"Transversal de las Américas" road concession[c]	Colombia	Transportation	3.050
7	Interocean corridor Chile-Argentina[d]	Chile-Argentina	Transportation	3.000
8	"Autopistas de la Montaña" road concession[a]	Colombia	Transportation	2.800
9	"Ruta del Sol" road project[e]	Colombia	Transportation	2.600
10	Reconfiguration of the Salina Cruz refinery[e]	Mexico	Hydrocarbon	2.517
11	Topolobampo I, II, and III and coal terminal[b]	Mexico	Energy	2.164
12	Bolivia-Brazil binational hydroelectric[e]	Bolivia-Brazil	Energy	2.000

Table 2.2 (*continued*)

	Project Name	Country	Sector	Investment (US$ Billion)
13	Reconfiguration of the Tula refinery[e]	Mexico	Hydrocarbon	1.937
14	Pécem thermoelectric power station[b]	Brazil	Energy	1.853
15	Garabí hydroelectric[e]	Argentina-Brazil	Energy	1.700
16	Punta Colonet–Mexicali[b]	Mexico	Transportation	1.639
17	West Ring Road[b]	Brazil	Transportation	1.500
18	Enlarging Campinas airport[b]	Brazil	Transportation	1.400
19	Paving Iñapari-Puerto Maldonado[b]	Peru	Transportation	1.393
20	Duplication of the Belo Horizonte–São Paulo road[b]	Brazil	Transportation	1.300
21	Yacyretá hydroelectric dam[b]	Argentina-Paraguay	Energy	1.200
22	Duplication of the Palhoça–Osorio road[b]	Brazil	Transportation	1.200
23	Cachuela–Esperanza hydroelectric[a]	Bolivia	Energy	1.200
24	Carare train[a]	Colombia	Transportation	1.200
25	Guanajuato interurban train[b]	Mexico	Transportation	1.121
26	Installation of LNG regasification plant[b]	Uruguay	Energy	1.090
27	Termomaranha thermo-electric power station[c]	Brazil	Energy	1.087

Table 2.2 (*continued*)

	Project Name	Country	Sector	Investment (US$ Billion)
28	Bogotá transit projects (local train)[a]	Colombia	Transportation	1.050
29	Transmission between Río Madeira hydroelectric stations[b]	Brazil	Energy	1.000
30	Northwest Argentina gas pipeline[b]	Argentina	Energy	1.000

[a]Under study.
[b]Under construction.
[c]Approved.
[d]Bidding in process.
[e]Preconstruction.

The information in the descriptions shown below is formatted to show for each country:

1. **GDP.**[44] Adjusted for purchasing power, gross domestic product measures internal economic output and can suggest whether a market may be large enough to be interesting—or small enough to escape the attention of large competitors.

2. **GDP/capita.**[45] Per capita income, adjusted for purchasing power, is a shorthand measure of the level of economic development and affordability of your product by the average consumer. Remember that the region's high income inequality weakens this measure's ability to represent a country's income "center."

3. **GINI Index.**[46] GINI is a shorthand way to measure how unequal incomes are in an economy. It ranges from 0.00 to 1.00. A GINI score of 0.00 (a socialist's utopia, but nonexistent anywhere in the world) would indicate total income equality, that is, an economy in which there are no differences in wealth. As GINI rises, income disparity grows, the market for middle-class consumer goods shrinks, and the greater inequity in wealth could fuel more potential for social instability.

4. **Ease of Doing Business.**[47] Identifies an economy's rank in the world, from 1 to 183, on its ease of doing business, with first place being the best. It can give you some feeling for the level of costs and aggravations your Latin customer or supplier experiences, or those that you would face if you were to become immersed in the local business environment.

5. **Corruption Perceptions Index.**[48] Identifies a country's rank in the world, from 1 to 180, on the perception of corruption, with first place being the least corrupt. Based on 13 independent surveys, it makes more transparent the prevalence of bribery.

6. **Competitiveness Ranking.**[49] This measure is calculated from both publicly available data and executives' opinions. It indicates an economy's relative potential to compete in world markets. The ranking ranges from 1 to 137, with first place being the most competitive. More competitive economies tend to grow more rapidly and to be less protectionist.

7. **Country Credit Risk.**[50] This measure classifies countries into eight risk categories (0 to 7, with 0 being least risky) to assess the likelihood that a country will service its external debt. Developed by a committee of experts appointed by the OECD (Organization for Economic Cooperation and Development) and in effect since 1999, this system is not perfect, but it may be the best available rough estimate of the risk of nonpayment a U.S. exporter or investor faces, even if its customer is willing and able to pay in local currency.

8. **Economic Freedom Index.**[51] This measure ranks countries (1 to 178, with 1 being most free) on the right to control one's labor and property. Economic freedom is positively correlated with per capita income, economic growth, human development, democracy, the elimination of poverty, and environmental protection. For comparison purposes, the United States is ranked number 8.

9. **Best Prospects for U.S. Exports.**[52] These are selected, edited excerpts of prospects observed by the author, or (more commonly) identified by the Commercial Office of the country's U.S. Embassy, typically following an analysis of customs data, firsthand and published market research, and forecasting of industrial trends. In addition to identifying favorable sales prospects for specific products, this section provides some useful insights

into the economic, political, legal, or social forces that underpin those market estimates.

10. **Business Note(s).**[53] This entry provides you with a handy fact, a warning, or a suggestion about a country's business environment.

QUICK NOTES: COUNTRY BUSINESS

ARGENTINA GDP: $575 billion. **GDP/capita:** $11,500. **GINI Index:** 50.0. **Ease of Doing Business:** 118. **Corruption Perceptions Index:** 106. **Competitiveness Ranking:** 85. **Country Credit Risk:** 7. **Economic Freedom Index:** 135. **Best Prospects:** ALTERNATIVE ENERGY EQUIPMENT. One of the world's top three wind corridors is in Argentina's southern Patagonia region. This region holds potential for approximately 500 gigawatts (GW) of electricity generation. Although Argentina's huge wind energy potential is only likely to be developed as transmission lines between Patagonia and the national system evolve, wind generation has increased significantly during the last decade, with current operating capacity estimated above 30 megawatts (MW). Solar power generation can be found in remote and rural areas and is approximately 100 MW, less than 0.2 percent of total electricity production. Spanish and Danish firms have penetrated the market and are steadily increasing market share. Although both wind and solar energy sectors hold high potential in Argentina, the market for wind generation seems to be more promising. Direct sales to municipal governments, electric cooperatives, and private companies are common, but local financing is scarce. ELECTRONIC SECURITY EQUIPMENT. High-tech imports play a significant role in the overall security market, as domestic manufacturing is primarily focused on the production of basic security equipment and safety supplies. The niche sale opportunity for U.S. exporters is in closed-circuit television (CCTV) and access control equipment on Internet provider (IP) networks. Market growth in recent years reflects the rising crime rate in Argentina. In the past five years, there has been a growing trend to import fire-safety product parts and to assemble alarms, detectors, and electronic fire systems locally in order to offer lower prices and to profit from "made in Argentina" tax benefits. Additionally, high-tech imports play a significant role in the overall security market, as domestic manufacturers hasten to satisfy a niche that, until recently, was supplied almost entirely by imported goods. These firms will continue to import high-tech components and products to be used in the production of antitheft electronic systems and alarms over cellular and wire-line telephone networks, including cameras, monitors, indicator panels, and signaling devices and also CCTV and other related areas, since local firms do not manufacture these types of products. FOOD-PROCESSING AND -PACKAGING EQUIPMENT AND PARTS. Argentina's strength in agricultural and food products presents opportunities for U.S. exporters in niche industries such as fat and vegetable oil processing, poultry processing equipment, and machines for cleaning, sorting, or grading eggs, fruit, or other agricultural produce. Parts for food processing and packaging equipment are also good prospects for U.S. exports, given the current trend to repair existing machines due to the rising cost of imports in pesos and the scarcity of local credit for capital goods. MEDICAL EQUIPMENT AND INSTRUMENTS. To alleviate costs, the government exempts from taxes and duties imports of some critical new medical products that are not manufactured in Argentina. Niche opportunities for U.S. exports include ultrasound diagnostic equipment, implants, stents, cardiac valves, pacemakers, hearing aids, specialized disposables, and intraocular lenses. Components and medical equipment parts offer a strong sales potential, in large part because market conditions require the reconditioning of equipment already in use. SPORTING GOODS. Historically, Argentina has earned a reputation for its soccer players, but it is also the homeland of world-class athletes in sports such as basketball, tennis, rugby, field hockey, biking, polo, golf, yachting, skiing, and rowing. Equipment demand for golf, camping, fishing, skiing, and fitness activities has been strong in recent years. Products with significant sales potential include soccer balls; basketballs; skateboards; roller-skates; ice-skates; skis and skiing gear; golf clubs, bags, balls, and gloves; tennis rackets and balls; bowling balls; extreme-sports gear and accessories; underwater breathing devices; goggles; fins; sailboards; and surfboards. **Business Notes:** (1) Although consumer preferences have long leaned in the direction of Europe, the rapidly growing trade ties with MERCOSUR are extending the reach of many brands from Brazil, Argentina's top trading partner. Nonetheless, the United States remains its second trading partner, and consumers have adopted many U.S. values and consumption patterns, seeing U.S. products as being of high quality and innovative. (2) Opening a branch, instead of a legally separate subsidiary, to do business in Argentina may expose your entire firm's assets to potential liability.[54]

BOLIVIA GDP: $43.4 billion. **GDP/capita:** $4,500. **GINI Index:** 58.2. **Ease of Doing Business:** 161. **Corruption Perceptions Index:** 120. **Competitiveness Ranking:** 120. **Country Credit Risk:** 7. **Economic Freedom**

Index: 146. **Best Prospects:** Bolivia can be a tough place to do business. Economic activity is often disrupted by political violence and social unrest traceable to centuries of economic, political, and social inequality. Indigenous, labor, and antiglobalization groups have targeted private investment, particularly foreign investment, as the reason underlying Bolivia's status as South America's poorest country. MINING. Mining is an important economic activity, accounting for some 25 percent of Bolivia's exports. Despite more than 500 years of systematic mining, only an estimated 10 percent of Bolivia's mineral resources have been exploited. Modifications to the mining code, together with tax increases and a new system of royalties, have reduced interest in the mining sector. The private sector purchases virtually all mining equipment imports. Top sales prospects for medium-size open pit operations are drills, crushers, pulverizers, conveyors, compressors, front-loaders, bulldozers, 15- to 30-ton heavy-duty trucks, gravimetric or flotation concentrators, and pumps. In the small-scale sector, the best prospects include small jack-leg drills, front-loaders, crushers, concentration tables, flotation concentrators, hand tools, and explosives. WOOD PRODUCTS. Forests cover almost half of Bolivia's surface area. Thirty-two million of the country's 53 million hectares of forest are set aside for permanent forest production, with approximately 8 million hectares managed under concessions. Bolivia leads the world in sustainable natural forest management, with more than 2 million hectares of certified natural tropical forest. Bolivia has more than 200 varieties of wood, 172 of which are considered fine or exotic, including moradillo, rosewood, and jacaranda. Mahogany represents 77 percent of total wood production, followed by oak at eight percent. Wood exports consist primarily of furniture and value-added parts made of wood, rather than sawn timber. Bolivian producers are experienced in finished products made of mahogany, and new technologies have recently been introduced into sawing and drying processes. The best sales prospects involve related equipment and processing techniques. **Business Note:** Because Bolivia is landlocked, goods are usually trans-shipped through Argentine, Brazilian, Chilean, or Peruvian seaports. Handling delays, roadblocks, and floods can make air shipment a preferable option.

BRAZIL GDP: $2 trillion. **GDP/capita:** $10,200. **GINI Index:** 55.0. **Ease of Doing Business:** 129. **Corruption Perceptions Index:** 75. **Competitiveness Ranking:** 56. **Country Credit Risk:** 3. **Economic Freedom Index:** 113. **Best Prospects:** As Latin America's largest economy and population, Brazil poses countless export opportunities. AIRCRAFT AND

PARTS. Embraer is the 800-pound gorilla in this sector. Its key suppliers include GE Engine Company, Honeywell, Hamilton Sundstrand, C&D, and BF Goodrich. The helicopter market is booming, and its suppliers' main challenge is to reduce delivery time. Products with the best potential for U.S. companies are helicopters, parts and components for helicopters, avionics and systems, aircraft control systems, and aircraft accessories. AIRPORTS. Brazil's stimulus program for airports foresees expenditures of US$20 billion through 2012. Best prospects are flight protection systems, passenger bridges, equipment for drug and explosive detectors, baggage X-rays, radar systems, and baggage-handling equipment. ELECTRICAL POWER SYSTEMS. Brazil's power transmission subsector is investing some US$1.3 billion in 2009–2013 to build 1,500 miles of transmission lines and 22 substations. The most promising export sales prospects are electrical switches to open circuits, circuit breakers, capacitor banks, relays, and electrical protection panels. Brazil plans to invest $US1.2 billion during the present decade in power distribution. Best prospects are lightning arresters, relays, insulated electric conductors, surge suppressors, and technologies to reduce stealing and technical losses. ENVIRONMENTAL. The most promising sales prospects are in soil and water contamination treatment equipment and services, health care waste treatment technologies, laboratory instruments, odor control products, and recycling technologies. INSURANCE. Best prospects include property and casualty lines, especially automobile (high growth potential here: in 2002 Brazil had one car for every 8.8 inhabitants; by 2009 the ratio was one car for every 4.0 inhabitants), life, health, pension, and reinsurance. An interesting niche opportunity may exist in the energy sector: some power utilities in Brazil wish to cover contingencies, such as excessive power loads, with policies that cover power blackouts. MINING. Brazil has a very limited import market for turnkey machinery, as many leading multinationals manufacture locally. These equipment manufacturers, though, provide excellent opportunities to sell U.S. parts and components for earth-moving equipment, belt conveyors, crushers and grinding equipment, laboratory instruments, and drill bits and equipment. OIL AND GAS. The huge discoveries that Brazil has made since 2007 could make it one of the world's top exporters of oil and gas in the current decade. During the 2009–2013 timeframe, Petrobras plans to invest US$174.4 billion to increase production capacity. By 2012, 22 new oil-drilling platforms will explore for oil in Brazil, and 175 new vessels will be added to its fleet, including 122 supply ships and 44 very large crude-oil carriers. Opportunities in offshore equipment and services include flexible pipes, oil well completion systems, pumps, valves, drill pipes, and undersea services. PHARMACEUTICALS. Approximately 85 percent of the raw materials used in the production of generic drugs in Brazil are imported. Also, there is a major demand for equipment and services used in the construction of pharmaceutical manufacturing plants. Best prospects are for products related to modern lifestyle problems, such as contraceptives, erectile dysfunction medicines, cholesterol and weight control medicines, diabetes medicines, and medicines for chronic disease treatment. SAFETY AND SECURITY. Best prospects include access control technology, CCTVs, alarm systems, surveillance technology, drug and explosive detectors, metal detectors, fire prevention and detection systems, cellular telephone blockers, biometrics, and home security equipment. Financial institutions are the market's mainstay, spending approximately US$1 billion per year on security. This is the most sophisticated consumer niche, demanding quality, warranty, and after-sales service. Port and airport security also offer excellent opportunities. Vehicle surveillance has seen rapid growth in recent years, with more than 300,000 cars being stolen every year. To minimize cargo robbery, transportation companies have invested approximately US$1.4 billion in security equipment and personnel. Other promising niches are small businesses and private homes. Although these end-users usually buy less expensive equipment, they can be numerous: Brazil has around 5 million homes that should have some type of security device, but only seven percent are equipped with electronic security systems. In the public sector, the best prospects include surveillance cameras, bulletproof vests, night vision goggles, helmets, munitions, nonlethal weapons, and handcuffs. TRAVEL AND TOURISM. U.S.-bound Brazilians are among the biggest spenders, averaging $3,557 per traveler. Business travelers are especially lucrative, as they often include some leisure days during their trip and spend more than most travelers. Argentina and Chile are the most popular ski destinations during Brazil's winter (June–August), the United States during Brazil's summer (December–February). Colorado, particularly Aspen, is popular, and many Brazilians have bought houses there. AGRICULTURE. Brazil is the world's number one producer of coffee, sugarcane, and oranges; number two of soybeans, beef, poultry, tobacco, bananas, and Brazil nuts; and number three of corn, pineapples, pepper, and cashew nuts. And it still has room to grow, having more unused commercially viable agricultural land than any other country in the world. Top U.S. export prospects in this sector include state-of-the-art postharvest machinery like field refrigeration units and storage for tropical fruits; fruit, grain, seed, and vegetable cleaning and sorting and grading machinery; and global positioning system (GPS) devices. **Business Notes:** (1) For a century, Brazilians have endured the widespread (at least, in the rest of Latin America), derisory saying that "Brazil is the country of the future . . . and always will be." But there are unmistakable signs that Brazil has already begun living its heralded future: inflation is down, wages are up, politics are stable, and the country has been chosen to host the World Cup in 2014 and the Summer Olympics in 2016. The corner that finally has been turned has lifted millions from poverty and created a flourishing middle class.[55] Brazil's high, but probably underreported, average income level can mask an impressively high purchasing power for consumer products. Using data on ownership of cars and TVs, the country's middle-class market may be some 40 percent of the population.[56] (2) As a management style to resolve difficulties, Brazilians are famous for using *jeitinho* (roguery): circumventing obstacles or interpreting rules ambiguously.[57]

CHILE GDP: $245 billion. **GDP/capita:** $14,900. **GINI Index:** 52.0. **Ease of Doing Business:** 49. **Corruption Perceptions Index:** 25. **Competitiveness Ranking:** 30. **Country Credit Risk:** 2. **Economic Freedom Index:** 10. **Best Prospects:** COMPUTER SOFTWARE. Good prospects exist for data-processing programs, navigators, and e-mail systems aimed at small and medium-size companies. CONSTRUCTION. As Chile manufactures a limited range of construction equipment, it must import the majority of its needs. Even where domestic producers exist, imports, especially from the United States, are often preferred for their quality and advanced technology. The most promising opportunities for U.S. exporters are earth-moving equipment, concrete technology for high-rise building construction, and consumables that accelerate the building process. ELECTRIC POWER EQUIPMENT. Thanks to an investment surge that promises to exceed $15 billion between 2009 and 2015, prospects are bright for U.S. exporters of clean coal technologies, wind generation plants, and high-efficiency transmission equipment and supplies (aimed at transferring electric energy more than 1,000 miles). FOOD-PROCESSING AND -PACKAGING EQUIPMENT. Chile enjoys excellent natural conditions for food production. In addition to its Mediterranean climate and long north–south geography, Chile is a disease-isolated phytosanitary island (desert in the north, the Andes Mountain range to the east, the Pacific Ocean to the west and south). Another advantage is its Southern Hemisphere location, which enables it to supply the Northern

Hemisphere markets during their off-season. As these markets have exacting quality, cleanliness, and delivery standards, Chilean exporters represent an ongoing demand for product tracking, food safety, best practices programs, and certification. Moreover, to reach its goal of becoming a top-ten world food supplier, the industry must invest heavily in research and technology (R&D), technology, and reliable energy sources. Most of the products required in this industry are imported, since local production is limited. Good prospects exist for U.S.-made food-processing equipment, especially freezing and refrigeration equipment, skinning machines, meat and bone separators, filleting equipment, meat grinders, dehydrating equipment, industrial microwave ovens, waste-recycling systems, and vacuum packaging machinery. HEALTH CARE AND MEDICAL EQUIPMENT. Thanks to the Free Trade Agreement between the United States and Chile, most U.S.-made medical equipment enters Chile duty-free. The United States has long been Chile's most important supplier of medical equipment and devices, accounting for 30 percent of all imports. Many medical professionals study or receive training in the United States and prefer U.S.-made equipment. Since the Ministry of Health will be investing $600 million in hospital infrastructure between 2009 and 2014, solid opportunities exist for U.S. companies to supply the necessary equipment. MINING EQUIPMENT. Although there is almost no U.S. presence in mining exploitation, the United States is the single largest supplier of mining equipment. Chile plans to invest about $18 billion in mining equipment by 2014. POLLUTION CONTROL EQUIPMENT. Many Latin American countries follow the environmental model that Chile is using or has already tested. As a result, Chile has become a platform country for the transfer of environmental technology and expertise to other Latin American countries. The water and waste management sectors offer the best market potential for U.S. companies. SAFETY AND SECURITY EQUIPMENT. There are good opportunities for U.S. exporters of security equipment to the commercial and industrial sectors. Demand for residential security products has also increased, largely due to the increase in violent crime. Personal safety and security products, with an emphasis on access control, fire detection, home automation, CCTV, and outdoor photoelectric beam detectors for perimeter protection, are among the best prospects. TELECOMMUNICATIONS EQUIPMENT. The telecommunications equipment sector has grown at an annual rate of 14 percent over recent years. The mobile telephony market should achieve 100 percent penetration in 2010. By 2011, Internet market penetration is expected to be 40 percent. Chile's fixed-line market will decline in 2011. Because of the high rate of Internet penetration and the competitive Internet service provider market, the country has the ability to rapidly absorb new technologies, such as equipment for 3G WiMax, WiFi, and other state-of-the-art technologies. Mobile telephony and broadband services (Internet, cable, and telephone) are the areas where investment demand is highest. A third of Chile's telecommunication investments have gone into the mobile telephony market. **Business Notes:** (1) Geography molds business behavior in Chile. The Andes and the desert isolate it from the rest of the continent, giving it a Pacific-facing orientation that supports a ready acceptance of Asian products. Its extreme length separates it into different climate zones, each having a unique consumer profile and demand pattern; covering the national market requires distributors to maintain traveling sales forces. (2) Chileans are known for being socially conservative and ethical in business dealings. (3) Chile's admission in 2010 into the Organization for Economic Cooperation and Development represents a first step toward tightening the bond between the OECD founding countries and flourishing emerging economies.[58]

COLOMBIA GDP: $396 billion. **GDP/capita:** $9,200. **GINI Index:** 58.5. **Ease of Doing Business:** 37. **Corruption Perceptions Index:** 75. **Competitiveness Ranking:** 69. **Country Credit Risk:** 4. **Economic Freedom Index:** 58. **Best Prospects:** PLASTIC MATERIALS AND RESINS. By Colombian law, all products used in food processing, health, cosmetics, home cleaning, industrial products, and lubricating markets must be protected from external elements by plastic materials. Best prospects for materials include polyethylene, polypropylene, polyvinyl chloride emulsions and suspensions, and polyesters. There is no local manufacturing of plastics machinery and equipment. Consequently, Colombia imports almost all the required equipment, and the best prospects for U.S. exporters are injection molding, extruders, blow molding machinery, and vacuum molding. MINING EQUIPMENT. Colombia has 40 percent of Latin America's coal reserves and is the fifth-largest thermal coal exporter in the world. By 2019, the government plans to enhance the sector's share of the national economy by producing up to 200 million tons of coal. As a result, mining equipment sales, including boring machinery, sinking machinery, parts, dumpers, lifting machinery, bulldozers, and mechanical shovels, will grow. SAFETY AND SECURITY. From 1994 until 2009, growth in this sector has averaged 15 percent annually. The vast majority of local companies are merely security guard companies whose equipment encompasses only uniforms, firearms, and communications devices. It is important to note that during the last 10 years, security departments within companies have increased by 39 percent and vehicle armoring has increased by 446 percent, with the number of armored vehicles increasing from 2,255 in 1997 to 12,321 in 2007. U.S. exporters should consider focusing on transportation of cash and securities, security departments within companies, armoring companies, consultancy firms, and biometric equipment. The main surveillance and antitheft system used in Colombia is CCTV. However, institutions and households are quick to pick up on new trends and devices. Biometrics is increasingly being used and also silent panic-button systems. In the mid 1990s, satellite location technology (GPS) emerged as the principal tool for managing and securing vehicle fleets, and it is now increasingly being used for personal navigational purposes. U.S. suppliers of GPS technology have entered the Colombian market, with the more expensive lines of equipment targeted to business use. Also, almost all consulting opportunities are focused on this segment of the market. Because Colombian law states that foreign security companies may not participate directly in security-related enterprises, joint-venture partnerships with local companies are a requirement. AUTOMOTIVE PARTS AND ACCESSORIES. Colombia has over 3 million cars, trucks, and buses and is considered an important auto assembler in Latin America. The average age of motor vehicles in circulation is at least 15 years, which makes Colombia an excellent market for spare parts for older cars. Despite the global crisis in this sector, the outlook for the auto sector continues to be excellent, with industry observers projecting a steady growth in demand until at least 2014. AIR CARGO SERVICES. Air cargo from Colombia to the United States has recently averaged 218,000 tons per year, with flowers accounting for approximately 80 percent of this amount. The main cargo gateway is Miami, followed by Los Angeles, New York, and Atlanta. Best prospects are airport security and safety equipment, material-handling equipment, inspection equipment and security devices, forklifts, cold storage facilities for flowers and perishable products, consulting services, and leasing, insurance, and finance. FOOD AND BEVERAGE PROCESSING. Colombia is the third-largest producer of dairy products in Latin America, after Brazil and Mexico. By 2009, the growth of the dairy industry had already surpassed the projections estimated for 2011. The best dairy market potential for U.S. exporters is in production equipment, bottling services, heat exchangers, and filling, sealing, and capping. MEDICAL EQUIPMENT. Colombia has one of the most extensive insurance systems and medical financial protection in Latin America, second only to Chile. Although universal coverage was achieved in 2010, studies show that the current supply of diagnostics-imaging equipment does not meet current demand, and reputable suppliers are lacking. The Colombian government plans to double the acquisition of diagnostics-imaging equipment within 10 years. Other best prospects for U.S. medical equipment suppliers are prosthetic devices; laboratory equipment and consumables; ultrasound, mammography, and cardiovascular equipment; and dermatological and laser treatment apparel (boosted by medical tourism and expanding plastic surgery demand). POLLUTION CONTROL EQUIPMENT. Government sources estimate that the country needs to make environmental investments in the range of US$3.3 to 3.4 billion per year to maintain an adequate level of protection against all sources of pollution, and that close to 80 percent of Colombia's municipal entities dispose of untreated wastewater into rivers or lakes. Best prospects include water and wastewater treatment plants, water pollution monitoring and control equipment, pumps, valves, solid waste hauling and disposal equipment, air pollution monitoring and control equipment, and consulting services. **Business Note:** Because of Colombia's reputation, many U.S. companies were not inclined just 10 years ago to even consider doing business there. At that same time, however, many savvy global companies clearly understood the country's strategic potential and have become well established in its market. As noted in Quick Notes: Country Visit in Chapter 1, Colombia has turned an important corner and now ranks as a progressive, diversified, and stable industrializing country.

COSTA RICA GDP: $49 billion. **GDP/capita:** $11,600. **GINI Index:** 47.2. **Ease of Doing Business:** 121. **Corruption Perceptions Index:** 43. **Competitiveness Ranking:** 55. **Country Credit Risk:** 3. **Economic Freedom Index:** 54. **Best Prospects:** AUTOMOTIVE PARTS AND ACCESSORIES. Many of the cars on Costa Rican roads are imported as "used" from the United States, due to high taxes on new cars. Thus, Costa Rican importers of automotive parts and accessories do much of their buying in the United States. Quality, availability, wide selection, fast delivery, and low prices constitute strong selling propositions for U.S. exporters. The price advantage is helped by CAFTA-DR, which enables U.S. suppliers to enjoy the low costs made possible by avoiding import taxes on automotive parts of up to 29.5 percent. HOTEL AND RESTAURANT EQUIPMENT. Costa Rica has experienced a dramatic increase in the hotel and restaurant industry because of growth in tourism. The Costa

Rican industry is very receptive to purchasing from U.S. companies because of the availability of local service and parts, price, excellent quality and reputation, and fast delivery. Good sales prospects exist for virtually all categories of products, but particularly strong are cooking equipment, industrial freezers and accessories for the restaurant sector, industrial laundry equipment, bedding, amenities, and decorative designs. The growing awareness and appreciation by tourists for environmentally friendly hotels and restaurants is driving a corresponding growth in demand for environmentally friendly services. In addition to finished products, U.S. exporters should be aware of strong demand for imported parts and components by local producers of electric, commercial, and industrial stoves; ovens and ranges; fryers; freezers; and refrigerating equipment. Direct investment, joint-venture, or licensing opportunities may exist in local production of refreshment dispensers, ice cube makers, blenders, commercial microwaves, and food processors. ELECTRONIC SECURITY EQUIPMENT. As rising crime rates drive demand, Costa Rican electronic security equipment importers are very receptive to purchasing electronic security products. The United States is a preferred source because it offers a wide assortment of products, availability of local service and parts, competitive prices, excellent quality and reputation, and fast delivery. AGRICULTURE. Fresh fruit imports to Costa Rica (grapes, apples, pears, peaches and nectarines, plums, and cherries) amount to some 50 metric tons, of which the United States supplies about 28 percent. It is of interest that the United States and Chile export almost the same fresh fruit products to Costa Rica, but during different seasons. Imports from Chile take place from January to July. During the rest of the year, imports come mostly from the United States, except for those fruits available year-round. Costa Rica imports fresh fruits year-round, but about 70 percent of domestic consumption of nontropical fruits occurs during the October–December Christmas season. Both the United States (under CAFTA) and Chile (under another free-trade agreement) enjoy duty-free access to the Costa Rican market for fresh fruits. **Business Note:** Costa Rica's gracious people, pleasant climate, eco-friendly projects, widespread understanding of English, and law-abiding behavior are magnets to legions of U.S. retirees and transients. If you tarry a little in parks, hotel lobbies, or bars, you will meet too many of the latter who have a well-polished story about an investment or business deal that will pay many millions in profits tomorrow, but requires "just a few thousand" in investment today. Beware: the other hand you feel in your pocket may not be your own!

CUBA GDP: $25.5 billion. **GDP/capita:** $2,300. **GINI Index:** (no data available, but probably low). **Ease of Doing Business:** (not ranked). **Corruption Perceptions Index:** 61. **Competitiveness Ranking:** (not ranked). **Country Credit Risk:** 7. **Economic Freedom Index:** 177. **Best Prospects:** The economic embargo that the United States has maintained since 1962 against Cuba decrees that "except for publications . . . certain licensed legal and telecommunications services, and certain goods licensed for export or re-export by the U.S. Department of Commerce (such as medicine and medical devices, food, agricultural commodities, and gift parcels), no products, technology, or services may be exported from the United States to Cuba . . . absent a specific license from OFAC [Office of Foreign Asset Control]."[59] Yet, the limited trade between U.S. companies and Cuba's communist government has been quietly growing as Cuban imports of U.S. goods have increased from $7 million in 2001 to $710 million in 2008[60] (making the United States Cuba's top source of agricultural goods[61]), and scheduled cargo shipments to the island sail regularly from U.S. Gulf ports.[62] Nevertheless, selling to Cuba can be a complicated process, in which foreign companies cannot directly access Cuban wholesale and retail distribution channels,[63] and political forces on both sides of the Straits of Florida add a large measure of uncertainty to any business venture with the island.[64] But, in September 2009, the United States relaxed travel limitations, making it easier for U.S. vendors of cellular and satellite communications gear, agricultural goods, and food, medicine, and medical devices to sell their goods in Cuba.[65] Some see this policy change as an auspicious sign, foreshadowing a normalization of economic and political ties between the United States and Cuba.[66] Already, some 158 U.S. companies do business with the island, and more than 5,000 (including Sprite, Kmart, and Café Pilon), having registered their brands in Cuba, are prepared to launch sales.[67] U.S. regulations, such as those that require the Cuban government to pay for U.S. agriculture products in cash or through letters of credit drawn on third-country banks, raise the cost of U.S. goods for Cubans. If such self-imposed restrictions were lifted, U.S. exports to Cuba could almost double from their 2006 level. The largest absolute gains would be for fresh fruits and vegetables, milk powder, processed foods, poultry, beef, and pork.[68] As King Dollar works to break down ideological barriers to trade with Cuba, there should also be a surge in U.S. nonagricultural exports, including energy products, medical supplies and equipment, hotel and restaurant equipment, mining machinery, automobiles and auto parts, building materials, and construction equipment. **Business Notes:** (1) Cuba's maze of regulations often discourages smaller exporters, whose patience and pockets give them less staying power than agricultural giants like Archer Daniels Midland, Cargill, and Tyson Foods.[69] (2) Although you know how pointless and ill-advised it can be to discuss politics with Cubans (whether in Havana or Miami), and may feel that wider business opportunities with Cuba lie far in the future, do not underestimate the power of economic gravity to bring outmoded political policies back to ground-level and restore normal trade relations across the Straits of Florida.

DOMINICAN REPUBLIC GDP: $51 billion. **GDP/capita:** $5,800. **GINI Index:** 50.0. **Ease of Doing Business:** 86. **Corruption Perceptions Index:** 99. **Competitiveness Ranking:** 95. **Country Credit Risk:** 5. **Economic Freedom Index:** 86. **Best Prospects:** AUTOMOBILE PARTS. In the Dominican Republic, the demand for automotive spare parts is linked to the aging car population, the growth in total vehicle population (now numbering 1.9 million), and the deterioration of Dominican streets and roads. Because of a tendency to overextend the useful life of vehicles, due to their high cost, there is a high demand for automotive parts. Although the market for these products is expected to increase by only five percent, imports from the United States should increase by 10 percent. This rise in U.S. market share may be attributable to price advantages gained under the CAFTA-DR, which decreased the import tax levied on most U.S. automobile parts from 20 to 0 percent. For U.S. manufacturers, best sales are shock absorbers, brakes, batteries, electrical parts, and parts for Japanese-made light vehicles. Used automotive spare parts also have good prospects. AIR-CONDITIONING AND REFRIGERATION EQUIPMENT. Growth in tourist-oriented hotels, resorts, and restaurants is helping to drive demand in this sector. Because of increased demand for labor- and time-saving products and services, the number of mini-supermarkets and convenience stores (*colmados*) has increased markedly, as has their demand for refrigeration. PRINTING AND GRAPHICS INDUSTRY. The Dominican printing and graphic arts industry is the largest in the Caribbean. Among the approximately 2,500 companies operating in the local market, some 80 percent are small enterprises. As there is no local production of printing and graphic arts equipment or supplies in the Dominican Republic, the demand is entirely supplied by imports. The United States is the absolute market leader in this sector. It is likely that the demand for printing and graphics products will grow in large part because of advertising campaigns held every two years for the congressional and presidential elections, as well as the implementation of the fiscal expense vouchers (*comprobante fiscal*) by the government for all asset transfer operations. This new procedure has increased the demand for printing paper and numbering machines. COMPUTERS AND PERIPHERALS. The Dominican government organizes two trade fairs annually to promote the use of PCs in the country. One of the trade fairs is oriented to Dominican teachers and the other to government employees. The trade fairs provide to their target clients an RD$5,000 subsidy (approximately US$150) to be used toward the purchase of a complete set of equipment that includes a PC and a printer, as well as a free one-year subscription to the Internet. The offer also includes five-year financing with no down payment. RENEWABLE ENERGY. The Dominican Republic experiences frequent electrical blackouts that can last from 2 to more than 12 hours a day. Supply shortfalls in the sector are mainly attributable to customer nonpayment, theft, payment delays from the government, and system inefficiencies. Energy sector problems threaten economic competitiveness and create widespread public dissatisfaction. The government's response has included a push to increase lower cost generating capacity. Although the Dominican Republic's installed generation capacity is over 3,000 MW and the average daily peak demand is around only 1,900 MW, technical and nontechnical losses averaging 45 to 50 percent result in energy shortages. The Renewable Energy Incentives Law of 2007 provides a number of incentives to businesses developing renewable energy technologies. This law was passed as part of the government's efforts to stimulate the local production of renewable energy, as well as the production of renewable energy products. The incentives include a 100 percent exemption from taxation on imported inputs and a 10-year exemption from all taxation on profits up to, but not beyond, the year 2020. **Business Notes:** (1) In general, U.S. products are perceived to be of the best quality. (2) The Dominican government encourages "backward linkages," projects designed to increase the local content of inputs to the country's in-bond assembly sector.

ECUADOR GDP: $39 billion. **GDP/capita:** $3,100. **GINI Index:** 54.4. **Ease of Doing Business:** 138. **Corruption Perceptions Index:** 146. **Competitiveness Ranking:** 105. **Country Credit Risk:** 7. **Economic Freedom Index:** 147. **Best Prospects:** PRINTING AND GRAPHIC ARTS. Recent changes in technology are forcing printers to purchase modern equipment capable of handling today's needs. Best prospects include digital presses and spare parts for offset printing equipment. PLASTICS MACHINERY, MATERIALS, AND RESINS. Most companies in the plastics industry manufacture packaging products, including plastic bags, bottles, plastic boxes, and food-packaging products. Raw materials used for these products are in great demand, including polyethylene terephthalate, polypropylene, high-density polyethylene, and low-density polyethylene. DECONTAMINATION EQUIPMENT. Ecuador is an oil-producing country. Exploitation and production practices have resulted in major spills. Although basic remediation has been provided to momentarily solve the contamination, an in-depth solution is required. Such a situation has created the need for decontamination equipment to fully mitigate the environmental damage. The market is yet to be developed for decontamination equipment and products. In addition, the government is enforcing a law that requires all ports and harbors to have contingency equipment. The market is served mainly by imports because there is no local manufacturer. The United States is a major supplier. The best prospects in this sector are skimmers, containment booms, pads, and rolls as well as organic absorption materials. AGRICULTURE. Ecuador's major imports of agricultural goods (in metric tons) in 2008 and the amounts supplied from the United States are as follows: wheat = 441, U.S. = 148; corn = 336, U.S. = 233; soybean meal = 470, U.S. = 90; and fresh fruit (peaches, nectarines, cherries, apples, plums, oranges, and pears) = 86, U.S. = 4. Although the U.S. share of imported fresh fruits is currently not of great consequence, it is heartening to note that Ecuadorian families continue to follow the trend toward healthier food consumption habits. As dollarization has brought price stability to the economy, prices of national products have also risen, now reaching levels approximating those of imported products. Ecuador's increased consumption of higher quality imported fruit has principally benefited Chile, with a commanding 85 to 90 percent market share based on a price advantage resulting from a favorable bilateral agreement with Ecuador. U.S. participation has experienced relative growth, reflecting strong consumer acceptance and perceptions that U.S. fruit is of high quality. Under more favorable trade conditions, fresh fruit would be one of the products with the highest growth potential in Ecuador. Products subject to the safeguard measure that are imported from Ecuador's trade agreement partners, such as Chile, must also pay MFN (most favored nation) tariffs, which eliminate any tariff advantage over U.S. products while the measure is in force. **Business Notes:** (1) U.S. exporters and investors incur no currency risk or exchange costs in Ecuador's dollarized economy. (2) Ecuador's antiquated system of laws and arbitrary court rulings can frustrate the conduct of business. Its Decree 1038-A bars foreign firms "from unilaterally modifying, terminating, or failing to renew a contractual agreement with its local agent without just cause . . . what constitutes 'just cause' is up to the Ecuadorian courts."[70] (3) Avoid discussing Ecuador's president, Rafael Correa, with Ecuadorians. He is a polarizing figure, and your opinion of his socialist policies—whatever they are—could soon find their way to unfriendly ears.

EL SALVADOR GDP: $28.4 billion. **GDP/capita:** $4,400. **GINI Index:** 54.4. **Ease of Doing Business:** 84. **Corruption Perceptions Index:** 84. **Competitiveness Ranking:** 77. **Country Credit Risk:** 4. **Economic Freedom Index:** 32. **Best Prospects:** CONSUMER-READY FOODS. Consumers are increasingly purchasing in supermarkets and moving away from the traditional open-air markets or mom-and-pop stores. About 40 percent of food sales are made in supermarkets. With an increase of housewives joining the labor force and a decline in the number of domestic employees to assist in food preparation, the demand for convenience and fast foods will increase. The positive association with U.S. brands is a major advantage over non-U.S. brands. AUTOMOBILE PARTS AND SERVICE EQUIPMENT. As El Salvador imports almost all of its vehicles, and as Salvadorans are very interested in learning about business opportunities with U.S. companies, this sector is one of the most important for U.S. exporters. "Tuning," the aesthetic and mechanical modification of vehicles, has become a familiar term to most Salvadorans and is a true passion for many vehicle owners. Another trend that favors this sector is "drifting": each time automobile and motorcycle owners gather to show off their new accoutrements, new demand is created. Several local automotive magazines feature the latest vehicle updates and products. The market has evolved to a new phase that requires that the vehicle not only transports the owner but also reflects his or her personality. This sector also is an excellent business opportunity because Salvadoran vehicles deteriorate rapidly. Because of poor road maintenance, increasing traffic, disorganized public transportation, aging vehicles, and importation of used vehicles, more parts are needed. Currently, 90 percent of used vehicles purchased in El Salvador are imported from the United States and are bought directly from salvaged car auctions to be repaired locally and then sold. These cars require continuous maintenance and replacement services. Mechanic and repair shops are frequently purchasing parts and accessories from local automobile parts importers, as well as buying automotive equipment, usually imported directly for use in their shops. The demand for used imported vehicles has decreased somewhat because well-established, reliable distributors are now selling new Chinese brands of low-cost vehicles, such as Chery, Great Wall, Jinbei, Zot Ye, Dongfeng, and JMC, on credit terms. **Business Notes:** (1) Salvadorans are reputed to be the most entrepreneurial businesspersons in Central America. (2) As a dollar-based economy, El Salvador presents no currency risk or foreign exchange commission cost to U.S. exporters and investors. (3) Major Salvadoran retailers maintain their own distribution systems and buy much of their consumer goods merchandise directly from foreign producers.

GUATEMALA GDP: $48.3 billion. **GDP/capita:** $3,700. **GINI Index:** 53.7. **Ease of Doing Business:** 110. **Corruption Perceptions Index:** 84. **Competitiveness Ranking:** 80. **Country Credit Risk:** 5. **Economic Freedom Index:** 83. **Best Prospects:** AUTOMOTIVE PARTS, ACCESSORIES, AND SERVICE EQUIPMENT. This includes bumpers, spoilers, tail lights, wheels, sound systems, alarms, tires, batteries, suspension kits, mufflers, filters, chips, exhaust systems, brakes, windshield wipers, spark plugs, wheel covers, and steering wheels. CONSTRUCTION AND BUILDING PRODUCTS. These include tractors, road construction and paving equipment, supplies for heavy infrastructure and residential housing projects, structural metals, bathroom wares and accessories, ceramic floors and tiles, shingle and roof products, doors and window frames, kitchen cabinets and countertops, kitchen and laundry appliances, plastic pipes and fixtures, electrical wiring, accessories and fixtures, and dry wall. FOOD-PROCESSING AND -PACKAGING EQUIPMENT. This includes cleaning, bottling, filling, and sealing machines for bottles and cans; parts and supplies for use to cleanse, dry, and seal containers; machinery and parts for food and beverage processing; machinery for filling, closing, and labeling plastic bags, and thermo-sealing; milling, grinding, and handling machines for grains, cereals, and legumes; machinery for the baking industry and for the preparation of candy, chocolate, sugar, dairy, beer, meat, fish, fruits, and vegetables; cooking stoves, ranges, ovens, and microwave ovens; and automatic beverage vending machines with refrigerating and heating devices. FRANCHISING. Opportunities exist for fast food, dry cleaning, gyms, lawn and garden, professional painters, fast shoe repair, cosmetics, casual clothing, pest control, day-care and learning centers, computer centers, security, advertising, real estate, auto repair and shops, discount stores, fitness centers, beauty and aesthetic shops, and convenience stores and pharmacies. COMPUTERS AND PE-RIPHERALS. These include motherboards, microprocessors, hard drives, CD-R/RW units, DVD units, RAM, and notebooks. AGRICULTURAL

PRODUCTS. Opportunities exist for apples, beef, poultry, pork, grapes, rice, and processed foods. **Business Notes:** (1) Guatemala is an excellent market for U.S. products with high name recognition. (2) Franchisors should know that when Guatemalan or other Central American investors consider a franchise, they look for a franchisor that has a worldwide presence, is new to this region but is solidly accepted in other markets, is honorable and reputable, and provides extensive training and backup. These investors often do not know a great deal about the specific industry. They look for known trademarks because consumers equate recognizable U.S. trademarks with quality. Potential franchisees are often young, wealthy executives familiar with the United States and other countries, or are large corporations that already own more than one franchise in different industry sectors, such as fast food, clothing, or health.

HONDURAS GDP: $17 billion. **GDP/capita:** $2,650. **GINI Index:** 55.3. **Ease of Doing Business:** 141. **Corruption Perceptions Index:** 130. **Competitiveness Ranking:** 89. **Country Credit Risk:** 6. **Economic Freedom Index:** 99. **Best Prospects:** AUTOMOTIVE PARTS AND SERVICE EQUIPMENT. Recent tariff changes included a ban on the importation of used automobiles and passenger motor vehicles that are more than 10 and 13 years old, respectively (from prior limits of 7 and 10 years, respectively). These measures should increase the country's used vehicle population. A 2001 automobile emissions law requires all passenger motor vehicles to be fitted with an emissions control system or catalytic converter. That requirement should stimulate the demand for automotive parts and accessories through local repair shop services. FOOD-PROCESSING AND -PACKAGING MACHINERY. This market has grown steadily over the last five years. Producers are expanding capacity and improving the quality of their exports, particularly of nontraditional agricultural products such as melons, watermelons, mangoes, winter vegetables, shrimp, jalapeno peppers, fruits, and flowers. Under CAFTA-DR, producers will be exporting new products to U.S. markets, especially processed products such as tortillas, dehydrated fruits and vegetables, Individual Quick Frost fruits and vegetables, and milk cooling tanks. Opportunities also exist in the pharmaceutical industry, as local manufacturers seek new markets and innovative packaging solutions. FRANCHISING. Recent projects in tourism, commercial construction, and social infrastructure should create solid prospects for U.S. franchises. An indicator of potential opportunities in franchising is the country's emphasis on making tourism a key cluster for economic growth. Future investments in large-scale projects, such as the Tela Bay tourism complex, should spur franchising related to hotels, restaurants, and beach resorts. Other high-growth tourism locales are the Bay Islands (where an important new cruise terminal project is underway) and Copán Valley. Urban modernization and a highly consumer-oriented society have encouraged investments in large shopping malls and retail outlets throughout the country's largest cities, providing additional chances for securing strategically located franchise outlets. SECURITY EQUIPMENT. High urban crime rates have increased demand for security equipment among personal, residential, commercial, and law enforcement users. The general market for security equipment should grow 25 percent between 2010 and 2013 as many users replace guards with technology. The security equipment market is supplied entirely by imports, with the United States claiming over 80 percent. Residential demand is growing. Most new private housing projects incorporate alarms, sensors, smoke and fire detectors, water sprinklers, or automated home security systems. Demand is up for personal security, as kidnappings have increased over the past three years. Additionally, demand for electronic alarm systems, CCTV, one-way mirrors, bulletproof windows, and armored vehicles is on the rise for commercial and banking installations. Securing a local distributor in the local market is critical, particularly for installation, maintenance, and after-sale services. The National Port Authority has obtained U.S. maritime certification, which requires technology to prescreen cargo containers before they arrive at U.S. ports as well as to counter illegal activities at the ports. The equipment needed to raise port security includes X-ray inspection and security cameras. Additionally, Honduras's four international airports are undergoing a series of security improvements. **Business Note:** Honduras's small geographic size makes it practical to appoint a single representative to handle your product. Its small market size also means that a distributor will often carry a number of complementary and even competitive lines, most on a nonexclusive basis and with small inventory stocks.

MEXICO GDP: $920 billion. **GDP/capita:** $9,100. **GINI Index:** 48.1. **Ease of Doing Business:** 51. **Corruption Perceptions Index:** 89. **Competitiveness Ranking:** 60. **Country Credit Risk:** 3. **Economic Freedom Index:** 41. **Best Prospects:** MODERN AGRICULTURAL MACHINERY AND TECHNOLOGY. Agricultural machinery poses a strong potential for U.S. suppliers, as 70 percent of Mexican agriculture is still harvested through manual labor utilizing rudimentary tools. Less than 20 percent of croplands are irrigated, leaving 80 percent of crops dependent on seasonal rains or irrigation through mobile water pumps. Modern agricultural technologies have enabled some to cultivate crops to reduce time and guarantee supply for the market at stable prices. This trend has been most visible with tequila producers who have begun cultivating the agave plant in greenhouses to reduce the cultivation period by at least 40 percent. This project has been successful and is being expanded. There is virtually no national competition for agribusiness technology and equipment, as 90 percent of products are imported. Because of their reputation for quality, innovation, and efficiency, U.S. products are most often the first choice for Mexican companies. FRANCHISING. The Mexican franchise sector has maintained growth rates of between 14 and 17 percent in recent years. It generates 600,000 jobs and represents six percent of the total GDP. Services franchising, such as entertainment concepts for children, personal care services, and repair shops, has surpassed food and restaurant franchising. Mexico offers excellent business opportunities for U.S. franchise concepts because of the recognition and acceptance of U.S. brands by Mexicans. Low-cost investment franchise concepts will be in demand in the next few years, as investors will be looking for innovative concepts to open in secondary markets. RESTAURANT EQUIPMENT AND SUPPLIES. Boasting 250,000 restaurants, this sector is constantly evolving, creating a constant demand for new technology. The lack of technology, especially in cold chain equipment, and the increasing sophistication of the Mexican consumer generate business opportunities for U.S. restaurant equipment exporters. Most specialized manufacturing equipment is imported. Under NAFTA, most equipment for hotels and restaurants manufactured in the United States can be imported duty-free. TRANSPORTATION INFRASTRUCTURE EQUIPMENT AND SERVICES. The growth in Mexican foreign trade, combined with the increase in cargo arriving at Mexican ports en route to the United States and Canada, requires a transformed logistics system to improve efficiency, cost savings, and cargo security. Railroads are intensively working to offer better services to attract new clients. They are buying more locomotives, replacing equipment, and improving the nation's 68 intermodal terminals. The goal of President Calderon is to increase the volume of cargo using railroad transportation by at least 18 to 20 percent by the year 2012. Most maritime ports are expanding their container terminals' capacity or planning to build additional facilities. In particular, the Mexican Pacific coast ports of Lázaro Cárdenas, Manzanillo, Guaymas, and Topolobampo offer an alternative to U.S. importers that are using the overloaded ports of Los Angeles and Long Beach. The Mexican ports are aggressively preparing for a sizeable increase in cargo traffic to the United States. President Calderon announced a National Infrastructure Program describing the projects that will receive priority between 2007 and 2012. The plan proposes investments of US$6 billion for the construction of five new ports and 22 modernizations. It also includes projects for new cargo facilities at several airports, the construction and modernization of 10,500 miles of roadways, US$4 billion to increase rail track speeds from 15 to 25 miles per hour on key routes, the implementation of 10 new multimodal corridors, the construction of 12 new intermodal terminals, and the modernization of existing terminals. These projects have created an important demand for intermodal equipment and services. Under NAFTA, most equipment for intermodal transportation manufactured in the United States can be imported duty-free. TOURISM. After Canada, Mexico is the largest source of international travelers to the United States. Spending by Mexican travelers in the United States totals approximately $9 billion, of which some 75 percent is tied to the 1.9 million Mexicans who travel by air. There are important differences between Mexican land and air travelers. Mexican land tourists usually travel to the southern states for a short time period in order to visit relatives or friends and to shop. In contrast, air travelers are more lucrative, as they usually stay longer and buy packages that include transportation, lodging, shopping, and recreational activities. The top "first-intended" destinations, that are not strictly border visits, are California, Texas, Arizona, and Nevada. Mexicans enjoy destinations that offer shopping, gaming, entertainment, amusement parks, a cosmopolitan environment, and skiing, flocking to ski resorts in Colorado and New Mexico in the winter months. Mexicans prefer to make their travel arrangements through a travel agent, due to apprehension about providing their credit card information through the Internet. Nonetheless, U.S. wholesalers and tour operators are becoming key players in the Mexican market because they negotiate directly with U.S. tourism companies and can offer better prices and packages. **Business Notes:** (1) U.S. firms interested in capitalizing on the huge market opportunities in Mexico should keep in mind that Mexico's size and diversity are often underappreciated by U.S. exporters. It can be difficult to find a single representative to cover this vast market. (2) Although not routinely reported as a single category by the U.S. International Trade Administration, environmental technology and products are attractive sales possibilities. Especially in Mexico City, one of the planet's most polluted cities, but also in Guadalajara, Monterrey, and elsewhere, vehicle exhaust, untreated sewage, and industrial emissions reach toxic levels. Preferential financing may be available through the U.S. Ex-Im Bank, the Inter-American Development Bank, or the North American Development Bank to promote environmental technology deals by smaller U.S. firms. (3) NAFTA is making the legal aspects of doing business in Mexico increasingly similar to those in the United States. (4) Exports constitute some 25 percent of Mexico's GDP. Since about 80 percent of Mexico's exports are to the United States, in normal times Mexico's economic fate is tied closely to the U.S. economy. Thus, it would ordinarily be expected that, as economic recovery takes hold in the United States, growth in Mexico would soon follow. But these are not ordinary times, for at least two reasons: first, scarce resources are being diverted away from productive uses to combat the narco-violence that has gripped the country. Second, cash flows from Pemex, the national petroleum company that has served as the Mexican government's *piñata* since the mid 1970s, are drying up as dwindling deposits and continued mismanagement take their toll. Although these two factors may be be hurting Mexico's economy, they could represent profitable opportunities for U.S. exporters offering products that could alleviate their adverse effects.

NICARAGUA GDP: $12.3 billion. **GDP/capita:** $2,400. **GINI Index:** 52.3. **Ease of Doing Business:** 117. **Corruption Perceptions Index:** 130. **Competitiveness Ranking:** 115. **Country Credit Risk:** 7. **Economic Freedom Index:** 98. **Best Prospects:** VEHICLES, AUTO PARTS, AND EQUIPMENT. The most popular cars are small, four- or six-cylinder, U.S., Japanese, or Korean models. Many people find four-wheel-drive vehicles very useful on Nicaragua's road system. High ground clearance for speed bumps and potholes is also an asset. Good gas mileage is a priority for many consumers, and there is considerable demand for the servicing of vehicles. There is also a high demand for heavy and light U.S. trucks, buses, and sport-utility vehicles, and tires for all motor vehicles. Vehicles with standard transmissions are preferred over automatic transmissions. There is no production of automotive parts and accessories for local consumption. Thus, good sales opportunities exist for virtually all categories of automotive products. PLASTICS. There are opportunities for plastic containers, plastic screens, plastic flower pots, plastic seals, plastic toys, and plastic key chains. COMPUTER EQUIPMENT. Sales of finished computers are growing, but sales of parts and accessories are growing at an even faster pace. Sales over the Internet of competitively priced information technology are likely to expand in the near future, particularly for the personal user segment, provided that reliable local after-sales dealer support is available for consumers. Demand for specialized hardware and accessories is gradually increasing in the professional services sector. The use of wireless computer networks is also increasing. TELECOMMUNICATIONS EQUIPMENT. The most promising subsectors in the telecommunications market are digital, cellular, and wireless telephone systems; data transmission equipment; and fiber-optic networks. FOOD-PROCESSING AND REFRIGERATION EQUIPMENT. Refrigeration equipment, such as refrigerated trucks, containers, and cold storage rooms, and laboratory equipment for testing and product certification are in high demand. Demand is highest for used equipment in good condition. AGRICULTURAL GOODS. Wheat, yellow corn, and rice are in demand. **Business Note:** The enforcement of contracts is uneven and somewhat cumbersome, as is the enforcement of judicial rulings. The rules of the game can be changed by sudden government proclamations or political factors, significantly disrupting business planning. Despite the anticorruption efforts, bribery and requests for bribes remain prevalent.

PANAMA GDP: $17 billion. **GDP/capita:** $5,500. **GINI Index:** 54.9. **Ease of Doing Business:** 77. **Corruption Perceptions Index:** 84. **Competitiveness Ranking:** 59. **Country Credit Risk:** 3. **Economic Freedom Index:** 60. **Best Prospects:** WAREHOUSING AND DISTRIBUTION. The Colon Free Zone (CFZ) is second only to Hong Kong. Within the CFZ, goods may be imported, stored, modified, repacked, and re-exported without being subject to any customs regulations. The huge assortment of Asian merchandise stored in CFZ warehouses attracts wholesalers from all of Latin America. And Panama's state-of-the-art logistics enables it to trans-ship products to its home market reliably and inexpensively, thus avoiding costly buying trips to Asia. Companies operating from the CFZ enjoy numerous tax breaks. Best prospects for CFZ operations are clothing, consumer electronics, shoes, pharmaceutical and medical products, cosmetics and perfumes, liquor and cigarettes, watches, and jewelry. The CFZ offers excellent opportunities for companies trying to get exposure to the Latin American market from a single location. BUILDING PRODUCTS. Whereas much of the construction in recent years was concentrated on middle- to high-income apartments and commercial buildings, new construction is expected to focus on low-cost urban housing and infrastructure, especially the expansion of the Panama Canal locks that began in 2010. Much of the growth in the construction sector has been fed by retiring U.S. baby boomers. U.S. building products enjoy a market share of over 60 percent and are well received because of their perceived quality and competitive price. Demand is especially strong for gypsum board, lighting, and roofing and flooring products. TRAVEL AND TOURISM. The United States is by far the preferred travel destination of Panamanians. There are growing niche markets for travel to the United States. One is for medical care, with Houston as a preferred destination. Other emerging segments are travel for religious reasons, for *quinceañeras* (girls who are celebrated by their families during the year of their fifteenth birthday) on cruises, and for business meetings and conventions. Popular products are low-cost packages with airfare, car, and hotel included, especially if they coincide with Panama's peak travel periods. CONSTRUCTION EQUIPMENT. The construction sector in Panama continues to lead growth in the national economy. The US$5.25 billion expansion of the Panama Canal, the completion of Panama's bay-cleaning project, and the construction of a number of tourism and housing projects will keep the demand strong for heavy equipment and construction machinery for at least the next few years. U.S. products enjoy a market share of over 50 percent, and they are well received because of their perceived quality and competitive price. Best prospects are earth-moving machinery, hydraulic excavators, off-road trucks, wheel loaders, and cranes. AIR-CONDITIONING AND REFRIGERATION EQUIPMENT. Panama's climatic conditions make cooling equipment a good prospect. Increased activity in the fisheries export sector and continued growth in the consumption of perishable goods, especially frozen items, should represent excellent market opportunities for U.S. exporters. Additionally, Panama's two major breweries, three large dairy plants, and three large soft-drink bottlers are important users of refrigeration equipment. Demand has also been stimulated by new supermarkets and the continuous growth of the construction sector, especially residential high-rise buildings and suburban housing. U.S. products are well liked, considered to be of excellent quality, and are competitively priced. Energy efficiency has become a key factor when choosing refrigeration and air-conditioning equipment. Best prospects are commercial and household air-conditioning and industrial refrigeration. **Business Notes:** (1) Consumer attitudes and many brand preferences are similar to those in the United States. U.S. television, radio programs, and magazines are all available and popular in Panama. Panamanians frequently travel to U.S. destinations for vacation, medical care, study, and business. Their buying patterns and tastes are similar to those found in the United States, so U.S. goods and services are well accepted and highly competitive in most product sectors. (2) The movers and shakers of Panama are the *rabiblancos* (white-tails), who dominate business and politics as a white elite.

PARAGUAY **GDP:** $26.2 billion. **GDP/capita:** $4,500. **GINI Index:** 53.2. **Ease of Doing Business:** 124. **Corruption Perceptions Index:** 154. **Competitiveness Ranking:** 124. **Country Credit Risk:** 5. **Economic Freedom Index:** 81. **Best Prospects:** Because of widespread underinvoicing and contraband, Paraguayan government trade records often economize on factual accuracy in recording imports.[71] COMPUTERS AND ACCESSORIES. While imports of computers and accessories are shifting toward inexpensive items from Asia (including counterfeit goods), buyers from Latin America coming to Paraguay are still drawn to shop for quality goods imported from the United States at lower prices than in their home countries. Computers and computer accessories are the major exports from the United States to Paraguay. PARAGUAY-PARANÁ WATERWAY SYSTEM OR HIDROVÍA. The Hidrovía Paraguay-Paraná is a 2,045-mile waterway system comprising the Paraguay and Paraná rivers. The governments of Argentina, Brazil, Bolivia, Paraguay, and Uruguay are working jointly to make the waterway into a major route to transport goods from the continent's interior to the Atlantic Ocean and vice-versa through the Río de la Plata. The present movement of goods on the Hidrovía comprises cereals, oilseeds, oils, metallic ores, steel, and petroleum. In the next 15 years, the 1.2 million square miles of the Hidrovía regional area will likely hold 40 million people. The Hidrovía river system carries over 51 million tons of produce, which, by year 2025, will reach an estimated 146 million tons, representing a business volume of US$46 billion. The ongoing Hidrovía project includes subprojects, such as deepening riverbeds, constructing ports, improving navigability and safety, and increasing capacity in terms of vessels, maintenance, and services. ATLANTIC-PACIFIC HIGHWAY PROJECT (CORREDOR BIOCEÁNICO) The Paraguayan government is working on projects to improve the roads throughout the country, especially those in the western region of Chaco. Development banks are financing over US$1.55 billion in new road works in the period 2008–2013. The project's aim is to increase the volume of goods transported by road and rail between the Atlantic and Pacific Ocean coasts. Best sales prospects include road and possibly rail construction and engineering services. MAQUILA ASSEMBLY AND DISTRIBUTION OPERATIONS. Paraguay has interesting possibilities for assembly and distribution operations, with attractive investment incentives (tax breaks, duty-free import of capital goods, unlimited repatriation of capital) and the lowest factor costs (especially energy) in the region. The government has been encouraging the development of this sector, which it sees as an alternative to the unregulated contraband economy in Paraguay's border region with Brazil and Argentina, and it has experienced rapid growth. HYDROPOWER. Paraguay is the top exporter of electric power in the world, with Argentina and Brazil receiving the majority of the power. Hydropower constitutes nearly 100 percent of electricity in Paraguay. Having the cheapest electric power in MERCOSUR, Paraguay offers good prospects for electricity-intensive industries. Opportunities for U.S. exporters exist in various upcoming projects, such as the completion of the Ana-Cua branch of the Yacyretá dam and the expansion of the power transmission grids. Paraguay also has unexplored potential for microhydro plants. AGRICULTURE. Paraguay has the potential to become an important world player in biofuels, and legislation is in place to support that potential. Focus is currently on sugar-based ethanol production for domestic and export markets, and on biodiesel production for local consumption. Seven biodiesel plants began operating in 2009, producing some 8 million gallons. There are also 10 ethanol plants, which produced about 32 million gallons in 2009. Plant construction and expansion projects present sales opportunities for U.S. suppliers of building and construction materials and biofuels-processing machinery. Paraguay is also the second-largest world producer of stevia after China. The food and beverage industry represents the largest demand for stevia, where it is chiefly employed as a sweetener and a flavoring agent. The health market is second in importance. In third place are byproducts made from the plant remains, such as teas and other extractive uses. Demand for imported machinery to process stevia should increase because of the FDA's approval of that product in 2008 and local companies' competitiveness in world markets. **Business Notes:** (1) A significant portion of the economy involves black and gray market activities, such as smuggling both legitimate and illicit goods to and from neighboring countries. Such transactions can complicate price schedules, commission plans, and distribution control. (2) Intellectual property rights are notoriously unprotected.

PERU GDP: $132 billion. **GDP/capita:** $4,600. **GINI Index:** 49.6. **Ease of Doing Business:** 56. **Corruption Perceptions Index:** 75. **Competitiveness Ranking:** 78. **Country Credit Risk:** 3. **Economic Freedom Index:** 45. **Best Prospects:** MINING EQUIPMENT. A number of top international firms operate major mining activities throughout Peru's Andean region. Both international and local firms hold plans to expand operations in Peru, making investments as high as $20 billion. Promising products for U.S. exporters include large dumpers for off-highway use; front-end shovel loaders; air or vacuum pumps; air and other gas compressors and fans; ventilating or recycling hoods; mechanical shovels, excavators, and shovel loaders; self-propelled track-laying bulldozers and angle dozers; and parts of sorting, screening, separating, or washing machines. PLASTIC MATERIALS. The plastic industry, almost 99 percent dependent on imports, is expected to continue to grow. Items with the highest current demand are PET containers and PVC pipes. The sector is quite competitive and price sensitive, but the quality, reliability, and punctuality of U.S. suppliers have allowed them to capture a leading share of the market. Some prominent market opportunities in this sector include flexible containers in different shapes to be used for agribusiness exports; rigid containers with humidity and gas barriers; sealed containers with plastic film or aluminum foil; and manufacture of "doy pack" containers. CONSTRUCTION EQUIPMENT. Most machinery used in the construction sector is imported. Consequently, all heavy machinery, including spare parts, is a best prospect. INDUSTRIAL CHEMICALS. Industrial chemical production has expanded in recent years, but local production has been unable to keep pace with the increasing demand. This industry supplies some of Peru's largest sectors, including mining, agribusiness, and fishing. TELECOMMUNICATIONS EQUIPMENT. Peru's telecommunications sector continues to expand rapidly, but competition for some US$2.2 billion of imports is strong. China, Mexico, and Brazil each control more than the U.S. share of nine percent. The sectors that have been most active in recent years include Internet, cable TV, and mobile telephony. While fixed telephony went from 6.1 lines per 100 inhabitants in 1998 to 9.8 by the end of 2008, mobile services rose from 2.9 lines per 100 inhabitants to 68.4 in the same period. In 2008, the average waiting time to receive a new telephone connection was 7.9 days, whereas in 1998, it was 3 months. Mobile service coverage reached 76 percent of Peru's national territory in 2008, a significant achievement given the inaccessibility of many of Peru's jungle and mountain regions. POLLUTION CONTROL EQUIPMENT. Government project plans call for an investment of US$2.7 billion through 2015 in water resources, water treatment, and wastewater treatment. Equipment in high demand includes soil and water remediation and monitoring equipment, industrial filters, garbage trucks, recyclers, water and sewerage monitoring systems, water filters, and wastewater treatment. AIR-CONDITIONING AND REFRIGERATION EQUIPMENT. Expectations that Peru's agricultural and fisheries sectors will continue to generate strong growth suggest promising markets for U.S. suppliers. COMPUTERS. Computer ownership in Peru remains low but is expanding quickly. In 2000, 4.4 percent of Peruvian households had computers. By the end of 2008, this proportion had increased to 15.5 percent. The government's "One Laptop per Child" program has bolstered demand for computer hardware, having delivered computers to 38,238 students and 1,765 teachers just in 2008. This initiative creates suitable learning environments for students by providing access to information technology, thus increasing the number of lecture hours, developing lasting training, and fostering creative competition. SECURITY EQUIPMENT. Demand for residential, industrial, and office security equipment remains strong in Peru, with 66 percent of Lima's population believing that the city's largest problems are delinquency, lack of security, gangs, and robberies. Private and public entities invest in security equipment designed to prevent break-ins by intruders and to make security guards more effective. Such equipment includes alarms, lights, mesh netting, and barbed wire. These products are also used by the majority of citizens for their homes. **Business Note:** U.S. products are well regarded in Peru. Nonetheless (and similar to neighboring Chile in this respect), its orientation to the Pacific makes competition from Asia a significant factor.

PUERTO RICO GDP: $48 billion. **GDP/capita:** $12,000. **GINI Index:** (no data available). **Ease of Doing Business:** 35. **Corruption Perceptions Index:** 35. **Competitiveness Ranking:** 42. **Country Credit Risk:** 0. **Economic Freedom Index:** (not ranked, likely similar to U.S.—no. 8). **Best Prospects:** Whereas the 1980s were a "Lost Decade" for most of the rest of Latin America, Puerto Rico's lost decade was the first decade of the 21st century, a period in which its economy contracted at an annual average rate of 2.8 percent. To restore economic growth and employment, Puerto Rico will undertake infrastructure and regional development projects, investing $4.537 billion by 2013 and $6.214 billion by 2017.[72] Puerto Rico annually imports approximately $30 billion, led by chemicals, machinery and equipment, clothing, food, fish, and petroleum products. **Business Note:** The hurricane season peaks between July and September. Check weather forecasts prior to traveling. Aside from the personal discomfort they occasion, hurricanes can seriously disrupt business appointments.

URUGUAY GDP: $32 billion. **GDP/capita:** $10,000. **GINI Index:** 46.2. **Ease of Doing Business:** 114. **Corruption Perceptions Index:** 25. **Competitiveness Ranking:** 65. **Country Credit Risk:** 4. **Economic Freedom**

Index: 33. **Best Prospects:** RENEWABLE ENERGY EQUIPMENT. Uruguay has no known oil resources and must import 100 percent of its fuel needs. Although the majority of the energy in Uruguay is hydroelectric, recurring droughts have caused major energy crises. All of the projects in the pipeline, both public and private, predict a high growth rate with a clear need for imports. Potential buyers are turning to U.S. sources because the Brazilian industry is focused only on sugarcane and the equipment available is too large for the Uruguayan market. Government policies will drive further equipment sales to meet requirements for five percent biodiesel and five percent bioethanol motor fuel blends by 2012 and 2014, respectively. The government is focused on promoting the installation of small power plants (wind, hydroelectric, and biomass) throughout the country. CONSTRUCTION EQUIPMENT. Construction is one of Uruguay's most promising sectors today. The capital city of Montevideo and the resort of Punta del Este are the most important areas for construction. Uruguay is an attractive market for U.S. construction machinery companies wanting to explore new opportunities in South America. Investment in heavy construction machinery is likely to continue over the next few years to support a rapid growth in infrastructure construction. The highest demand is likely to be for mobile cranes, public works equipment, off-highway dumpers, bulldozers, graders and levelers, forklifts, tractors, mechanical shovels, excavators, and road rollers. Used construction machinery has good market opportunities in Uruguay because it competes in price with new equipment from Japan and China. U.S. suppliers offering flexible, innovative, and competitive credit terms fare best in achieving export sales to Uruguay. **Business Note:** Because of its distance from the United States and its small population, Uruguay has been overlooked by many U.S. companies. U.S. exporters that try to develop a position in the Uruguayan market may find that their primary competition is from MERCOSUR (especially Brazilian and Argentine) and, more recently, Asian (especially Chinese) suppliers.

VENEZUELA GDP: $151 billion. **GDP/capita:** $6,200. **GINI Index:** 43.4. **Ease of Doing Business:** 177. **Corruption Perceptions Index:** 162. **Competitiveness Ranking:** 113. **Country Credit Risk:** 7. **Economic Freedom Index:** 174. **Best Prospects:** MEDICAL EQUIPMENT. U.S. imports have more than 50 percent of the medical equipment market because of geographic proximity, quality, pricing, and technical support. Apart from some disposable items and hospital linen, there is no manufacturing of medical equipment in Venezuela. The bulk of medical equipment purchases remain in the private sector. Because of a fear of nationalization, many clinics (as hospitals are referred to) postponed or cancelled major purchases in the recent past. However, the lack of recent government threats as well as the failure of some government proposals may mean that private buyers are reconsidering their investment plans in new technology, diagnostic equipment, and treatment equipment. Private-sector activity is supported by the medical insurance and social security coverage normally offered as part of labor benefits by most companies and by the government. It is estimated that the previous 15 to 20 percent of the medical insured population has increased to 50 percent, adding to the big deficit of hospital beds. The situation is so dramatic that Venezuela suffers a considerable shortage of available hospital capacity. It is estimated that there are 1.35 hospital beds per 1,000 inhabitants, whereas the minimum recommended by the World Health Organization is 3 to 4 hospital beds. The situation is such that in some clinics patients have to wait two or three days to get a bed. Given the lack of resources in the public sector and the rise of private health insurance, major private hospitals (clinics) are undertaking ambitious expansion programs and have already initiated infrastructure works to offer nearly 500 additional hospital beds. Health care goods and services enjoy priority for foreign exchange under the government's tightly controlled currency control regime, so the health care sector represents a solid opportunity for American exporters. SECURITY AND SAFETY EQUIPMENT. Distribution experts estimate the size of the Venezuelan market for industrial safety equipment to be about US$100 million per year. This sector has been growing considerably in recent years, achieving high levels of professionalism and applying the newest technologies. There are two main reasons for this growth. (1) A recent labor law has forced local companies to acquire new safety and security equipment and supplies to protect their workers, thus creating a big demand for fire alarm and protection systems, evacuation systems, and personnel safety accessories such as boots, gloves, and hard hats. (2) Crime rates have increased with the proliferation of malls, bank branches, office buildings, parking lots, and other facilities that serve large numbers of people. This growth has driven demand for access control equipment, CCTV, metal detectors for banks, and drug and explosives detection equipment. U.S. companies have proved particularly competitive in the supply of equipment for intelligent fire detection and alarm systems, fire pumps, valves and accessories, and personal safety items. Local production of security and safety equipment and systems is limited. Local companies are competitive as suppliers of safety accessories like boots, gloves, hard hats, and first aid kits, and in providing services to assemble intelligent systems. Virtually all other equipment for industrial security and safety is imported. Many local firms have associations with U.S. companies as a way both to broaden their product offerings and to acquire technology. Venezuela has traditionally been a captive market for the United States, although European and Taiwanese competition is increasing. The United States has the largest share of the import market because of its multiple advantages. U.S. equipment suppliers normally work closely with the local and foreign engineering, petroleum, and manufacturing companies involved in design and engineering to ensure that their equipment will be specified and considered. In addition, there are high recognition of U.S. brand names, lower transportation costs due to geographic proximity, and a strong local representation by U.S. agents and dealers. **Business Notes:** (1) As sales support, service, and spare parts are essential to success in equipment sales, it is important to use a representative that can provide them. (2) Franchisors will find that Venezuelans are used to U.S. services and that this sector has been especially strong, even during the recent economic crises. (3) In early 2010, there was speculation that the devaluation of the Bolívar and continued nationalization of private enterprise by the Chávez regime would lead to shortages and social unrest.[73] (4) The U.S. Department of Commerce advises that:

> In light of current conditions, particularly President Chavez's nationalizations of many sectors of the Venezuelan economy, antimarket orientation, and virulent anti-U.S. rhetoric, U.S. exporters to and investors in Venezuela are well-advised to perform their risk-return calculations carefully, mindful of the uncertainties, but aware of the opportunities in the Venezuelan market.[74]

Notes

1. "GDP Shares by Country and Region," International Macroeconomic Data Set, U.S. Department of Agriculture, November 2009, 4.

2. "Global Economic Prospects 2010," World Bank, December 10, 2009, http://web.worldbank.org/external/default/main?theSitePK=612501&pagePK=2904583&contentMDK=20665990&menuPK=612532&piPK=2904598 (accessed January 21, 2010).

3. Author's calculation, based on World Bank data, 2010.

4. Eduardo Lora, "Should Latin America Fear China?" Inter-American Development Bank, May 2005, 28.

5. Neil Shister, "Near-sourcing: The Way Forward," *World Trade*, April 2009, 16–20.

6. Guillaume Corpart Muller and Enrique Orellana, "A Mexican Industry Whose Time Has Come," *Kroll Tendencias*, 2009, http://mx.mc383./mc/welcome?.gx=1&.tm=1256780512&.rand (accessed February 14, 2010).

7. Jeremy N. Smith, "What Comes after Just-in-Time?" *World Trade*, April 2009, 21–26.

8. "Latin America More Competitive for Outsourcing," *World Trade*, January 2009, 17.

9. "América Latina Avanza Hacia la Recuperación," *América Economía*, September 29, 2009, http://www.americaeconomia.com/NotePrint.aspx?Note=342514 (accessed February 14, 2010).

10. Gregory Zuckerman, "Emerging Stock Markets Are Looking Better," *Wall Street Journal*, September 26, 2009, B1.

11. "Latin America: Oil for China," *Latin Business Chronicle*, October 14, 2009, http://www.latin businesschronicle.co/app/article.aspx?id=3753 (accessed February 14, 2010).

12. John Lyons, "Brazil Turns to China to Help Finance Oil Projects," *Wall Street Journal*, May 18, 2009, A6.

13. "China Ofrece Nuevos Créditos a Cuba," *América Economía*, September 2, 2009, http://www. americaeconomia.com/NotePrint.aspx?Note=330775 (accessed February 14, 2010).

14. Barack Obama, "State of the Union Address," Washington, DC, January 27, 2010.

15. "America Leaves Itself Behind," *Wall Street Journal*, November 11, 2009, A20.

16. Ibid.

17. "One Obama Cheer on Trade," *Wall Street Journal*, February 1, 2010, A20.

18. "Free Trade Agreements," U.S. International Trade Administration, c. 2008, http://www.trade.gov/fta/index.asp (accessed February 15, 2010).

19. Robert Zoellick, "Unleashing the Trade Winds," *The Economist*, December 10, 2002, 67.

20. "Weekly Trade Spotlight: U.S.-Mexico Trade Relations," Office of the U.S. Trade Representative, February 9, 2010, http://www.ustr.gov/about-us/press-office/blog/2010/february/weekly-trade-spotlight-us-mexico-trade-relations (accessed February 15, 2010).

21. Reprinted from "NAFTA Facts," Office of the U.S. Trade Representative, March 2008, http://www.ustr.gov/sites/default/files/uploads/factsheets/2008/asset_upload_file71_14540.pdf (accessed February 15, 2010).

22. Ibid.

23. Ibid.

24. Ibid.

25. Ibid.

26. "Mexican Corn: The Effects of NAFTA," World Bank Group, September 24, 2004, http://siteresources.worldbank.org/INTRANETTRADE/Resources/Pubs/TradeNote18.pdf (accessed February 16, 2010).

27. "MERCOSUR Eludes Chávez as Paraguay Demurs," *UPI*, January 7, 2010.

28. Joanna Klonsky and Stephanie Hanson, "MERCOSUR: South America's Fractious Trade Bloc," Council on Foreign Relations, August 20, 2009, http://www.cfr.org/publication/12762/mercosur.html (accessed February 16, 2010).

29. "Dominican Republic—Central America FTA," U.S. International Trade Administration, May 31, 2009, http://www.ustr.gov/trade-agreements/free-trade-agreements/cafta-dr-dominican-republic-central-america-fta (accessed February 15, 2010).

30. "U.S.-CAFTA-DR Free Trade Agreement: Benefits to Small and Medium-Sized Exporters (SMEs)," International Trade Administration, c. 2007, http://www.export.gov/static/cafta_sme_Latest_eg_main_017560.pdf (accessed February 16, 2010).

31. Hans Bader, "U.S. Stimulus: Patronage and Waste," *Financial Post*, May 15, 2009, http://network.nationalpost.com/np/blogs/fpcomment/archive/2009/05/15/u-s-stimulus-patronage-and-waste.aspx (accessed February 17, 2010).

32. Michael Reid, *Forgotten Continent* (New Haven: Yale University Press, 2007), 120–121.

33. Solange Montero, "Subconectados," *América Economía*, January 30, 2009, http://www.americaeconomia.com/revista/NotePrint.aspx?Note=214107 (accessed June 12, 2009).

34. Dante Di Gregorio, Martina Musteen, and Douglas E. Thomas, "Offshore Outsourcing as a Source of International Competitiveness for SMEs," *Journal of International Business Studies* 40 (2009): 969–988.

35. "Sunset over the River Plate," *The Economist*, June 6, 1998.

36. Marianne Fay and Mary Morrison, "Infrastructure in Latin America and the Caribbean," World Bank, August 31, 2005, http://siteresources.worldbank.org/INTLAC/Resources/LAC_Infrastructure_complete.pdf (accessed August 11, 2010).

37. *Latin American Logistics,* c. 2006, http://www.latinamericanlogistics.org/articles/the-state-of-latin-american-infrastructure-and-logistics.htm (accessed February 20, 2010).

38. Ibid.

39. Ibid.

40. "Higher Education Finance and Cost-sharing in Brazil," c. 2005, Working Paper, University of Buffalo, gse.buffalo.edu/org/inthigheredfinance/files/Country/Brazil (accessed February 20, 2010).

41. Fay and Morrison, "Infrastructure."

42. "KPMG MD Moves to Brazil," *Euromoney Institutional Investor Online Network*, August 20, 2009, http://www.silobreaker.com/kpmg-md-moves-to-brazil-5_2262541348651401253 (accessed August 20, 2009).

43. "Infraestructura en América Latina," *América Economía*, January 7, 2010 (author's translation), http://www.americaeconomia.com/notas/infraestructura-en-america-latina-paradoja-de-largo-plazo (accessed January 15, 2010).

44. "Country Profiles," in *CIA World Factbook 2010* (Washington, DC: Central Intelligence Agency, 2010).

45. *The World Factbook 2009.* Washington, DC: Central Intelligence Agency, 2009. https://www.cia.gov/library/publications/the-world-factbook/index.html (accessed August 11, 2010).

46. "World Development Indicators," Washington, DC: World Bank, 2007, http://data.worldbank.org/indicator (accessed August 11, 2010).

47. "Doing Business 2010," World Bank, November 2010, http://www.doing business.org/ (accessed August 11, 2010).

48. "Corruption Perceptions Index 2009," Transparency International, 2009, http://www.transparency.org/policy_research/surveys_indices/cpi/2009/cpi_2009_table (accessed January 6, 2010).

49. *The Global Competitiveness Rankings: 2009–2010 Report,* World Economic Forum, September 8, 2009, http://www.weforum.org/pdf/GCR09/GCR20092010 fullrankings.pdf (accessed January 15, 2010).

50. "Country Risk Classifications of the Participants to the Arrangement on Officially Supported Export Credits," Organization for Economic Cooperation and Development, October 23, 2009, http://www.oecd.org/dataoecd/47/29/3782900.pdf (accessed January 16, 2010).

51. "The 2010 Index of Economic Freedom," The Heritage Foundation, 2010, http://www.heritage.org/index/Ranking.aspx (accessed January 21, 2010).

52. *Country Commercial Guides,* various countries, U.S. Department of Commerce, 2009 and 2010.

53. Author's experience and other sources (as noted).

54. Terri Morrison and Wayne A. Conway, *The International Traveler's Guide to Doing Business in Latin America* (New York: Macmillan, 1997).

55. Antonio Regalado, "Don't Rock the Boat," *Wall Street Journal,*" March 29, 2010, R1, R3.

56. Doreen Hemlock, "Getting to Know Brazil," *Sun-Sentinel,* July 17, 2000.

57. Alfredo Behrens, *Culture and Management in the Americas* (Stanford, CA: Stanford University Press, 2009), 246, 251, 259.

58. Yolanda Morales (quoting remarks made by José Ángel Gurría, secretary general of the OECD), "OCDE Abre Puertas a Países Emergentes Pujantes Como Chile," *El Economista* (Mexico City), January 12, 2010, 8.

59. "An Overview of the Cuban Assets Control Regulations," Office of Foreign Assets Control, U.S. Department of Treasury, September 3, 2009, 12–13.

60. "2009–2010 U.S. Export Statistics for Cuba," U.S.-Cuba Trade and Economic Council, Inc., May 2009, http://www.cubatrade.org/ (accessed February 2, 2010).

61. Martha Brannigan, "From Truffles to Furs, U.S. Ships More Food to Cuba," *Miami Herald,* September 7, 2009, http:/www.miamiherald.com/news/top-stories/v-print/story1220161.html (accessed September 9, 2009).

62. Jenalia Moreno, "Port of Houston Begins Weekly Cargo Shipments to Cuba," *Havana Journal,* January 16, 2010, http://havanajournal.com/business/print/8893/ (accessed February 2, 2010).

63. "Selling and Buying in Cuba," Federation of International Trade Associations, 2009, http://www.fita.org/countries/cuba.html (accessed February 2, 2010).

64. "Cuba Risk Assessment," *Global Edge,* Michigan State University, 2009, http://globaledge.msu.edu/countries/cuba/risk/ (accessed February 2, 2010).

65. Alan M. Field, "U.S. Amends Cuba Trade Regulations," *Washington Post,* September 8, 2009, http://www.joc.com/node/413275 (accessed February 2, 2010).

66. Nick Miroff, "Cuba's Undersea Oil Could Help Thaw Trade with U.S." *Washington Post,* May 16, 2009, http://www.washingtonpost.com/wp-dyn/content/article/2009/05/15/AR2009051503416.html (accessed February 2, 2010).

67. Miami Herald staff, "How to do Business in Cuba," *Havana Journal,* September 14, 2009, http://havanajournal.com/business/entry/how-to-do-business-in-cuba/ (accessed February 2, 2010).

68. "U.S. Agricultural Sales to Cuba: Certain Economic Effects of Agricultural Restrictions," U.S. International Trade Commission, July 19, 2007, http://www.usitc.gov/press_room/news release/2007/er0719ee1.htm (accessed February 3, 2010).

69. Brannigan, "From Truffles to Furs."

70. Morrison and Conway, *International Traveler's Guide,* 159.

71. The author recalls a 1983 meeting with a high-level Paraguayan government official, in which the official unintentionally revealed that the country's domestic production and recorded imports of soybeans were about one-fourth of the official amount exported from Paraguay to other countries.

72. "Strategic Model for a New Economy," Government of Puerto Rico, September 2009, http://www.bgfpr.com/investors_resources/documents/2009-10-09-MENE-IngEXECSUMMARY-REVISED-.pdf (accessed February 2, 2010).

73. Enrique Suarez Campos, "Socialismo del siglo XXI," *El Economista* (Mexico City), January 12, 2010, 8.

74. "Doing Business in Venezuela: 2010," *Country Commercial Guide*, U.S. Department of Commerce, 2010, http://www.buyusa.gov/venezuela/en/ccg.html (accessed August 11, 2010).

Part II

WHY AND HOW LATIN AMERICANS DO BUSINESS DIFFERENTLY

In business, as in war, understanding the terms of engagement is the first step toward winning the battle. But make no mistake about it: business in Latin America is conducted under different terms of engagement than you will customarily encounter in the United States. Understanding those different terms of engagement, and how they can affect you, is the pivotal factor controlling the success or failure of your Latin American business venture.

Differences between the Latin American and the U.S. approaches to doing business flow from differences in regional mindsets. Those mindset differences, in turn, can be most easily understood and used to advantage if they are considered as springing from two separate but continuously interacting forces: history and culture. Quality studies conclude that history and culture are the fundamental determinants of national well-being and the conduct of business.[1,2] Even though the line dividing those intertwining forces is seldom sharply defined, history and culture represent conceptually legitimate, as well as comfortably familiar, categories into which a large and complex body of information may be conveniently partitioned for easy understanding.

Thus, this part of the book is organized around the roles that history (Chapter 3) and culture (Chapter 4) play in shaping the terms of business engagement in Latin America. The aim, in these two chapters, is to provide a working understanding of the differences in mindset that are at the front lines of business engagement between U.S. and Latin American executives. Toward that end, Chapters 3 and 4 draw judiciously from a massive body of literature on Latin American history and culture, selecting and describing those forces that make sense from a business perspective. Thus, the intent here is not to extract a full core sample of the geology that underlies the terrain on which business forces engage one another in the Americas, but to describe the overall lay of the land. Only by understanding how your Latin American business associates think, live, and do business will you be able to engage them under terms most advantageous to you.

Notes

1. Lawrence E. Harrison, *Who Prospers? How Cultural Values Shape Economic and Political Success* (New York: Basic Books, 1992).

2. David S. Landes, *The Wealth and Poverty of Nations: Why Some Are So Rich and Some So Poor* (New York: Norton, 1998).

Chapter 3 ———————————————

The Historic Legacy

The further backward you look, the further forward you can see.
—Winston Churchill

It is not by chance that reforms are so difficult.
—Fernando Henrique Cardoso, former president of Brazil

What should we call that historic footfall on a Bahamian beach that was destined to shake the entire earth? That 1492 event could scarcely qualify as a discovery to the tens of millions of native souls who already inhabited the Western Hemisphere. Indeed, their Asian ancestors may have preceded by 30,000 years[1] the appearance of any European in what came to be called the New World. Nor does the label "encounter" capture the scope and power of the epochal reverberations set in motion by that first European arrival.

CIVILIZATIONS IN COLLISION

No single word comes close to describing how that first Spanish footfall hit our planet with the force of an asteroid. Trade patterns were shifted forever, while ages-old social and economic systems were turned upside-down and inside-out throughout the Old and the New Worlds. The impact of the Europeans' arrival was as jolting, massive, and unceasing as have been the tectonic collisions that continue to thrust the snow-capped Andes high above the steamy Amazon basin.

As with those seismic collisions, the early and ongoing effects of Iberian peoples colliding with the indigenous societies of the Americas resembled a forcible rape more than a consensual union. The sheer violence of that savagely invasive encounter gave rise to a complex cultural topography that is still evolving. The historical perspective taken here describes how cultural collisions and blending in the New World caused the business environments of the two Americas to evolve in markedly divergent directions.

Among the countless reasons given to explain the different business environments, none is more compelling than the ways in which differences in market systems shape differences in business mindsets. The mindset determined by market structure pervades the spectrum of business decision making, spanning issues as elemental as competitive positioning, corruption, distribution strategy, customer service, target-market selection, quality management, organizational structure, and share value.

Historical incidents provide us with a visible record of invisible economic processes. The challenge is to track those invisible processes through time, discovering in them the forces that shape the way business is done today and will be done tomorrow. The historical record is purposely telescoped in this chapter, limiting the incidents described to those directly relevant to whether markets are inward looking and protectionist or outward looking and open. As the difference in orientation accounts for the most durable differences in business practice in Latin America, the distinction will keep our story concise and to the point.

1492–1981: SELF-DETERMINATION IN CHAINS

During much of Latin America's first 490 years of existence, business practices were shaped by inward-looking, government-regulated markets that contrasted with the *laissez-faire* policy directions then evolving in the United States. Three intertwined forces were responsible for steering Latin America onto the state-controlled economic path that would diverge so sharply from the market-controlled economy of the United States: (1) the tenacious heritage of the region's colonial past, (2) its post-independence oligarchies, and (3) its long-standing love-hate relationship with the United States.

The Cultural and Institutional Imprints of Colonialism

The paths taken by colonialism left deep imprints that survive today to mark as unique the cultures and institutions of Latin America.

The Cultural Legacy of Colonialism

Through the mysterious workings of an unexpected destiny, our New World society was catapulted into existence from a springboard of exotic circumstances. Not since the birth of Christ had the course of human history been so irreversibly redirected as it was in 1492. To understand the effects that long-ago event had on the ways of doing business in Latin America today, you must first appreciate the very different natures of the four cultures that were about to collide in the New World.

1. The Iberian. Spain and Portugal had the distinction of remaining the last battlefield in Europe where the Christian Crusade continued to be waged against the Muslim infidel. As the rest of Europe entered the Renaissance, embracing religious freedom and individual worth, Spain and Portugal remained church-state bastions in the religious war against the godless Moors. The inseparable institutions of war and religion that had defined the earlier medieval Christian world throughout Europe during the Middle Ages continued unabated in the Iberian peninsula. It was in 1492 that the fusion between the Roman Catholic Church and the feudal authority that had been building in Spain for eight centuries reached a historic fulfillment. As if the year 1492 were a coiled spring suddenly released, the world saw in Spain a climactic series of events that was to shape the destiny of nations and men for the remainder of recorded history. The compression limits of history were surely tested as, in that single fateful year of 1492, Spain:

- Triumphed in its 10-year siege of Granada, the last Moorish stronghold in Europe, thus achieving the final goal of eight centuries of crusading
- Watched as Columbus set sail for the spice islands of the Orient and later blundered haplessly into the unimaginably greater wealth of the New World
- Consolidated, under the single rule of Ferdinand and Isabella, the five independent kingdoms that made up the core of what was to become the modern Spanish state

- Sent its pope, Alexander V, to direct the Holy See in Rome as the pontificus maximus; one year later, that compliant church leader granted Spain exclusive rights to conquer the New World, west of Portugal's possessions

- Expelled from its territory those Jews who had survived the fires of the Inquisition, many of whom would soon follow Columbus to the New World as Christian converts

- Produced the first grammar of a romance language; its author, Antonio de Nebrija, would comment prophetically that language was the most powerful weapon of empire

The confluence of those events had the effect in Spain, and to no lesser degree in Portugal, for analogous reasons, of prolonging the momentum of the Crusade mentality, making the conquest of the New World pagans simply an extension of the conquest of the Islamic Moors. As in that earlier epoch, Spain and Portugal committed themselves wholly to securing the Americas for God and for king. Their zeal to defend the religious doctrine was viewed as nothing less than defending the cause of civilization in its age-old struggle against barbarism. The nobility of their cause left no latitude for non-Christian beliefs.

To maintain the purity of the faith in the colonies, Spain permitted no one to migrate who was not Christian and a loyal citizen. Spain's strict emigration policies produced a far more homogeneous group of European settlers than did England's policies, which caused the lands of the future United States to be settled by a diverse collection of English, French, German, Danish, Dutch, Chinese, and other nationalities. The difference between Spain's and England's policies stemmed from the different aims they had for their respective American possessions.

As Spanish America was already inhabited by civilized peoples whose numbers exceeded the population of Spain, there was little reason to encourage massive emigration. Spain simply needed to reorganize the exploitation of the new colonies' wealth by replacing the native ruling class with loyal Spaniards. In the English colonies, a different set of conditions dictated a different immigration policy. The small population of Stone Age natives and scarce deposits of mineral wealth shaped the crown's need to send large numbers of hard-working Europeans to convert the vast wilderness to agriculture. The manufactures needed by that large population of farmers would then create a captive market for the products of English industry. Accordingly, England set no restrictions on number, nationality, or religion of immigrants to Anglo America.[2] It could hardly have been foreseen at the time that those differing colonial immigration policies were to create attitudes toward manual labor, individual achievement and worth, and civic responsibility in Anglo America that would diverge sharply from those that evolved in Spanish America.

In colonial Latin America, it was unrealistic to believe that life outside of a feudal, militaristic Christianity could exist. Today, we feel the same way about the existence of a civilized society without an organized national economic and political structure. Such pervasive and uncompromising intolerance helps to explain why, in Spain and Portugal, there remained much greater popular acceptance of autocratic and feudal rule than in the rest of Europe. Iberian claims to nobility were invariably traceable to the bloody exploits of some ancestral warrior who had wrested by force lands that he then settled and ruled. The exalted figure of the soldier led to contempt for manual labor and a readiness to resort to military means to achieve political ends. The glorification of the exploiter left neither compassion for the exploited nor support for the rule of impartial law. In addition to engendering the cult of an authoritarian military, Spain's and Portugal's mediocre records as economists and statesmen were also transferred to the New World, thus perpetuating for almost five more centuries a legacy of feeble economic and political institutions. That legacy is fundamental to understanding why that first Spanish footfall on a remote Bahamian beach was to doom all further economic and social advance of the New World's indigenous peoples that, over the previous 30,000 years, had evolved into such remarkable civilizations as the Inca, the Maya, and the Aztec.

2. The Indian. "Indian," as a term to describe the native residents of the New World, is used advisedly. Whereas the term "Indian" has no unusually pejorative connotation in English, the term *indio* in Latin America (at least implicitly) refers to an uneducated and socially inferior individual. To avoid being offensive, *indígena* (indigenous) should be used.

Living indigenous traditions in countries like Bolivia, Peru, Ecuador, Guatemala, and Mexico form the cultural cornerstone of their modern life. Pre-Columbian feelings of harmony with nature and stoicism clashed with the Iberian drive for wealth and domination under the triple-threat banners of God, Gold, and Glory.

Nevertheless, the pre-Columbians' intimacy with the forces of nature in no way diminished an intense involvement in distant commerce.

Numerous curious discoveries found throughout the Americas attest to a long-established, remarkable trading prowess: artifacts, unearthed from ancient Peruvian tombs, that were fashioned from turquoise and that were traced to the U.S. Southwest; emeralds from Colombia that had been used ritually in Mexico before the time of the Aztecs; and amber from the Dominican Republic buried in pre-Inca Andean sites.

Even the local trading patterns found today in Latin America are the surviving features of a far-distant past. Today's open-air markets held in small towns and villages have their origin in age-old networks of interlocking village markets. Highland buyers of lowland-grown cacao beans, for example, were sellers of potatoes, and spirited haggling would take place as the terms of exchange were settled. Because local markets also functioned as a place to exchange gossip and the news of the day, they became centers of social activity for natives who led otherwise isolated existences. Open-air markets are a common and colorful mainstay of the Latin American lifestyle, shaping the instruments and instincts with which Latins approach business situations. Consequently, it is not surprising that today many Latins are gregarious and move naturally and effortlessly along a spectrum of roles: at one moment bargaining aggressively, at another displaying an infectious sense of humor, and at yet another serving as gracious hosts. Anglos who have not been exposed since an early age to the same freewheeling marketplace atmosphere may at first be disconcerted as their Latin opposite shifts fluidly between parts seemingly scripted for different business and social situations.

3. The Mestizo.   The descendants of European conquistador fathers and Indian mothers, called mestizos, are the most visible and important social evidence of the conquest. The hybrid child of the Old and New Worlds soon became the dominant element in the social fabric of Latin America. Today's factory worker, national president, small farmer, army general, barber, cabinet minister, taxi driver, corporate CEO, artist, university professor, or physician is statistically likely to be a mestizo. Exceptions to mestizo dominance in Latin America are found in Argentina, Uruguay, and Chile, countries in which, prior to the massive waves of European immigration that began in the mid 19th century, peoples of mixed European and Indian blood constituted the majority.

During three centuries of colonial rule, mestizos were viewed as combining the worst traits of the Iberian and the Indian, deplored as being deceitful, lazy, and unstable. Unrecognized by his father and raised neither as an Indian nor a European by his mother, the mestizo yearned to be part of the world of wealth and status in which his European father lived. The ferment of a century of wars of independence and civil uprisings gave him that opportunity. Between the early 19th and early 20th centuries, he won status by moving upward into roles of military and political leadership. As he gained power through allegedly liberal revolutions, the mestizo partially displaced the *criollo* (creole, of Spanish blood, but born in the New World) oligarchies and took over their businesses and property, their European ways, and their disdain for the Indian.

4. *The African.* Of the some 12 million Africans brought to the Western Hemisphere between 1500 and 1850, the greatest number went to Latin America.[3] Brought chained and branded as chattel to both Anglo America and Latin America, the African arrivals occupied the social status of slaves in both societies. Over time, it became common for the African in Latin America to gain his freedom peacefully and become integrated with the rest of society. By contrast, the African who won freedom in the United States was segregated from white society.

That does not mean that there was and is no color-based prejudice in Latin America. Rather, it is differently defined, based on the amount of color. In slave-era Latin America, the pure African was regarded as inferior, but every drop of white blood raised his status. That tradition continues today in countries like Brazil and the Dominican Republic, where most of the populace can claim some African ancestry. In those societies, nearly imperceptible differences in skin coloration are the central determinant of one's position within the social hierarchy. The converse applies to the United States, where Africans were an unalloyed minority and possessing a single drop of African blood was sufficient to taint one's social status.[4]

The Institutional Legacy of Colonialism

Spain's colonization of the Americas was an enterprise of epic proportions. The costs of maintaining the sword and the cross as the two front lines of conquest were sizeable. To finance the immense expenses of its military and missionary advances in the New World, Spain organized her new colonies as cash cows. They were exploited as captive subsidiaries with the aim of providing for their own operating costs and of paying dividends to the crown. The colonies' huge surpluses were drained off to support the royal treasury, rather than reinvested to further their own economic development. In his order "Get gold, humanely if possible, but at all hazards—get gold,"[5] King Ferdinand succinctly expressed colonial Spain's equivalent of a business plan.

Spain imposed pervasive controls over virtually every aspect of commercial activity in the colonies. If you wanted to export cacao, for example, you would have to grow it in Venezuela. Sugarcane could only be raised in the Caribbean. Chilean colonists were not permitted to raise tobacco, but they could grow wheat.[6] Five hundred years ago, Spain's efforts to control every minute detail of economic life in the colonies gave rise to five durable institutions that shaped the business system of the New World. Although now gradually yielding to the forces of globalization, those institutions—statism, civil law, corruption, personalism, and the cult of power—still survive as the strongest strands of the common business culture found throughout the republics of Latin America. Let us trace the origin of each of those historic strands and the path it has taken to arrive at today's business practices.

1. Statism. Just as the visible legacies of the Iberian conquerors survive today as imposing churches, plazas, and fortresses, so has the less visible imprint of statism lasted into our own time. Whereas, in the United States, the capitalist government's role is to provide an environment to stimulate market-driven, bottom-up economic forces, in statist Latin America the role of government has been to control the economy through top-down mandates. Rigid, crown-controlled monopolies have curbed the ability of private business initiatives to respond to market opportunities. Then, and for most of 500 years thereafter, private enterprise was assigned to a seat at the back of the bus. Where statism has held sway, private enterprise and economic growth have suffered. By transferring its feudal version of statism to the colonies 500 years ago, Spain forged an antibusiness mold that still shapes the perceptions many Latin Americans have of the private sector.

Spain's bias against private enterprise had its roots thrust deeply into the soil of elitist tradition. The condescension accorded to business activity is reflected in the etymology of *negocio,* the Spanish and Portuguese word for business. *Negocio* is derived from *negación del ocio,* literally, "negation of leisure." The word reflects the classic Greek belief that nothing of creatively redeeming value could be achieved in the absence of leisure. In contrast to the Anglo concept of business ("busy-ness") as the antithesis of leisure, the Spanish and Portuguese concept indicates a predisposition to view those who engage in business as pursuing ends that are somehow intellectually empty, socially suspect, or ethically bankrupt.

Over time, the Iberians' arrogantly elitist disdain for business became the cornerstone of Latin America's traditional scorn for capitalism. It is ironic that the antibusiness (and antimanual labor) attitude of an elitist European aristocracy became the anticapitalist and anti-U.S. ideological rallying cry of Latin American populists. The emotionally inflated economic nationalism and contempt for capitalism they espoused discouraged the very international trade and investment that held the key to alleviating Latin America's massive poverty.

By allowing politicians and bureaucrats to control the business of the New World, Spain let slip between its fingers the wealthiest windfall discovery of all time. By wasting its New World bonanza on frivolous consumption and dynastic wars, Spain forfeited the opportunity to invest productively in developing its economy at home. Having coupled political paralysis with economic impotence, Spain became the pauper of the major Old World empires by the early years of the 17th century, creating an enduring image of economic ineptitude and prompting commentary like the following: "A City friend has confided to me the secret of his successful investment policy. Never, he says, invest in a country which has been previously governed by Spain. This principle has kept him out of trouble."[7] Spain's antifree enterprise posture was transferred to Latin America, where state-run economies became a bitter recipe for bloated payrolls and inefficient companies, saddling consumers with overpriced, shoddy goods and choking off individual initiative. The resulting economic sclerosis reinforced and perpetuated the spectacle of poverty that has plagued the human condition in Latin America for centuries.

2. Civil Law and the Legal Labyrinth. The legal system and institutions that are familiar to Anglo executives are not the same ones practiced in three-fourths of the rest of the world, including Latin America. Whereas the English colonists carried with them the common-law system practiced in England, the Iberian conquerors brought into the New World a Napoleonic Code version of the Roman civil-law system that had been evolving in Europe for almost 20 centuries. In this manner, two very distinct systems of law developed in the New World: common law in Anglo America and civil (or code) law in Latin America.

A key difference between civil law and common law is that, under the former, the presumption of a right to act always rests on a judicial ruling. Thus, the limits of what is permissible are predefined under a strict code of legal behavior. Under common law, it is presumed that a right to act exists unless otherwise restricted by law. As the codified norms of what constitutes legitimate action under civil law seldom change, over time civil law becomes increasingly distant from currently accepted behavior. Common law, on the other hand, is founded upon a continually unfolding series of rulings that constitute recent precedent, thus enabling the law and human behavior to evolve in parallel paths.

Because legislation under civil law is considered to be all-embracing, a Latin American lawyer will first search for argument in the statutes, then to scholarly commentary on the statutes, and finally to cases. In contrast, a U.S. common-law lawyer will first look to cases, then to statutes. The primacy of legislated statute under civil law reduces the discretionary authority of judges who take office soon after graduating from law school and passing a lenient qualifying examination.[8] Enjoying more power than judges are prestigious legal scholars, whose influential written opinions may represent a major factor in the success (and cost) of a legal action.

The sheer number of regulations and rules in a civil-law system means that legal actions that would be straightforward and uncomplicated under U.S. common law can be onerous in Latin America. Even the simplest document must be notarized and attached with the appropriate paid stamps, seals, and signatures. Table 3.1 uses World Bank data[9] to compare various Latin American countries with the United States on selected legal obstacles to doing business.

Because virtually every conceivable human act has already been spelled out under civil-law codes, contracts tend to be shorter than under common law. That does not make civil-law contracts any less subject to careful review by a qualified lawyer who can alert you to unintended infractions. For example, because not all Latin American countries allow their citizens to maintain unauthorized accounts outside the country, you must be cautious about making payments outside the country of your Latin associate. You should also be cautious when defining what constitutes an act of God as a basis for excusing nonperformance. Whereas an earthquake could be a pardonable event for not meeting a production delivery or contract deadline in both the United States and Latin America, the same symmetry may not apply if a workers' strike caused the delay. Latin American laws are so protective of labor that a nonperforming party might well prevail in a Latin American court with the argument that it was beyond the reasonable ability of management to avoid the strike and its consequences.

Given the rigidity of the colonial civil-law system, it was virtually impossible to accomplish any productive economic undertaking if one acted in full compliance with the law. Indeed, 16th-century colonial officials, knowing the irrelevance of crown laws to the reality of life in the colonies, commonly operated under the maxim "Obedezco, pero no cumplo" (I obey, but I do not carry out). The colonial practice of maintaining an inflexible but unenforceable system of rules encouraged the widespread disregard of law that has plagued Latin America for centuries. The ongoing practical effect of that lengthy tradition can be seen today in Latins' highly evolved, almost innate sense of *olfato político* (political nose or "smarts"). It is that sharp nose for politics that enables Latins to know, in a given situation and at a given moment, where the constantly shifting line is drawn that separates the written law from the real law that is being enforced.

Whereas litigation can be a viable, cost-effective means for a company to protect its interests in the United States, as Table 3.1 suggests, it is usually a less satisfactory option in Latin America. The likelihood of delays in congested court systems, low tort recoveries, high potential for

Table 3.1

Ease in Complying with Procedural Regulations

Procedure	U.S.	Latin American Countries
Time to import (days)	5	71 (Venezuela), 33 (Paraguay), 29 (Nicaragua, Ecuador)
Documents to import (number)	5	10 (Guatemala, Honduras, Paraguay, Puerto Rico, Uruguay)
Starting a business (days)	6	141 (Venezuela), 120 (Brazil), 65 (Uruguay), 64 (Ecuador)
Starting a business (% of income per capita)	0.7	111.7 (Nicaragua), 99.2 (Bolivia), 56.7 (Paraguay), 47.3 (Honduras)
Enforcing contracts (days)	300	1,459 (Guatemala), 1,346 (Colombia), 900 (Honduras), 852 (Costa Rica)
Enforcing contracts (cost as % of claim)	14.4	52.6 (Colombia), 50.0 (Panama), 43.7 (Venezuela)
Disclosure to investors (index, 0–10)	7	0 (Honduras), 1 (Bolivia, Ecuador, Panama), 2 (Costa Rica)

"losing" files, and absence of a discovery process combine to make one wary about bringing suit in Latin America. If differences may not be settled amicably or by mediation, it is wise to write into your agreement a clause that provides for dispute resolution under the jurisdiction of a U.S. court or arbitration process. Prior to relying on that clause, however, you should verify that the decision of the U.S. court or arbitration panel will be recognized and enforceable in Latin America.

Many disputes can be avoided simply through a clear understanding of the differences between common-law and civil-law terminology. For example, U.S. executives looking to set up joint-venture operations in Latin America may misinterpret what the term "corporation" signifies under civil law. Under common law, a corporation is a sovereign creation. As such, it is common for legal counsel to be in attendance during its establishment, and extensive clauses to protect the parties are written into the formal agreement. Under civil law, however, a corporation is simply a product of an agreement between two or more parties. The Spanish term *Sociedad Anónima* (anonymous society) expresses the confidential partnership nature of a relationship based on personal trust, rather than on legalistic formality. The resulting contrast in interpretations can create unwanted conflict when, in an attempt to put an agreement in place based on the rule of law, U.S. executives surround themselves with lawyers. The presence of so much legal firepower at a meeting presumably intended to cement a relationship based on mutual trust may not be understood by Latin executives. They may feel that there would be no more need to bring a lawyer to a meeting between trusted friends than there would be to use legal counsel in a meeting between husband and wife—unless one of the spouses was not acting out of trust.

As Latin American courts have often favored the rights of a lender over those of a stockholder (particularly if a minority, foreign stockholder), some experienced investors use an innovative financial mechanism to protect a minority equity position. To establish their investment as debt, instead of equity, they exchange their cash injection for bonds convertible to preferred stock of the Latin firm. As the bond issue carries covenants (e.g., a minimum liquidity ratio of 2:1) that Latin firms would not ordinarily meet, the investor is in a legally tenable position to declare the borrower in default. The ability to pull the rug out from under their majority partners' weak or unscrupulously managed operation at any time levers minority investors into a controlling position at the same time that it increases the security of their principal and current cash flow.

Later, when propitious to do so, investors can exercise their option to become shareholders.

3. Corruption. A common challenge to doing business in Latin America is learning how to detect and respond to sometimes flexible ethical standards. Although it is especially prevalent in government procurement, revenue-collecting, and permit-issuing functions, corruption is difficult to countenance anywhere. The money that lines a corrupt official's pocket could otherwise have been invested in education, health services, or infrastructure to bolster economic productivity and social well-being. Additionally, the mere image of corruption keeps away the legitimate investment needed to bring Latin American economies into the global mainstream.

Although business profit is often the victim of corruption, the business's profit orientation is also its source. As profit margins grew narrower under the pressure from competitive world markets in recent years, the high cost and risk of making payoffs or kickbacks became less affordable. As bad business practices acted to drive out good ones, firms that refused to be parties to unscrupulous transactions stayed out of markets where payoffs were required to do business. While multinational firms had the luxury of being able to leave one country and relocate operations in another, the far more numerous smaller local firms were under pressure to go along with bribes demanded by sticky-fingered officials. Because most Latin firms lack the luxury of having an alternative to living with corruption, the unwanted operating reality they face should serve to moderate the voices of those who would criticize them for being less virtuous than U.S. firms.

The profit opportunities created by the appalling inefficiencies of the state-owned enterprises (SOEs) were an especially fertile field for corrupt officials to demand payoffs or kickbacks. The sky-high duty rates protecting SOEs created strong incentives to smuggle foreign-made goods into local black markets where quality-starved consumers would pay premium prices. The key factor underpinning the smugglers' success was law enforcement officials who agreed to turn a blind eye in exchange for a portion of the illicit profits.

Neither U.S. citizens nor Latins enjoy being shaken down by either a petty bureaucrat or a powerful political figure. But, among Latin Americans, corruption at both levels of public office came to be widely, but grudgingly, countenanced, for different motives. Contributing to the tolerance of corruption at the lower levels of government was the fact that payoffs performed an income-redistribution function. Bureaucrats, clerks, and police were usually paid low wages because they were politically or socially blocked from gaining higher paying jobs in the public or private sectors. Hence, the proceeds from payoffs supplemented their meager salaries, allowing them to afford their lower-middle-class existence. Because those who used frequent public services belonged to the privileged class of wealthy landowners or industrialists, receiving a payoff from the powerful was sanctioned by social justice. Viewing payoffs as a mechanism to redress the sprawling inequalities of income distribution in Latin America had a ring of legitimacy in a society where the rich regularly evaded paying taxes and the poor had little access to social benefits.

As a U.S. business executive, your refusal to make a payoff may trigger outrage on the part of the public official who solicited it. Moral disdain and hostility are common, understandable Anglo reactions when a Latin official attempts to put the "bite" (known in Spanish by its literal equivalent, *mordida*) on them. Offending a public official by curtly rejecting his modest (at least, to him) request for a gratuity may be only marginally more productive than provoking an armed terrorist by insulting his religion or questioning his parentage. It is more fruitful to view the occasional expectation of a gratuity as belonging to the same moral category as tipping waiters. In each case, you are supplementing the low wages paid by their employer.

A different ethical norm attaches to payoffs made to high-level government officials. Wholesale corruption existed in colonial times in Latin America, and it was quietly tolerated at the uppermost levels of government. The reason it was tolerated is qualitatively different than the rationale for sanctioning corruption at the lower levels. During colonial times, a bankrupt crown routinely auctioned public offices. It was implicitly understood that the winning bidder had the right to recoup his investment. Therefore, once installed, the new officeholder's first priority was to use any means possible (short of daytime looting) to accelerate his payback. The attitude that an official was tacitly entitled to charge others for access to the prerogatives of his office was normal for the time, and helped to perpetuate the popular view that authority was a license to steal.

So it happened that generations of Latin Americans grew up with the view that corruption was a natural condition of power, and it was normal for anyone in a position of authority to expect a payoff in return for bestowing favors. But although Latins may understand and be resigned to official corruption, they do not do so without protesting. Indeed, heated complaining about pervasive payoffs and the outrageous behavior of greedy officials is a national pastime. At odds with today's broad public displeasure with the murky financial behavior of public officials is the telling fact that no simple translation exists in Spanish for "accountability." Awkward efforts to coin an equivalent exist, such as *obligación de rendir cuentas* (obligation to render accounts). But the inability of the Spanish and Portuguese languages to produce a succinct, one-word description to express an expectation of transparency and honesty in financial dealings testifies to a mindset still hobbled by a centuries-old toleration of corrupt authorities.

It is an unpleasant fact that ethically offensive people will be found in public offices in both Latin America and the United States. The incidence of corruption among public officials in Latin America, however, is less than one would believe. Nonetheless, payoffs happen and, at the lower levels of officialdom, are a routine cost of doing business in parts of Latin America. But payoff decisions involving higher level authorities are more atypical and are weighed by a different set of ethical and legal norms. In the realm of ethics, your decision about whether to make payoffs to high-level officials is a moral choice, and thus a discretionary decision subject to your own personal standards. In the realm of law, however, the act of bribery is much less ambiguous. Making payoffs to high-level foreign officials or political figures is strictly prohibited by U.S. law, and it can trigger criminal charges against your company and against you personally.

The U.S. Foreign Corrupt Practices Act (FCPA) of 1977 prohibits any U.S. firm's employees or agents from paying any foreign government official, political leader, or political candidate to gain or retain business by influencing the discretionary decisions made by that individual. The U.S. Justice Department has recently brought FCPA charges against prominent companies, such as Siemens, Alcatel, Willbros, Tyco, and IBM.[10] But the FCPA is reasonable and bends to companies making payments to (usually lower level) public officials to expedite normal transactions, such as providing security services, issuing work permits, or loading perishable goods into a refrigerated hold. In brief, the FCPA allows you to speed or ease routine transactions by oiling the smaller cogs of bureaucracy. But beware of trying to lubricate the big wheels to gain a business advantage, such as a contract award. Disgruntled losing bidders can smell grease a continent away, and they may be delighted to report to U.S. authorities their suspicions of a U.S. competitor's bribe-won business. Even if such suspicions are unfounded, the expense entailed in legal defense, disruption to operations, and negative publicity could be ruinous for smaller companies.

Smaller U.S. exporters may find the FCPA particularly vexing. This can occur because, although they have little direct control over the daily activities of their Latin American agents or distributors, these representatives may be in direct contact with government officials and may be violating FCPA standards to gain business for you. In such cases, the U.S. company could be held fully liable for its representatives' infractions.[11]

4. Personalism. The institution of personalism in colonial Latin America has its roots thrust deeply in the feudal system of land tenure and patrimony that prevailed in Spain and Portugal since the eighth century. That durable system was transferred virtually intact to the New World.

Just as a drunk uses a lamppost for support instead of illumination, the Iberians used religion as a rationale to justify their feudal-like depredation of the Indians. As the conquest advanced, new lands wrested from the Indians, along with the right to exact labor tribute from the same Indians, were granted to the conquerors. The labor tribute was awarded to compensate the landowners' cost of bringing the Indians to a Christian salvation.

By gaining simultaneous awards of land and cheap Indian labor, the Iberians could exploit the valuable mining and agricultural potential of the land. Because those cash-cow concessions were granted by royal favor, being part of a network of influential social and family alliances was critical to success. As one's official position in the colonial hierarchy was directly related to one's personal position in the colonial social order, there was no separation between the person and his prerogative to exercise the authority of his position. To this day, business relationships in Latin America are predicated on doing business with members of the same social class and with friends whom one can trust.

As a result, organizations in the Spanish and Portuguese colonies were highly centralized and staffed on the basis of know-who rather than know-how. Except at the pinnacle of these steep pyramids of power, lines of communication were vertical, from subordinates to their *patrones* (masters). Organizations were rigid, incapable of engendering horizontal information flows, delegating decision making, and responding flexibly— the hallmarks of today's competitive flat-form organizations.

Iberian personalism was a system built on oppressive regulations enforced by entrenched bureaucrats, responsive only to their *patrones.*

Public service was an unknown concept. Information was brokered, not disseminated. Authority was exercised for personal privilege, and common people were subjects who must obey, rather than citizens who could claim rights. The resulting fusion of economic and social power among the elite lives on as a system of concentrated wealth, making income distribution in Latin America the most unequal in today's world.

5. *The Cult of Power.*   The origins of divergent attitudes toward political authority in Latin America and the United States reach much further back in history than the colonization of the New World by Europeans. The advanced indigenous civilizations encountered by the Spanish were stratified societies, organized around powerful castes of noble birth. In contrast, the natives that English colonists found on the North American frontier were more democratic societies, fragmented into small groups and governed by consensus.[12] Oddly, as dissimilar as were the attitudes toward authority held by the New World native groups, each was to find its own attitude matched in the attitude of the Old World invaders who were to become its master. As an accident of history, those self-reinforcing pairings would have far-reaching effects.

One of the first effects of those contrasting social attitudes was felt in the economic realm. The Spanish were able to force the Indians to work in the mines because those Indians already were accustomed to rule by an iron hand. As no similar class-based tradition existed among the more egalitarian red men of the North American frontier, attempts made by English settlers to subjugate them to labor servitude met with failure.

As power was transferred from the conquered to the conquerors in Latin America, the indigenous authority structures remained largely intact, the primary change being the substitution of Iberian autocrats for the native variety. To maintain their faraway system of colonial autocrats under centralized crown control, the Iberian monarchies found it essential to decentralize authority in the New World. Appointees to all key posts were selected by Iberian emperors. The possibility that any colonial authority would accumulate too much power was blunted by the checks and balances produced by the jealousies the rival appointees felt toward one another.

The cost of centralizing control at home by decentralizing control in the New World was high. The power struggles set in motion by atomizing authority among and within the political, military, and judicial realms laid the groundwork for the heavy-handed dictators, inefficient economies, and arbitrary individual rights that have darkened so much of Latin

America's history. Not surprisingly, micromanagement and information hoarding are still more commonly practiced than are delegation and empowerment in Latin American organizations.

Reinforcing the tradition of rule by an absolute monarchy was the Iberian philosophic legacy of natural law. Under natural law, if a ruler acts unjustly, the citizens have a right and duty to rebel. As every citizen feels empowered to adjudicate any law, a built-in disposition toward anarchy results.[13] That tradition helps explain why, until recent times, Latin governments were more often overthrown by force than overhauled by votes. It also explains why Latins, to protect themselves against their own penchant for anarchy, were willing to tolerate strong rule as a necessary evil.[14] So it was that "the faithlessness of politicians [and] the faithful stubbornness with which people seek to believe"[15] made betrayal synonymous with political life for centuries. Until recently, democracy was a fledgling experiment in a region where every man was his own political party, idealistic rhetoric obscured venal reality, and the force of custom legitimized the custom of force.

Independence: Revolution from the Top

Independence from Spain and Portugal, early in the 19th century, had little effect on the economic and political life of most Latin Americans. The movers and shakers behind independence were the creole elite (born in the colonies) who acted to wrest greater economic and political power from the dominant peninsular class (born in Spain or Portugal).

The postindependence power struggle among the creole elite gave rise to the rival liberal and conservative political movements that, to this day, vie with one another to impose their own economic policies. What movement represents which policy can be confusing to Anglos, because the labels used to describe them in the United States do not signify what they mean in Latin America (and, for that matter, in Europe). In general, liberals were members of the commercial class who supported free trade, foreign investment, and minimal government interference in the economy. Clinging to colonial traditions, the conservatives were more nationalistic, supporting protectionist economic policies to shield local producers from foreign competition.

The Birth of Import-Substitution Industrialization

While power changed hands between liberal and conservative political factions for much of the latter 19th century and until about 1930, economic policy in most of the region was dominated by liberals. But, for economies dependent on exporting a narrow range of raw materials to meet the demand of the high-growth markets of the United States and Europe, the Great Depression that gripped the world in the 1930s was a death sentence. The liberal era ended abruptly as world demand for Latin America's sugar, meat, wool, coffee, copper, and other commodities plummeted. Turning away from outward-oriented trade policies, Latin America embraced the conservative gospel of becoming self-sufficient in the industrial goods it previously had imported from the United States and Europe, paid for with the earnings generated by its raw material exports. That inward-oriented policy came to be known as import-substitution industrialization (ISI), and it continued long after the Great Depression ended. As the developed economies focused on fighting World War II, industrial output was diverted away from peacetime uses, international commerce shriveled, and Latin America was cut off from normal trade flows. High world prices for manufactures, combined with low prices for primary goods, helped ISI policies continue after the war ended in 1945. But the greatest postwar impetus for Latin America's infatuation with ISI was the pronationalist fervor that grew in the 1950s and that made ISI dominant until 1982—the onset of the Lost Decade.

What was ISI's effect on business strategy? Because competition based on price, quality, and customer service was almost nonexistent in Latin America during ISI's closed-market reign, the consumer-oriented marketing that became king in the United States during the latter 20th century was unnecessary. Industry was plagued by poor infrastructure, rigid labor codes, unreliable suppliers, and corrupt bureaucracies. The trick for managers was simply to get product to the plant's shipping dock, even if that process regularly took place with the finesse of a blind butcher. As protected monopolies, SOEs and large family-owned companies made shoddy products, sold them at inflated prices, and relied on product-starved consumers to beat a path to their door. It is no mystery why, even now, a commonly used Spanish term for marketing is *ingeniería comercial*, or commercial engineering. The term connotes the primacy of producers and the low priority assigned to consumers.

Personalism and the Family-Owned Business

Your first impressions of the business system of Latin America are unlikely to produce many high amazement-level surprises. You will note, for example, that financial institutions are similar to, and may well be branch operations of, banks you deal with in the United States. Moreover, you will find that chambers of commerce and trade associations operate along familiar lines. Furthermore, you will recognize that the legal forms of business organization are roughly analogous to structures used in the United States. But as your experience accumulates and you peel back the surface layers, you may find that your first impressions were misleading.

A unique and widespread feature of the Latin American business system is the prevalence of family-owned firms. They have flourished because they are well adapted to survive in a closed society that trusts only in-group members, and in a legal system that offers few property guarantees to outside investors and traders. As that originally closed-society institution gives way to the modern open-market environment, the functioning of family-owned firms in today's Latin America reflects a spectrum of management attitudes ranging from traditional to modern. When you find yourself meeting with executives displaying the traditional inclinations, it may be crucial to recognize their managerial peculiarities and to estimate whether those peculiarities will (a) fade into the background as the traditional firm struggles to adapt to the competitive demands of globalization or (b) remain as vestiges of a managerial Jurassic Age that will put a firm on the extinct species list.

Meet the Family

When you deal at any length with a traditional family-owned business, you come to understand its strengths and weaknesses. Not surprisingly, each stems from the same underlying condition: ownership and management control held in the same hands. Family control of ownership and management carries undeniable business advantages:

- Family owner-operators know their business upside-down and inside-out because they grew up in it. That level of intimate knowledge is seldom observed among the footloose managers of publicly held firms in the United States who move from company to company as job opportunities of the moment beckon.
- Conflict-of-interest issues and managerial opportunism, occasioned by separation of management and ownership, are minimized.
- Because the family's reputation and power are so reliant on the success of the family business (which usually bears the family name), the family will give its all to ward off any threat to survival in troubled times.

- If the company is not independently unionized, labor-management relations are likely to be harmonious. It is not rare for longtime employees to enjoy favored *compadre* (trusted retainer) relationships with the family *patrón*.
- Although particular transactions are geared toward generating short-term paybacks, the overall orientation is long term. The complementary short-term and long-term goals impose a conservative perspective on planning.
- As family companies are not publicly held, their activities, performance, organization, and plans are not a matter of public record. The resulting opacity makes it difficult for competitors or tax authorities to gain access to sensitive information.
- With its large equity position, a family can make long-term bets on high-potential acquisitions or new ventures and not have to worry about losing control of the company if a wager does not pay off.

These strengths have made Latin America's traditional family-owned firms an enduring institution. But other traits of that venerable enterprise have left it especially vulnerable to survival threats during times of rapid change, like the present. The family firm's competitive vulnerability stems from several weaknesses:

- Although the scale of the family-owned business can become quite large, its scope is limited by the size of the family and the interests and capabilities of its individual members.
- Decision making can be intuitive and emotional.
- As a consequence of weak contingency planning, traditional family businesses become more reactive than proactive to changes in their operating environment.
- When the primary incentive to maintain the firm's viability is family prestige, that motivation may not be enough to achieve breakthrough innovations or lean management practices.
- The organizational structure that evolves in traditional family firms is more indicative of the power positions and interests of individual family members than it is of the firm's key functions or competencies.
- Reluctance to divulge operating results to nonfamily creditors and investors blocks access to capital.

At one time, the traditional family firm was well suited to a stable but weak competitive environment in which threats to the family business arose locally. In that confined setting of interlocking political, social, and business networks, the family could resolve difficulties by exercising its personal influence. In competitive global markets, however, capital, technology, and management trump family influence as determinants of success.

Capital, technology, and management, as requisites of success, can create a scenario that favors a prospective U.S. business associate of a family-owned Latin American firm. If the U.S. firm is slow to understand the nature of the Latin firm's longer term needs, it could inadvertently forfeit an auspicious opportunity. The possibility of developing a close relationship with a U.S. firm offers the traditional family-owned firm a means to overcome any or all of the three constraints that limit its future growth. Your firm's ability to help a Latin partner overcome its capital, technology, or management constraints could lock in access to a future that will pay dividends long after the profit from the initial transaction is booked.

Capital. Latin American capital markets have traditionally been weak mechanisms to transfer private savings into productive uses. Runaway inflation made fixed-income instruments a poor choice for savers to maintain their purchasing power. Small shareholders faired no better: deficiencies in civil-law systems,[16] corrupt courts, and company cultures of secrecy seldom favored minority investors. Unable to penetrate the shroud of secrecy, outside investors were left in the dark about the family firm's true operating performance or wrongdoings. An often-true story is told about the Latin patriarch who maintained three sets of books on the family business. The first was kept for investors and bankers. It showed stunning results. Profits almost equaled revenues, liquidity was overflowing, and the plant was operating on a 24/7/52 schedule to work through its huge order backlog. A second set of financials was kept for the tax authorities. It reflected a financial near-death experience. Massive losses had accumulated over the firm's 100-year history, even nonpaying customers had stopped buying, and the owner had to exit the building late at night, taking different routes home to avoid being assaulted by angry creditors. ("Could the kind examiner find it in his heart to lend the owner two dollars for lunch?") The third set of books, of course, reflected the firm's true condition, and it was furtively removed from beneath the mattress at night for the owner to examine in secrecy.

Consider the reality of realty and savings. Given the disadvantages of being a small holder of debt or equity, three common means survive to manage finances. The first, used by those of limited resources or financial sophistication, is whimsically called *banco colchón* (mattress bank). Those practicing this option simply convert their local-currency savings to U.S. dollars. They are betting on the greenback's loss of purchasing power being less than that of pesos held in a low-interest local savings account.

But two better alternatives are open to the bigger league players with whom you are more likely to deal. One alternative is to invest in real property. Because land ownership is an important source of social prestige and personal satisfaction in traditionally agricultural Latin America, it is no surprise that realty in Latin America often sells at prices higher than comparable property in the United States.

Tax evasion and wealth hiding are strong appeals for quietly shifting profits abroad. These are lures that could directly affect you as a U.S.-based supplier or buyer. The Latin firm plays this game with a willing U.S. partner by adjusting transfer prices. Cooperative vendors or buyers over- or underinvoice Latin firms. The difference between the real value and the invoice value of the transaction is deposited by the U.S. company into an accommodation account controlled by the Latins and, presumably, kept safe from the prying eyes of home-country tax authorities. The ruse allows profits to accumulate abroad that would otherwise have to be declared as taxable income and, often an even more important factor, be recorded at home as wealth. The wealth-hiding motive is strong in countries like Brazil, Colombia, Mexico, and Venezuela, where sophisticated kidnappers select their victims on the basis of their wealth as reflected in the "confidential" records of banks and official agencies.[17,18]

Your decision of whether to accede to your Latin associate's request to set up an accommodation account will probably hinge on both ethical and legal concerns. Whereas ethical concerns are a subjective matter, legal concerns entail four concrete considerations. First, keep your end of the deal above board. Engage in no off-the-books transactions. This precaution can protect you from skeptical executives, shareholders, or law enforcement officials. Second, be aware that the profit you helped to make disappear from Latin America may reappear on your own company's books as taxable income. This shift in the origin of the income could invite the attention of two tax authorities: (1) the Latin American fiscal enforcers, who may find your firm, and you individually, guilty of acting as a conspirator to evade tax liability; and (2) the U.S. Internal

Revenue Service, which, in applying Section 582 or other relevant sections of the U.S. Tax Code, may deny your accommodation payments as allowable business expenses. Third, you may become liable to federal money-laundering charges. Finally, if your Latin American buyer or supplier is a political figure or an SOE, you or your company could face criminal charges under the 1977 FCPA. In sum, consenting to set up an accommodation account should be neither done capriciously nor seen as a cost-free means to gain good-guy status with your Latin counterpart.

A unique body began to arise in Latin America during the 19th century as a direct consequence of both the personal character of business relationships and the inability of family firms to obtain capital through the normal channels of debt and equity financing. This body, often a banking, industrial, and/or trading cluster with interlocking ownership, came to be called an investment group. Investment groups have functioned in most Latin American countries to channel savings within the private sector toward investment opportunities.[19] They remain today as private-sector alternatives to government-financed experiments in socialist capitalism.

Membership in an investment group enables a family firm to grow more rapidly through access to capital, technology, and market information. The need and opportunity to grow rapidly became a significant factor in Latin America during the 19th century as production technologies became more complex and capital intensive. Access to capital from a member bank within its group enables a family-owned manufacturing firm to develop and market products, build inventory, and modernize its plant as it gears up production for world-class buyers. Such capital injections are seldom available at arm's length with a local commercial bank limited to short-term credits based on a conservative estimate of the liquidation value of pledged assets.

Dealing with a member firm of an investment group can be a rewarding experience. Your firm's high credit standing, reputation for honesty, and positive letter of introduction from a U.S. correspondent of the investment group's anchor bank can open doors that may lead you to the Latin American equivalent of business utopia: forthright negotiations, simple closings, and on-time payments.

Technology and Management. As Latin American economies grow, demands are placed on family firms that can outstrip their ability to respond with internal resources. The resulting performance gaps occasion the need for outside capabilities to meet the challenges of new product and process technologies, new markets, new sources of inputs, or new logistical systems. As a trusted U.S. supplier or buyer of proven competitive success, your firm may be seen by the Latin American firm as a reliable means to extend the latter's technological or managerial reach. Many U.S. suppliers or buyers have found this scenario to be a rewarding opportunity to enter into joint ventures or strategic alliances entailing licensing, market representation, or exclusive supplier relationships.

A final suggestion when dealing with family firms: avoid the mistake of underestimating their abilities just because they may appear managerially or technologically unsophisticated. Remember, the Titanic was built by professionals, the Ark by amateurs.

ISI: Yesterday's Economic Blessing, Today's Management Curse

Size Matters

At least it has in Latin American economic performance. Imagining that the law of comparative advantage could be repealed, small countries that continued the ISI policies into the 1950s learned in the 1980s that they had sacrificed competitiveness at the altar of economic nationalism. Falling into the trap of thinking they could be efficient in producing most of the goods they consumed, they found that scale disadvantages condemned them to being efficient in none. The lofty duties that protected high-cost local industry from cheap imports created an artificial economy that, in turn, created artificial rules of business.

The ISI era continued in Latin America much longer than necessary or helpful, because it coincided with record levels of macroeconomic performance. For two decades after the end of World War II, Latin America's economic growth far outpaced growth in the industrialized countries. Prospects seemed especially bright during the 1965–1980 period, when manufacturing surged ahead at annual gains, averaging seven percent. As if foreshadowing a dark period to come, however, inflation during the same years averaged over 30 percent, and export gains were meager.[20]

The region's rapid growth in output and inflation was driven internally by subsidies to bloated SOEs and by the entry of massive numbers of migrants from the ISI-impoverished countryside into the city's money economy (ISI's effect was to transfer wealth from efficient rural agriculture to inefficient urban industry, from where the votes were not to where the votes were). Those internal motors of industrialization were fueled externally by cash flows from a growing sea of foreign debt. The ability of the region to repay that debt was rooted in the assumption that prices for its raw material exports would rise forever. As export revenues plummeted during 1981 with the worldwide glut in oil and other commodities, the scene was set for the tragedy of the Lost Decade that moved to center stage in 1982.

The Arrogance of Authority

Latin America's fractured geography, combined with fractious postindependence politics, produced local *caudillos* (strongmen) throughout the region. As *caudillos* expanded their dominion by crushing or making alliances with neighboring *caudillos*, they became national dictators. Rule by armed force became the normal pattern of authority in Spanish America for 150 years after independence. It was not until the 1980s that more of the region's citizens lived under democratically elected governments than under dictatorships.

Today, all of Latin America except Cuba is a technical democracy. Although democracy does not guarantee good rule, an open political system is the natural ally of an open economy. Working in unison, free elections and free markets undermine corruption, advancing both social and business interests. As today's democratic regimes tend to be more technically oriented than their repressive predecessors, being right on policy is more vital than being right on politics. That is why the best rule for involvement in Latin American politics is not to be involved.

The Tangled Histories of Two Americas

The centuries-old background of European military and religious conflicts set the course that relationships between the English and the Iberian settlers in the Americas would follow. Largely detached in the colonial era, those relationships became increasingly intertwined and often conflictive after independence. This section explains how the distinct origin and evolution of the Western Hemisphere's dominant cultures created differences in the ways that business is conducted in those two realms.

The View from North to South: Shifting Latitudes and Attitudes

"Welcome to Latin America. Please set your watches back 50 years." These words formed a favorite greeting one of my 1960s-era U.S. bosses would use to welcome visitors from corporate headquarters to our Latin American subsidiary. The intention of his favorite one-line welcome was not to demean the people or the culture of the country in which the subsidiary was located. Rather, it was to prepare visitors for the different business practices and operating standards they would soon witness.

Fast-forwarding to the 2010s, U.S. visitors to Latin America will swiftly realize that the wheels of economic, social, and political development are turning in the region. Given a little more time, they will also perceive that those wheels are rolling in a direction and over terrain that are no longer under U.S. control.

The View from South to North: Image Change for the U.S. Corporation

Hardly praiseworthy were the corporate citizenship records of many U.S. companies that began migrating to Latin America in the late 1800s. The infamous habit of U.S. companies to become cozy with autocratic regimes remained evident for a half century. U.S. corporate comfort with the stable, controlled country environment provided by Latin American dictatorships fueled U.S. "banana diplomacy" policies that backed many brutally repressive despots.

But a 1960s incident exemplifies how times have changed. Auditors working in a Latin American country's office of corporate income-tax collections supplemented their meager official salaries by soliciting bribes to "correct" the returns of firms that had underpaid their income taxes. To decide who would win the chance to exact the largest payoff, auditors would auction among themselves the rights to examine the returns of those delinquent firms they judged to be the juiciest prospects for extortion. I was pleased to learn that, among the largest companies operating in the country, only two received no bids: my own employer and another U.S. multinational. The firms eliciting the highest bids, because they were deemed to be the largest evaders, were all locally owned. At least among that country's tax auditors, it was implicitly believed that corruption was a domestic product, not an imported behavior.

That incident is not an isolated example. Contrary to populist demagoguery—justified, in many cases, by socially reprehensible past behavior—the usual ethical behavior of U.S. firms now operating in Latin America is exemplary. Taxes owed are taxes paid, contracts are won on the basis of competitive offerings rather than bribes, workers are treated honestly and rewarded for productivity, and firms follow a hands-off policy toward local politics. Testimony that long-held feelings of resentment, envy, and jealousy of the United States are softening can be found in a remark recently made to me by a Latin intellectual: "The only thing worse than being exploited by U.S. multinational corporations is not being exploited by them."

The growing acceptance of U.S. firms during the latter decades of the 20th century was not based merely on their ability to deliver sorely needed capital and technology to Latin America, but on their undisputed lead in management. Even the most outspoken socialist cannot seriously question the marketing, financial, and production prowess of U.S. management. As Latin American executives become familiar with smaller U.S. firms, they gradually realize that management quality is not correlated with firm size. As a result, smaller U.S. firms and Latin firms of all sizes began to strike deals together, many of them rooted in expectations that interactions with the former would strengthen the management capabilities of the latter. The same motivation drove many Latin Americans to attend management seminars or to enroll in one of the many U.S.-style MBA programs being offered in the region.

By the close of the 20th century, business and political leaders in the two realms of the Americas had found common ground on which to build mutually advantageous alliances. But to take that step forward, Latin America had to take two steps backward, suffering a 10-year lesson in the high prices paid for its past policies of protectionist isolation.

1982–1991: THE LOST DECADE—SYSTEM SHOCK AS A DOUBLE-EDGE MACHETE

As a lesson in how to drive economic development in rapid reverse, few examples can beat the backward race record set by Latin America during its Lost Decade of 1982–1991. Mexico defaulted on its debt in 1982. The ensuing "Tequila Crisis" triggered the world's most severe financial crisis since 1929.[21] Misguided ISI policies had propelled the region's debt to eight times its 1973 level. Investor panic took over: annual private capital inflows, averaging $12 billion between 1976 and 1981, did an about-face, becoming capital outflows of over $26 billion per year between 1982 and 1987.[22] Unemployment soared and per capita income plunged, slashing 1990 middle-class purchasing power to 1972 levels. Social discontent fueled widespread violence and, as angry street mobs demanded more money, weak governments were quick to print it. The two-digit inflation rates of previous decades soared to three digits in the early years of the Lost Decade, then raged to four and even five digits during its later years.[23] Interest in the executive seminars and business consulting I was conducting in Argentina, Brazil, Costa Rica, Honduras, Mexico, and Peru shifted away from quality control, productivity improvement, and export marketing and toward practices for dealing with hyperinflation. Painful hangovers from the "Tequila Crisis" signaled that ISI's financial bankruptcy had caught up to its ideological bankruptcy. The toppling that followed set in motion a series of economic, social, and political upheavals that were to forever alter—mostly for the good—the region's business landscape.

Coming of Age

During the Lost Decade, it became clear that protecting high-cost, uncompetitive industry was out of step with the march toward globalization. By the end of the Lost Decade in 1991, the region had turned a crucial corner, embracing a neoliberal policy set that came to be known as the Washington Consensus: fiscal prudence, open economies, competitive exchange rates, institutional reform, and spending aimed at reducing income inequality.[24]

It was no coincidence that the end of the Cold War coincided with the end of Latin America's Lost Decade. Latin Americans muted their more extreme expressions of anti-U.S. sentiment and turned their attention toward the now-undeniable economic record of their neighbor to the north. They asked the obvious question: Why had the economic performance of Latin America lagged so far behind that of the United States? Table 3.2 synthesizes key historical factors that have made the economic and political paths taken by the two great cultural transplants of the New World diverge so sharply.

Rediscovering the Americas 500 Years after Columbus

By the end of 1991, the curtain was falling on both the Cold War and the Lost Decade. By 1992, the worst social agonies of the Lost Decade had disappeared, and the Washington Consensus was uprooting many of the economic behaviors that had typified Latin America during the previous 60 years: nationalistic resistance to foreign investment gave way to free capital flows, controlled economies evolved toward open trade and deregulated markets, and impulsive expansions of the money supply yielded to disciplined anti-inflationary measures. In the political sphere, except for Cuba, dictatorships had been replaced by popularly elected regimes. After 500 years of economic and political tyranny, Latin America had learned that it could not join the future by protecting the past. The Lost Decade had reset regional mindsets.

Statism Yields to Free Markets

In controlled markets, the state retained the authority to regulate key business variables such as retail prices, contract enforcement, product quality and cost, production technology, profits remitted abroad, and labor's role in

Table 3.2

Historical Basis of Contrasts between the Economic and Political Systems of the United States and Latin America

Historical Factors	United States	Latin America
Colonial emigration policy	Unrestricted as to nationality and religion	Limited to Roman Catholics loyal to crown
Profile of European colonists	Farmers and tradesmen; arrived with wives or families, prepared to settle permanently	Peasant soldiers; sought to return after making a quick fortune; intermarried with native women
Profile of indigenous inhabitants	Loosely organized, egalitarian; small population	Complex and stratified social structure; large population
Population growth	Rapid	Initially negative, then slow
Primary labor force	European colonists	Indigenous and African slaves
Religion permitted	Any Christian denomination	Roman Catholics only
Independence significance	Popular revolution against economic and political oppression	Changed only lyrics of economic tune; elitist musical score remained unchanged
Access to power	Through impartial law	Through personal patronage
Responsibility for one's welfare	Individual	*Patrón* and in-group
Hiring and promotion criteria	Performance and skills	Family and social background
Social governance basis	Rule of law	Rule of men
Primary role of military	Defend against external threat	Defend against internal threat

company decisions. Because politicians and bureaucrats controlled the economy, the key to business survival was to influence those government officials who wrote and enforced the rules of the game. Thus, executives focused on nurturing friendly contacts in local and national power circles who had the *palanca* (leverage) needed to put a company on the inside track. When compounded by decrepit infrastructures, political controls created a distorted business reality that forced companies to assign priority to influencing or circumventing government policy, and to struggle with supply and production bottlenecks. After dealing with political and production headaches, executives had little time or will to worry about raising customer satisfaction levels.

The misguided policies and official corruption that marked controlled economies widened the tension between the private and public sectors. Executives thumbed their noses at rules that they saw as having been made solely to undermine business or exact a payoff.

Among the worst offenders of efficient business practices were SOEs. The bloated payrolls and rigid, inward-looking organizational cultures typical of SOEs were the antithesis of what was required to become customer oriented and cost competitive. The policy pill prescribed to treat the competitive paralysis of Latin America's SOEs was privatization.

From State-Owned Enterprises to Privatization

After almost 500 years of sliding down the slippery slope of state-controlled markets, Latin America's economies hit bottom in the Lost Decade and began to climb the opposite bank by adopting the belt-tightening programs advocated by the International Monetary Fund. The policy thread of those neoliberal measures that had the most direct and dramatic effects on the conduct of business was the privatization of numerous SOEs. Airlines, railroads, sea and air ports, telecommunications, cigarette and food manufacturing, tourist resorts, and even a Mexican nightclub were among the gamut of public enterprises that Latin American governments turned over in whole or in part to private capital.

The demise of the SOEs as public institutions was a microlevel sequel to the death of ISIs at the macroeconomic level. Privatization was driven primarily by the prospect of fiscal benefits. By selling unprofitable SOEs to private investors, governments would no longer have to drain treasuries to bail losers out. Hungry budgets would be fed by tax proceeds received from enterprises that had become profitable under efficient private management. By combining the receipts received from the sales of SOEs, the savings from not having to support operating losses, and the new tax revenues, governments would gain the means to increase spending on their countries' desperate social needs and reduce their massive foreign debt.

Privatization gradually lowered the wall of distrust and misunderstanding that has always strained relations between the public and private sectors in Latin America. As financial objectives displaced political objectives in the former SOEs, Latin American industry gained competitive strength through sane capital investment, updated technology, professional management, and direct access to export markets. In the process, the role of the state became more cooperative and technically oriented toward private enterprise.

Civil Law Becomes More Business Friendly

Corporate governance can improve no faster than the legal environment in which corporations operate. A key improvement is narrowing the gap between yesterday's obsolete legal norms and today's business needs. For example, the procedural obstacles shown in Table 3.1, although still onerous, are notably more business friendly than they were prior to the reforms of the 1990s and 2000s.

An important topic on which civil law and common law once differed greatly, but now appears to be converging, is tax law. As open-market policies reduce import duties and export taxes, national budgets are increasingly financed by income taxes and value-added taxes (VATs). The United States is the model for the former, Europe for the latter. The U.S. Internal Revenue Service has been a strong influence on training Latin tax officials in matters of policy, audit, and enforcement. Whereas income-tax evasion was blatant just 25 years ago, it has steadily dropped since the Lost Decade. Nonetheless, a trend is building toward generating government revenues more from VATs than from income taxes. Whereas autonomous tax examiners used to pocket with impunity the settlements they negotiated with taxpayers, governments now find that the more straightforward VAT system lends itself to less perfidy between taxpayers and tax collectors. Taxation under the VAT system is less complex because a firm's tax liability is simply a flat percentage of its sales adjusted for the cumulative tax that was paid as the product advanced through the supply chain. A major benefit of the VAT system is that it is self-enforcing: it is in the interests of manufacturers and resellers to keep customers honest about reporting true invoice values.

Corruption on the Defensive

People who did much business in Latin America prior to the 1990s know that government corruption was a pervasive and unavoidable fact of business life. Bribery would flourish wherever there was an import duty to be levied, a routine permit to be signed, or a government purchasing contract to be awarded. Trying to conduct business in those times without engaging in bribery was like trying to nail Jell-O to a tree. But times are changing. Researchers show that as countries become more exposed to global trade, adopt more open markets, and become more democratic, they also experience lower levels of corruption.[25,26] Latin America is no exception. As Latin American governments became more decentralized in the 1990s and 2000s, local-government budgets and responsibilities grew commensurately. The passing of more power to the municipal level had countervailing effects on corruption: on the one hand, there were more resources available for ethically flexible local powers to plunder, but the greater visibility of those resources enabled more effective local oversight. A report by the Center for Strategic and International Studies described how, in Mexico and in Peru, corruption was combated as access to government information and efficiency in government services improved.[27]

In Mexico, the city of Torreón created a joint commission of citizens and public officials to oversee municipal processes, established a Web site for citizens to anonymously report corrupt officials, published online all-public contracting opportunities and bidding, and listed all public works and progress-tracking information on the Internet. As one indicator of progress in stamping out corruption, Torreón purged 70 percent of its police force, hiring prescreened employees to replace the fired officers.

A Peruvian civic organization, Ciudadanos al Día (Up-to-Date Citizens), battles corruption by surveying citizens' opinions about the quality of services they receive from various public agencies. Ranked and published in the media, survey results have spurred competition among municipalities to gain public approval by improving their service delivery.

The saying "Closed borders mean open palms" was rooted in the high import duties that fueled much of Latin America's corruption during the pre–Lost Decade period of ISI. When import duties were reaching 100 percent or more, an importer-friendly customs officer, unburdened by ethical restraint, could live off the fat of the land. He could accept an undervalued export invoice, or change a product's tariff classification to a lower duty rate, or ignore a few extra cartons of merchandise that somehow had escaped being included on the shipper's packing list. But when duty rates edged down to 20 percent, much of the fat had fallen from the bone. And when they slipped to five percent, even most of the bone vanished. As tariff barriers across Latin America fell in the 1990s and 2000s, customs corruption did not disappear, but it became less blatant. Helpfully, most Latin American governments wish to ensure that the process of clearing customs is one that will neither discourage investment and tourism nor despoil the image of their country. Recent evidence of this trend is Mexico's decision to fire all 700 of its customs inspectors, replacing them with better trained professionals.[28]

A 2009 study reported that 86 percent of companies in Argentina, Brazil, Chile, and Mexico consider corruption and legal insecurity to be their countries' greatest problems, and customs shakedowns were not the firms' only complaint.[29] A major source of corruption was connected to government purchasing. If you wanted to sell to the government (which still today is the largest single buyer in any Latin American country), you had to build the cost of *la mordida* (literally, the bite) into your bid price. Even though thousands of corrupt SOEs have been privatized, it would be naive to claim that corrupt officials and bureaucrats have disappeared from government purchasing offices in Latin America. It is more accurate to say that instead of being able to touch and taste today's routine bribery, as in the past, you now just smell it.

But, knowing how even the smell of corruption can undermine economic development and social inclusion goals, many responsible Latin American leaders are acting to make government purchasing more transparent. As an example, Mexico's president recently made a strong appeal to the private sector to denounce corruption in public-sector dealings, inviting reports of wrongdoing to be made directly to his office or by the Internet.[30]

The typical public tender process of today is clean and transparent. Bid documents are adequately advertised, although you may need to pick up the bidder's package in person at a designated government office, and have cash or a counter check drafted on a local bank to pay for the document copy fee. On the date and at the place and time specified, sealed bid envelopes are collected from the bidders physically present, opened in full view, and their contents announced publicly.

So, is there a catch? Well, even though the tender bidding process has become more open today, bidders can still pull the key levers that control award decisions by influencing the technical specifications written in the tender document. Being influential in the procurement process at an early stage is an advantage. Firms may underbid their services at the project definition, design, or engineering stages. Any profits they forego at these early stages may be offset by the gains made from being in a position to specify a set of project standards that favor themselves and place competitors at a disadvantage for the final construction or purchasing award.

A less legitimate variation on this same theme is to cultivate the goodwill of the government technicians responsible for specifying contract standards. Two notable developments make "friend-of-the-pen" approaches more difficult. The first is the increased oversight and auditing of the bid process on the part of bilateral (e.g., U.S. Agency for International Development) and multilateral (e.g., Inter-American Development Bank) donors that fund large projects. The second, and probably more far-reaching constraint, is the vastly greater access to project information available to alert competitors and media reporters through the Internet and other publicly accessible sources. Freely obtainable information is the most powerful deterrent available to curb corruption, bolster competitive markets, and encourage clean and open business dealings. Happily, those are the very conditions that create the potential for small businesses to thrive.

Personalism versus the Cult of Democracy

Latin America had turned an important corner by the 1990s. Five centuries of authoritarian rule had been replaced by popularly elected governments everywhere but Cuba. Replacing bullets with ballots is a strong boost for business growth and investment security. Latin Americans learned that, if it was difficult to attain freedom in the market arena without having freedom in the political arena, it is virtually impossible to have political freedom without market freedom. As popularly elected leaders replaced dictators, rule by law replaced rule by men. As this process matures, democracy deposes crony capitalism, and economic power passes to smaller firms that compete on the basis of customer service, ethical practice, and creative initiative.

Bumps, Detours, and U-Turns on the Road to "The New Normal"

Writing thousands of years ago, the poet Horace noted, "Adversity has the effect of eliciting talents which in prosperous circumstances would have lain dormant."[31] Horace's wisdom has lasted through the ages, and it seems directly applicable to Latin America's turnaround from the Lost Decade. The fiscal and monetary belt-tightening that Latin America had suffered during the Lost Decade of the 1980s began to pay off during the 1990s. Positive outlooks for business were evident in countless microlevel effects that could be traced directly to macrolevel reforms made after the

Lost Decade. An example is the gains made by Argentina as it deregulated its economy. Major cost savings were achieved between 1991 (the last year of the Lost Decade) and 1996. During that short period, unit manufacturing costs fell by 16 percent. Those impressive production gains were complemented by savings of 67 percent in the cost of port containers, 26 percent in electricity, 20 percent in water and sewage disposal, 30 percent in postal rates, and 43 percent in ocean freight.[32] Such positive results encouraged policy makers to redesign institutions and launch ambitious economic policy reforms.

To gain public backing, the raft of reforms they proposed after the Lost Decade was broadly promoted. Expectations for the new policies were high, and, indeed, the region enjoyed a heartening return to healthy economic growth between 1992 and 1997. But not all the promises carried in that raft of reforms were successful in reaching the opposite shore. Many of the promises failed because of the Asian financial crisis of 1997, declining terms of trade for non-oil-exporting economies, and the U.S. recession in 2001–2002. As Latin American economies contracted between 1998 and 2003, during what came to be called the Lost Half-Decade, social tensions grew. When coupled with events occurring outside of Latin America, the social stresses of the 1990s and 2000s created fresh conditions that were shaping a new normal for the region by the 2010s.

Moderates and Pink Populists

As the 2000s advanced, it became clear that the journey forward would not be smooth and straight. Many countries, such as Mexico and Brazil, elected leaders moderately to the right or left of the centerline, and those countries tended to heed the market-friendly and consensus-based investment and tax-policy lessons learned from the Lost Decade. But, capitalizing on the discontent sown by the Lost Half-Decade or by continuing social exclusion, a minority of national leaders took a U-turn, returning to the statist economic and social policies of earlier periods. United in their agreement on the evils of neoliberalism and U.S. domination, the back-to-the-past movement coalesced around Hugo Chávez, who assumed the presidency of Venezuela in 1998, and soon formed a tight bond with Castro's Cuba. In greater or lesser degrees, its adherents—presidents Nestor and Cristina Kirchner of Argentina, Evo Morales of Bolivia, Rafael Correa of Ecuador, and Manuel Ortega of Nicaragua—pursued populist policies of nationalization of private assets, government controls over markets and broadcast media, runaway public spending, and an anti-U.S. rhetoric.[33-41] As economic uncertainty and social turmoil came to a boil in these volatile populist environments in the early 2010s, confidence in the economy stalled, inflation rose, and new job-generating activity fell. Private capital took flight and showed few signs of soon returning. Indeed, the four "Bolivarian" countries of Venezuela, Ecuador, Bolivia, and Nicaragua, together with Argentina, accounted for almost 50 percent of the total number of pending complaints brought by world investors to the International Court for the Settlement of Investment Disputes.[42] In the past, internal discontent and lack of external investor confidence often have presaged a weakening of antibusiness regimes.

Crime Does Not Pay—It Costs

Latin America is a violent place. Next to sub-Saharan Africa, it has the highest murder rate in the world. Research by the Inter-American Development Bank concludes that the region could raise its per capita income by 25 percent merely by lowering its crime rate to the world's average.[43] While narco-violence and kidnapping in Colombia and Mexico and youth gang activity in Central America increasingly captured headlines in the 2000s, it was uneven education that underlay much of the region's lawlessness. The education of lower income Latin Americans often ends before they enter secondary school. Although their primary-school education makes them literate, it also makes them "educated enough to understand how unfit [they] are for modernity."[44] That awareness makes crime seem a rational career alternative to many. In response, business ramps up its anticrime measures: bodyguards are hired, armed escorts guard truck convoys, building security is hardened, employees are monitored and backgrounds are checked, kidnap insurance is purchased, and inventory and purchasing controls are tightened. As a result, the economic cost of crime is high, estimated to reach eight percent of GDP in Mexico,[45] for example—more than four times what that country spends on education.

The Oriental Express

By the 2010s, China had risen from obscurity to become the most well-known new actor on Latin America's trade and investment stage. Already displacing the United States as Brazil's largest trading partner and Chile's top destination for exports, China has become a "trade angel"[46] for the region. China's investments and loans to the region not only secure it a source to feed its hunger for raw materials, but also are an alternative to investing its massive cash surpluses in United States Treasury notes.[47] As natural resources flow from Latin America to China, finished goods flow back in the other direction. Most of China's exports to the region in the early 2000s were labor-intensive products, such as footwear, clothing, and toys. Today, China is exporting a growing amount of more sophisticated goods, such as consumer electronics, industrial machinery, motorcycles, and automobiles.[48] As the Chinese sell more high-end products to the region, and U.S. exporters find their traditional markets threatened, political pressure may build in the United States to regain lost market share by widening and deepening FTAs with Latin America.

20–21 VISION: THE PRESENCE OF THE FUTURE

Kierkegaard lamented that life could only be understood backward, but must be lived forward. But even if our hindsight understanding of Latin America has not always been a perfect 20–20, we are not condemned to be stone-blind to the future. We can claim some prescience by virtue of knowing that Latin America looks to the future with 20–21 vision: it sees its experience with 20th-century policy failure as a lesson to inform wiser policy choices in the 21st century.

It is already seeing concrete results of wise policy choices in such elemental determinants of economic development as labor productivity. During the preturnaround years of 1975–1990, annual changes in labor productivity in agriculture averaged 1.9 percent; in industry, a discouragingly negative 0.9 percent. The corresponding measures for the post–Lost Decade period 1990–2005 were 3.5 percent in agriculture and 2.0 percent in industry. Labor productivity gains made tangible are seen in the region's movement to add economic value by working smarter. From Brazil's world-class Embraer commercial jets to Mexico's vibrant aviation sector,[49] Latin America shows clear signs of turning away from its traditional but no longer viable model of competing with cheap hands. Although its movement up the value chain is not always steady or evenly distributed from country to country or sector to sector, the nearly universal shifts in the region's historical record are unmistakable signs that the Latin American policy genie is out of the bottle, and that there is no easy way to put it back in:

- Business-friendly governments
- Growing adherence to democracy and the rule of law

- Commitment to free trade and open markets
- Deregulated and consumer-oriented markets
- Legal systems geared for smaller businesses
- Less tolerance for corruption
- Improving telecommunication and road, port, and air transportation infrastructures

Those landmark shifts argue that the historic transformation sweeping Latin America is creating a range of business opportunities that has never been more varied, or more favorable, to small U.S. firms.

The Persistence of the Past

Like chewing gum sticking to a shoe sole, however, the business habits acquired during Latin America's protectionist past adhere to its present, slowing its progress toward the future. Using yesterday's controlled-economy market rules to do business in today's open markets is akin to playing night golf with meatballs on a crocodile farm. The powerful forces of improved competitiveness unleashed after the Lost Decade and the Lost Half-Decade are loosening the gluelike grip on the way business has traditionally been conducted in the region. Latin executives mired in that sticky tradition are fighting the last war. But there are occasions when you may be able to help yourself by helping them become unstuck. When an important business relationship is at stake, judicious nudges by trusted and experienced U.S. executives may help pull a Latin partner out of an unproductive rut. The key is for U.S. executives to be alert to the signs of the rut, and to know in what direction to nudge their Latin partners. The willingness of Latin executives to climb on board the modern management boat is an encouraging indicator of a firm's future prospects.

Table 3.3 summarizes the signs of tradition-bound companies, contrasting their management behavior with that of modern, globally competitive organizations.

Finding the Shoe That Fits

There is little question about the overall direction of change in Latin America's business environment. The reality of the ongoing transformation is mirrored in the evening news, in daily company operations, and in the content of management-development seminars. Larger questions concern

Table 3.3

Contrasts in Business Behaviors of Modern and Traditional Companies

Business Practice	Modern (Open-Market) Pattern	Traditional (ISI, Protected-Market) Pattern
Production planning	Produce for demand	Produce for inventory
Intraorganizational communication	Delegated decision making, vertical and horizontal information flows	Top-down decision making, vertical information flows
Organizational structure	Few management levels, stays flat as organization grows, flexible response	Steep pyramid, gains management levels as organization grows, rigid response
Organizational divisions	By integrated product lines, defined by final markets	By specialized function, defined by internal priorities
Personnel selection	By merit, past performance	By family or social standing
Labor force	Trainable for multiple functions	Low skills limit to specialized functions
Productivity measure	Total cost of each product, zero-defects quality standards as target, benchmarking practiced	Costing of each function (production, marketing, etc.), tolerant of defects, unaware of industry best practices
Research and development	Innovative, viewed as essential to competitive performance	Imitative, practiced on a limited, as-needed basis
Technology choice	Product and process optimization, carefully selected	Product imitation, process adaptation; adopted with limited information
Organizational focus	Market orientation	Production and political orientation

the different rates at which the new features are being transferred from country to country and, within countries, from cities to the countryside. But the largest and most incisive questions are rooted in the growing realization that, in the process of trading crony capitalism for market capitalism, there is no one-size-fits-all policy for doing business. At the regional level, management models that have worked in the United States and elsewhere must be adapted to fit conditions unique to Latin America. At the country level, strategies tailored to fit, say, Brazil, will seldom fit Nicaragua. At the corporate level, it is obvious that privately owned smaller firms will play a larger role in the new economy than will the state-owned megamonopolies of the past. The access those smaller firms have to capital, markets, and modern management and technology is pivotal to the region's economic future.

Latin America has come of age for smaller firms. The fall in tariff barriers, coupled with advances in transportation and communication technologies, now make it practical and profitable for smaller firms in both realms of the Americas to do business with each other. The similarities between Anglo American and Latin American smaller firms in terms of operating scales, company cultures, project time horizons, and product types make them natural business allies.

The Future Is Now

Benjamin Disraeli wrote that the key to business and political success was to understand the times in which one lives. But that wise statesman failed to tell us how to do it. Historians tell us that momentous turning points in the course of human events are seldom apparent to those living at the time they are happening. The unawareness that people have of the historic context in which they live is akin to the fish's indifference to the water that surrounds it. This analogy may help explain why the opportunities for smaller businesses that have been building in Latin America during the last two decades may still be one of today's best-kept secrets. By turning the page on a five-century tradition of an inward-looking mindset rooted in an indigenous and Iberian feudal past, Latin America has opened a new chapter on global integration. Today's historic turnaround is creating opportunities that give smaller U.S. firms access to the lucrative international deals that a close-fisted destiny had previously bestowed only on large multinational corporations.

Notes

1. Brian W. Blouet and Olwyn M. Blouet, "Historical Geography of Latin America," in *Latin America and the Caribbean*, ed. Brian W. Blouet and Olwyn M. Blouet, 4th ed. (New York: John Wiley, 2002), 51–96.

2. John Herman McElroy, *American Beliefs* (Chicago: Ivan R. Dee, 1999).

3. Frank Tannenbaum, *Ten Keys to Latin America* (New York: Knopf, 1962).

4. McElroy, *American Beliefs*.

5. Peter L Bernstein, *The Immortal Metal That Once Ruled the World* (New York: Wiley, 2000), 8.

6. P. C. Roberts and Karen LaFollette Araujo, *The Capitalist Revolution in Latin America* (New York: Oxford University Press, 1997).

7. Christopher Fildes, "Spanish Chestnut," *The Spectator,* November 19, 1988, 22.

8. K. S. Rosenn, "A Comparison of Latin American and North American Legal Traditions," in *Multinational Managers and Host Government Interactions,* ed. Lee A. Tavis (Notre Dame, IN: University of Notre Dame Press, 1988).

9. "Doing Business 2010," World Bank, Washington, DC, 2009, http://www.doingbusiness.org/economyrankings/?direction=Asc&sort=1 (accessed March 30, 2010).

10. James G. Tillen and J. Mattison Ellis, "Confronting Corruption in Latin America," *World Trade,* February 2009, 8.

11. Sam Anson, "Managing FCPA Risk from Third Party Agents," *Kroll Tendencias,* no. 86, August 2009, http://mx.mc383.mail.yahoo.com/mc/welcome?.gx=1&.tm=1271876459&.rand=0cvvvfgrooek1#_pg=showMessage&sMid=14&fid=C3&filterBy=&.rand=536109883&midIndex=14&mid=1_12024_ABN9v9E AAHivSpYK2Qdw9j30yAg&fromId=drbeckeris@yahoo.com&m=1_7370_ABR9v 9EAAH8sSwNvlAD62FeMtWg,1_8259_ABV9v9EAAPcqSti8sgpHWTMdn%2F8,1 _9050_ABF9v9EAAMPrSqbhPgB62kWlLMQ,1_10377_ABV9v9EAABoxSqC1Fwu3E RTS%2F%2F0,1_11185_ABZ9v9EAAXXNSqCoSQBorAC4VaU,1_12024_ABN9v9E AAHivSpYK2Qdw9j30yAg,1_12938_ABF9v9EAAA6fSpE8swr4H2yem6s,1_14084 _ABF9v9EAADZHSYRmKAmxdmdiLrQ,1_15031_AHd9v9EAAVjER4EnCwkVkD3 pEjc,&sort=date&order=down&startMid=0&hash=8d00f7395146e651acad8d5834 d781fb&.jsrand=3667890 (accessed December 9, 2009).

12. McElroy, *American Beliefs*.

13. R. Morse, "The Heritage of Latin America," in *The Founding of New Societies,* ed. L. Hartz, vol. 123 (New York: Harcourt, Brace, and World, 1964).

14. Emilio Willems, *Latin American Culture* (New York: Harper & Row, 1975).

15. Alma Guillermoprieto, *The Heart That Bleeds* (New York: Alfred Knopf, 1994), 54.

16. Alberto Chong and Florencio López de Silanes, "Corporate Governance in Latin America," Working Paper 591, Inter-American Development Bank, March 2007, 3.

17. Barbara Wall, "In Latin America, Unease Grows," *International Herald Tribune*, October 10, 2000, 11.

18. "Secuestros en Mexico," Instituto Ciudadano de Estudios Sobre la Inseguridad (Mexico City), August 2008.

19. José DelaCerda Gastélum, *La Estrategia de las Latinas* (Mexico City: LID Editorial, 2009), 125–134.

20. Economic Commission for Latin America, *Annual Report 1996*, Santiago, 1997.

21. Michael Reid, *Forgotten Continent: The Battle for Latin America's Soul* (New Haven: Yale University Press, 2007).

22. Sebastian Edwards, *Crisis and Reform in Latin America* (New York: Oxford University Press, 1995), 24.

23. Economic Commission for Latin America, *Annual Report 1996*.

24. John Williamson and Pedro Pablo Kuczynski, eds., *After the Washington Consensus: Restarting Growth and Reform in Latin America* (Washington, DC: Institute for International Economics, 2004).

25. Wayne Sandholtz and William Koetzle, "Accounting for Corruption: Economic Structure, Democracy, and Trade," *International Studies Quarterly* 44 (2000): 31–50.

26. Shang-Jin Wei, "Natural Openness and Good Government," National Bureau of Economic Research Working Paper (Washington, DC: June 2000).

27. Katherine Bliss and Peter DeShazo, "Controlling Corruption in Local Government in Latin America," *Policy Papers on the Americas*, vol. 20, study 1, 4–6 (Washington, DC: Center for Strategic and International Studies, January 2009).

28. "Mexico Replaces Customs Officials," *Philadelphia Enquirer: World & Nation*, August 17, 2009, 1, http://www.philly.com/inquirer/world_us/20090817 _In_the_World.html (accessed September 2, 2009).

29. Alejandro Clavería, "Corrupción Sería el Principal Problema en la Región," *América Economía*, May 13, 2009, http://www.americaeconomia.com/ 268341-Corrupcion-seria-elprincipal-problema-en-la-region (accessed February 15, 2010).

30. Jorge Ramos, "Calderon Pide Denunciar Corrupción," *El Universal* (Mexico City), April 21, 2010, M1.

31. Quotation appeared in Gerard J. Arpey, "Diversity Trumps Adversity," *American Way*, January 1, 2010, 6.

32. "International Notes," *Forbes*, September 1, 1998, 27.

33. Darcy Crowe and Dan Molinski, "Prices in Venezuela Surge after Devaluation," *Wall Street Journal*, January 13, 2010, A8.

34. Enrique Campos Suárez, "Socialismo del Siglo XXI," *El Economista* (Mexico City), January 12, 2010, 8.

35. "The Ortega-Chavez Axis," *Wall Street Journal*, February 22, 2010, A17.

36. "Bolivia: Gobierno Tomaría Control de Eléctricas," *América Economía*, 2009, http://www.americaeconomia.com/Note=376049 (accessed February 24, 2010).

37. "Ejército Evitará Alza de Precios," *Excelsior* (Mexico City), January 2010, 1.

38. "Argentina Seizes the Central Bank," *Wall Street Journal*, February 8, 2010, A19.

39. Dan Molinski, "Venezuela Jails Judge Who Freed Banker," *Wall Street Journal*, December 19, 2009, A9.

40. Francisco J. Nuñez de la Pena, "Necesidad y Urgencia," *El Economista* (Mexico City), January 12, 2010, 43.

41. "Another Test for the Chilean Model," *Wall Street Journal*, December 21, 2009, A18.

42. Antonio María Delgado, "¿Por Qué A. Latina Se Covirtió en la Meca de los Arbitrajes Por Incumplimiento?" *América Economía*, April 2010, http://www.americaeconomia.com/notas/se-buscan-abogados (accessed April 26, 2010).

43. Lawrence W. Tuller, *An American's Guide to Doing Business in Latin America* (Avon, MA: Adams Business, 2008), 35.

44. Javier Corrales, "Markets, States, and Neighbors," *Americas Quarterly*, Spring 2009, 28.

45. "Mexico: The Cost of Crime," *Latin Business Chronicle*, September 22, 2008, http://www.latinbusinesschronicle.com/app/article.aspx?id=2755 (accessed February 27, 2010).

46. Javier Santiso, "Can China Change Latin America?" *OECD Observer*, July 2007, http://www.oecdobserver.org/news/fullstory.php/aid/2281/Can_China_change_Latin_America? (accessed February 27, 2010).

47. Alex Pasternak, "China Goes to Latin America for Oil, Minerals—and Water," *Huffington Post*, April 17, 2009, http://www.huffingtonpost.com/alex-pasternack/china-goes-to-latin-ameri_b_188513.html (accessed February 27, 2010).

48. Evan Ellis, "China's Maturing Relationship with Latin America," *China Brief* 9, no. 6 (March 18, 2009), The Jamestown Foundation, http://www.jamestown.org/single/?no_cache=1&tx_ttnews[tt_news]=34723&tx (accessed February 28, 2010).

49. Marion Lloyd, "Mexico's Jet Set," *Latin Trade*, December 17, 2009, http://latintrade.com/2009/12/mexico%e2%80%/99s-jet-set (accessed December 23, 2009).

Chapter 4

Using Cultural Literacy to Hone Your Competitive Edge

Deep cultural undercurrents structure life in subtle but highly consistent ways that are not consciously formulated. Like the invisible jet streams in the skies that determine the course of a storm, these currents shape our lives; yet their influence is only beginning to be identified.[1]

CULTURE AS CAPITAL

Business everywhere is a race to beat the competition. To compete, you need enough financial capital to leave the starting gate. Besides enough financial capital, you need enough human capital to continue running the race and reach the finish line. But in Latin America, you will not even be allowed on the track until you have the right kind and the right amount of cultural capital. Cultural capital is as good as cash. Do not leave home without it. It is the surest means you have to earn trust. And trust is the most potent advantage you have to close today's deal, and to book repeat business tomorrow. Two propositions show the pivotal role of trust in making profitable deals happen in Latin America:

Proposition 1: *Rock-Bottom Price + Bell-Ringer Product = Sale*
Proposition 2: *Reasonable Price + Reasonable Product + Customer's Trust = Sale*

Proposition 1 describes a world that never was or will be. The premises underlying it are rooted in the "simplifying" assumptions that you had to learn to pass Economics 101. It is a flawed approach to doing business anywhere, especially in Latin America. It presumes that buyers are vendor neutral and will instantly issue a purchase order to any new supplier whenever that supplier offers a lower price or a better product. Those who have failed to lure a loyal customer away from a competitor simply by offering what they believed was a better deal know that it takes more than neat and tidy blackboard theory to land a new account. The sterility of economic theory flies in the face of human behavior when an unknown anybody, representing an unknown brand of an unknown company located in an unknown place, tells a prospect to abandon a supplier who has cultivated his or her trust over many years.

Proposition 2 mirrors the reality known to executives that are experienced in opening markets in Latin America. Veterans of successful Latin American marketing campaigns know that you do not have to engage in cutthroat pricing or offer bell-ringer products to prosper in Latin America. Nevertheless, it is essential to reassure customers that they can rely on your word because it is backed by your own personal integrity. When you motivate customers to buy only from you because you are trustworthy, you expand the envelope of what constitutes an acceptable price and product. That is why trust is such a precious currency in Latin America. Wise executives will try to earn, conserve, and invest it with the same discretion that controls their other business decisions.

You Cannot Afford to Ignore Your Customer's Cultural Roots

Anthropologists know that individuals who share a common culture also tend to exhibit similar personality traits, attitudes, and beliefs. This makes culture the chief determinant of the way individuals view the world about them, relate to others, and make decisions. Any force that has such an armlock on business decisions is worth understanding. Use the information that follows to jumpstart the process of making culture work for you.

What You Don't Know Can Hurt You

The cultural dissimilarities that evolved over five centuries have made the Anglo American and Latin American business systems diverge widely. Nonetheless, the thrust of globalization over the last 25 years is steadily nudging the traditional business systems of Latin America toward convergence with modern Western systems. In the 2010s, elements of both traditional and modern cultures coexist in Latin America. Your sales and earnings performance can hang on knowing how to discriminate between the old and new ways, and on knowing how to make them work together to your best advantage.

Tip O'Neill rose from obscurity to become Speaker of the U.S. House of Representatives by practicing a simple rule: "All politics is local." The former Speaker's rule for success in the political arena applies with equal force to the international trade arena, where "all business is local." Putting that rule into practice is easy: know the territory, and never believe anyone who claims that "people are alike and do business the same way everywhere." Blindness to local differences in culture can lead otherwise able executives to write ethnocentric checks that their firms cannot afford to cash.

Moving beyond Yesteryear's Path

John Herman McElroy[2] draws an analogy between the evolution of a culture and the formation of a path. He reasons that the first person to traverse a new landscape chose a route that seemed the most expedient course for the existing conditions. Later travelers followed that pioneer's track because they believed it would lead them where they wanted to go. Over time, that initial track evolved into a plainly marked path that all travelers now follow. Its constant use has confirmed it as the right course. Cultural traditions are formed similarly. Each generation takes on as its own the beliefs and values of the prior generation. As the established way of life is successively imitated over repeated generations, its behavioral patterns steadily take on the force of a mandated tradition. It is only when the original formative conditions undergo obvious and threatening change that the culture, like the path, becomes amenable to change. As the tide of globalization encroaches upon their habitual path, Latin Americans are exploring new paths. In the process, they are revolutionizing the way business is being done in the Americas.

The following two sections provide insights into Latin American culture from a U.S. business perspective. The first views how Latin American organizations are run and how decisions are made within them. The second views how culture affects the workings of the marketplace in Latin America. For convenience, those two perspectives are described from the viewpoint of a U.S. seller interacting with a buyer in Latin America. Even if your business in Latin America is not exporting, but importing, investing, licensing, or finding a strategic-alliance partner, these sections contain tips to help you put profitable deals together south of the border.

LATIN AMERICAN BUSINESS CULTURE: PROFILE OF MANAGEMENT AND ORGANIZATIONAL BEHAVIOR

When you arrive in Latin America from the United States, you instantly notice that you have crossed more than a mere national border. You have entered into another realm. You are assailed and invigorated by the strange sights, smells, and sounds of this new reality. So varied and intense are the changes in these unfamiliar surroundings, that your senses are overwhelmed. The obviousness of these surface contrasts masks a deeper truth: the forces underlying the business opportunities and challenges you will find in Latin America are not to be seen in the outward expressions of this new environment. Rather, the forces driving your business destiny are embedded in the more subtly sensed differences in traditions, values, and expectations. A veteran of many Latin American business campaigns sums it up this way: "Ignore what you can see" (that is, the sun, sand, and other attractive distractions), "and pay attention to what you can't see" (that is, the invisible cultural forces controlling human behavior).

This section discusses the cultural forces that shape the realm of human conduct where what you cannot see is key to how Latin American organizations and managers behave. Even though that realm is invisible, what happens in it is as real as bedrock, and it can make the difference between your venture's success or failure. To find your way in that invisible realm, think of it as being charted by seven guideposts. Knowing how to read these guideposts will give you the cultural literacy equivalent of night-vision goggles, letting you see the opportunities and avoid the traps to which your culturally illiterate competitors will be blind.

Seven Guideposts to Latin American Business Culture

Culture is both the paintbrush and the armor of the mind. It colors the way we view the world, and it protects us from those who are unlike us and could do us harm. The worldview shared by members of one culture is never arbitrarily different from another. Rather, it reflects the many forks in the path of human experience, where each has taken a different turn to set its own course. The central ways in which business cultures of Latin America and the United States have diverged can be traced to seven pivotal turning points that are identified by seven guideposts: power inequality, structure need, social orientation, universalism-particularism, communication, time and space, and formality. This section describes the guideposts and traces the different courses taken by the region's two dominant business cultures.

The first three guideposts are described by Geert Hofstede in his rigorous research on culture-determined management attitudes.[3,4] Hofstede found that over 50 percent of differences in managers' attitudes was due to national culture, a proportion far greater than could be explained by managers' profession, gender, race, or age. Hofstede's study included 13 Latin American national cultures, each of which displayed its own profile of attitudes. For simplicity, those 13 cultural scores have been reduced to a single composite for each of Hofstede's three attitudinal measures included here. Although using an average measure creates a loss of descriptive precision for individual national cultures, it allows us to portray broadly how Latin Americans view the world about them and behave in accordance with that view.

1. Power Inequality

Called power distance by Hofstede, power inequality reflects the degree to which less powerful individuals in a society accept that power is distributed unequally. Cultures ranking high in power inequality tend to concentrate decision making at the top. Hence, managers from countries that rank high on power inequality tend to seek decision-making approval from superiors more often and on more issues than do managers from lower ranking countries. That approval-seeking process delays progress on key decisions that must be taken within the short timeframe of a business trip or a production timetable. Those delays frequently frustrate executives from the United States, where power attitudes are lower.

(The scale on the next page and those that follow show how Latin America and the United States rank on key cultural measures. For purposes of comparison, they also show the national cultures that rank highest and lowest on each measure.)

Social Implications.   The rankings on the next page show that, relative to the typical Anglo, who tolerates authority, the Latin respects authority, accepting as a given Latin America's large differences in power. Those different attitudes translate to different management styles. In the United

POWER-INEQUALITY RANKING

Most Hierarchy			Most Equality	
1	27		58	74
Malaysia	Latin America		United States	Austria

States, managers are seen as problem solvers. In Latin America, managers are seen as experts. In the United States, a good manager refers an employee to an informed authority when the employee's task involves resolving a problem outside the manager's own expertise. In a traditional Latin American firm, a manager behaving in the same way is deemed incompetent. Similarly, the readiness of U.S. managers to roll up their sleeves and get their hands dirty to resolve an immediate problem on the factory floor is admired by their superiors, peers, and subordinates. In the traditional Latin American work setting, the same behavior might harm the manager's career. His superiors may question the social pedigree of anyone so ready to dirty his hands. Peers may fear his example, alarmed that his behavior could set a bad precedent. Subordinates might lose respect for someone whose low self-esteem would dispose him to engage in such a menial task. In traditional Latin organizations, especially, one shows respect for authority by, for example, addressing people formally and observing differences in status.

Anglos have long rallied around the banner of meritocracy. Their lower power-inequality ranking conditions them to view power as a privilege that must be acquired by legitimate means and used responsibly. They are uncomfortable with whatever they perceive to be unfair or demeaning treatment. The tolerance for high power inequality typical of traditional Latin societies plays a role in the ordinary citizen's feeling of being powerless to correct an overbearing or abusive authority and, thus, of being reluctant to rock the boat. To an Anglo, a frustrating example of this hesitancy to alter the established order could be the unwillingness of a smaller distributor to take aggressive steps to increase market share. His reluctance to act forcefully may stem from not wanting to confront the market leader if the smaller distributor perceives that the market leader occupies a higher position in the local business or social hierarchy.

Rather than feel smugly superior because of their lower tolerance for power differences, Anglos should examine the flip side of the power-inequality coin, which reveals some appealing features of high-power-inequality behavior. For example, Latin American children are raised to be obedient to parents. The view of parents as authority figures spills over into the workplace, where unequal power relationships are considered a part of the natural order, and subordinates expect to be told what to do, ideally by a benign paternal figure. The Latin's hierarchical perspective is at odds with attitudes commonly held in the United States, where children are encouraged to develop and exercise their own free will. Anglo children learn early on to treat their parents as equals (or even inferiors). Although Latins may acknowledge the creativity value of the U.S. free-will mandate instilled during childhood, they also view the drugs, promiscuity, and materialism that plague U.S. society as its unhealthy behavioral extensions.

Managerial Implications. Because of the emphasis placed on equality in the United States, it is not surprising that Anglo workers expect to be consulted about how to perform their jobs, and view hierarchy in the workplace as applicable to workers' roles, not to workers. It follows that participative management styles are widely practiced and that flat, rather than steeply pitched, organizational structures are common in the United States. Because work routinely bypasses managers, power-tolerant Anglos view hierarchy within organizations as a structure to help organize decisions and facilitate information flows. In contrast, power-respecting Latins view the purpose of a pecking order as a mechanism that lets each member of the organization know who has authority over whom.[5]

The cultural attitudes held by low-power-inequality Anglo managers explain the widespread use of participative management practices in U.S. firms, where a manager's operating decisions incorporate the experience and opinions of the employees who will carry out her decisions. This approach is predicated on providing employees with the responsibility and freedom to make work-related decisions that will cause them to be more productive. Essential to empowering employees is ensuring that they are aware of the planning decisions made by superiors.

That level of employee empowerment is seldom practiced in traditional Latin hierarchies.[6] Research comparing managerial behaviors in 12 cultural regions of the world showed that Latin American managers at all levels regarded being considerate to employees as relatively unimportant.[7] As a consequence, employees in traditional organizations work only in the way that management instructs them, because delegating decisions to lower level employees would undermine authority, creating discomfort and uncertainty.

Given the centralized structure of decision making in Latin American organizations, there are likely to be only a few people in a traditionally managed firm who have the clout to decide if that firm will buy your product. These key decision makers are the people with whom you want to be in contact. Going straight to those with purchasing authority will yield better results than beginning with mid-level, technically qualified employees who understand your product but who have no authority to make the buying decision. Once you have established rapport with the decision maker, you will be sent to the technical side of the house to verify if your product is what the firm needs. This makes your sales campaign a two-stage test. First, you must clear the personal relationship hurdle. Only then will your product be submitted for technical evaluation. Attempting to reverse the sequence by selling to the engineers first and then waiting to get referred to the top can cost you much lost time and effort in a traditional Latin American company culture.

2. Structure Need

Hofstede referred to this cultural variable as uncertainty avoidance. It describes the degree to which ambiguity, unknown situations, or unclear rules create discomfort in individuals. People from cultures with high structure need tend to be uneasy if discussions posted on a meeting agenda move into new territory or in unforeseen directions. It is common for them to resist innovative or "outside-of-the-box" solutions, or trying to run when they believe that walking will also get them where they want to go.

Social Implications. Despite their high need for structure, Latin Americans are entrepreneurial.[8] However, their risk-taking ventures have to meet a higher expected rate of return than similar projects would in the United States. The typical U.S. risk taker's attitude of "nothing ventured, nothing gained" is reversed in Latin America. Latins' attitude

STRUCTURE-NEED RANKING

Most			Least
1	20	62	74
Greece	Latin America	United States	Singapore

toward new ventures is "nothing gained, nothing ventured." The region's relatively high levels of economic and political risk tend to make Latins unwilling to commit resources to a new project until much of the uncertainty has been squeezed out, perhaps through leveraging personal contacts or making well-placed bribes.

Managerial Implications. Seeing what is different as curious, Anglos are likely to be open to uncustomary ideas. Seeing what is different as dangerous, Latins are more inclined to resist change. Because employees are protected by rigid work rules, seniority benefits, and severance penalties, efforts to raise performance by streamlining work practices are often blocked in Latin America. Relative to Anglo employees, Latins tend to place greater emphasis on retaining and consolidating their present position than on being promoted to a higher position.

Latins' need for structure in the workplace follows naturally from habits formed in childhood. Latin children are taught to adhere to traditional ways of doing things, and that what is different can be dangerous. The same tendency inclines Latins toward work rules, standardized job descriptions, and the security of seniority. Anglo managers in Latin America often are frustrated by the restraints imposed by customary practices when they seek to impose cross-functional training and work policies, eliminate obsolete work rules, or discharge employees for poor performance. Anglos view procedures and policies merely as guidelines that may be broken if the deviation is best for the company. Latins view those same procedures and policies as absolute, the sacrosanct foundation of the organization's stability and, not incidentally, their own job security.

The higher need of Latins for structure makes them more susceptible to fatalism than Anglos, who believe that people should take charge of their own destiny. In contrast, and at the other extreme, Latins believe that destiny is driven by chance. Accordingly, little can be done to alter a predetermined outcome. Some trace the Latins' predisposition toward fatalism to the region's natural environment[9]: devastating earthquakes, hurricanes, floods, landslides, volcanic eruptions, and tropical diseases breed an acceptance of the inevitable. Such submission to destiny is reflected in the ubiquitous use of the Spanish word *ojalá* (may God be willing) and implies that one should not accept too much personal responsibility for future outcomes. If, for example, a delivery date is missed or a cost overrun occurs, the Latin manager responsible for the failure may strenuously try to externalize the blame, finding excuses for nonperformance in everything except himself.

In Latin America, where high structure need coincides with high power inequality, lines of communication tend to run vertically instead of horizontally. Each subordinate will jealously guard sensitive information from coworkers, sharing it only with the *patrón* (sponsor) to whom he owes his job.[10] The weak horizontal information flow can make traditional Latin organizations slow to respond to market changes or competitive threats.

Family-owned firms are especially susceptible to the paralyzing effects of high structure need and high power inequality. As globalization advances, these organizations face a growing need to update and streamline their operations. In the case of family-owned firms, the two most common modernizing methods are upgrading the managerial skills of family members and hiring professional management from outside the family. As a result, business school enrollments in Latin America are breaking historical records.[11]

The combination of high structure need and high power inequality creates a special type of bureaucrat in Latin America's public sector, one who personifies C. Northcote Parkinson's observation that the man who is denied the opportunity of making decisions of importance regards as important the decisions he is allowed to take. Therefore, no matter how inane a bureaucrat's request for documentation or data may appear, it is essential not only to comply, but to do so with a smile. If you do not treat minor, detail-fixated functionaries with a deference bordering on worship, you may learn painfully that their ability to poison your deal is out of all proportion to the modest stations they occupy in life.

3. Social Orientation

As shown in the scale on the next page, one extreme of this dimension is individualism, defined by the degree to which a culture promotes the role of the individual over that of the group. Its opposite is collectivism, in which individual interests are subordinate to the welfare of the group.

Social Implications. No national culture ranks as high on individualism as the United States. Our natural tendency to project our own values onto other societies can turn our unnatural degree of individualism into a cocked gun, aimed to shoot ourselves in the foot when we do business in Latin America. Consider that most of today's management theories and concepts were formed in the United States during the last 60 years, in a place and time in which assumptions about high individualism

SOCIAL-ORIENTATION RANKING

Most Individualist	Most Group Oriented	
1	60	74
United States	Latin America	Guatemala

limited their relevance to the group-oriented cultures of Latin America. Therefore, wise U.S. executives will realize that much of their business savvy, based on their U.S. experiences, may not apply in Latin America. Their wisdom stems from knowing what they do not know about culture-driven differences in behavior.

As members of the most individualistic culture in the world, Anglos are weak on loyalty to employers, coworkers, communities, neighbors, relatives, and spouses. Because Anglo individualism involves fewer people in making decisions, less time and effort are involved in getting projects moving and responding swiftly to changing conditions than in group-oriented Latin organizations. This tendency has been pivotal in explaining U.S. industry's record level of creativity and the resulting power of the U.S. economy.

Latin American attitudes on individualism vary widely among groups belonging to the same organization. One study surveyed attitudes toward individualism and equality among 2,192 managers and workers in 20 Venezuelan organizations. It found that workers were much more collectivistic and tolerant of unequal power than were managers.[12]

Because collectivism assigns individuals to in-group or out-group membership, affinity circles are a key force in shaping how business is done in Latin America. Latin social relationships are like concentric circles, with an individual's nuclear and extended families occupying the two centermost circles. Moving outward, subsequent circles include more distant relatives, close friends, schoolmates, teammates in sports, and, eventually, everyone to whom the individual feels a degree of obligation or trust. All others lying outside the individual's affinity system are untrustworthy strangers to whom one feels no moral obligation. That detached attitude often leads to nepotism, tax evasion, littering, environmental neglect, and reluctance to cooperate to achieve a common goal.[13] It also helps explain the passiveness that some Latins display to the grinding poverty that surrounds them, and by extension, the region's weakly developed tradition of public charity.[14]

You are defined by others. Individuals within Latin societies may move from one affinity circle to another. But people located outside the circles will remain strangers until they can establish themselves within a circle. If you are on the outside, you must find a way to position yourself within one of the circles to gain the personal trust of its members. One of the surest and most direct ways to win in-group status is to be introduced by an in-group member. Here are some ways to gain in-group membership on at least a probationary basis:

- Have a letter of reference written on your behalf by a U.S. bank that has a correspondent relationship with a reputable bank in Latinoland.
- Take advantage of the bond provided by a common affiliation such as a membership in Rotary International or a religious organization.
- Participate in a trade show or mission sponsored by the U.S. Department of Commerce or your state's export promotion agency. Those functions typically enjoy the prestige of being hosted by U.S. embassies.
- Take every opportunity to make your face known to the widest possible range of businesspersons, bankers, chamber of commerce officers, industry association officials, government bureaucrats, media reporters, and civic leaders.

Managerial Implications. Collectivism emphasizes workplace harmony. When it combines with high power inequality, the conditions are present to create middle-management yes-men. Yes-men choke performance by failing to advise their superiors when something goes wrong on the job or when their superior's judgment is mistaken.

Social orientation affects how salespeople are assigned to territories. In the high-individualism United States, it is not unusual to reassign salespeople to work in a different sales territory. Because customer loyalties are to the product and the company, the appearance of a new salesperson will not disturb the client-vendor relationship. A different outcome may occur in a group-oriented Latin culture, where the constant nurturing of trust between buyer and seller is critical to keeping customers' loyal. In Latin America, you run the risk of losing key accounts if you regularly rotate salespeople.

Social orientation also has a strong effect on the way personnel are hired. The hiring policies of most U.S. firms stress bringing on board the best-qualified applicants because of their performance potential. Job candidates submit resumés emphasizing their professional skills, achievements, and education. Not surprisingly, hiring the best-qualified candidates is also the first concern in traditional group-oriented Latin American firms. The criteria of what constitutes best-qualified for the Latin American position, however, will center more on the applicant's family background, social class, or loyalty to an influential executive, because these are key indicators of a candidate's in-group status and, thus, trustworthiness. The ability to get along with coworkers, of course, is another price of entry to membership in the collegial in-group. Hence, candidates for responsible positions within traditional Latin organizations will focus on cultivating influential employees. So it is no mystery why personal relationships often take precedence over performance in Latin organizations. As a result, Anglo executives who set "getting the job done" as a priority can find it vexing when they must penetrate the barrier of personal relationships before they can approach performance issues. A common mistake made by Anglos, when dealing with blue-collar workers, is to reward individual performance. Such a practice dilutes the work ethic of the group[15] and can lead to lower performance in group-oriented Latin America.

Given the sharply different emphases on hiring and promotion criteria, it is no mystery why Anglo and Latin managers may see one another's personnel policies as misguided. Anglos disdain the nepotistic practices of Latin firms, believing that such policies undermine morale, democracy, and, ultimately, financial performance. Group-oriented Latin managers, on the other hand, believe that the only candidates who can be trusted in responsible positions are those who are known to other responsible employees or who have proved their trustworthiness in other organizations known to share company values. The moral force in collective societies that ties employees and companies together blurs the dividing line between personal lives and work lives. It is common for larger Latin American companies to care for employees' needs by providing them with low-cost food staples, family social and medical services, scholarships, and sports and recreational facilities.

To support their position, Latin managers can point to ample evidence of Anglos' lack of loyalty, as shown by their high turnover in employment, social positions, and matrimonial relationships. In short, the Latin model of the employer-employee relationship is based on the premise of mutual moral obligations. That noble view clashes with the cold and calculating Anglo model wherein employees view their skills and knowledge as marketable commodities and look to sell them to the highest bidder.

The traditions of long-term employment at the same company and loyalty to one's group can be obstacles when trying to recruit managers in Latin America. Prospective candidates for a job will seldom be open to the overtures of a headhunter unless the hiring company has a well-respected name in the business community. Candidates must feel comfortable that the confidentiality of the search process will safeguard their identity. For that reason, advertising an open position in newspapers or on the Internet may not yield the highest quality candidate for the job. More effective recruiting is done by directly and personally inviting a prospective hire to discuss a job possibility in confidence. This approach should be made by a trusted family member, friend, or professional associate, and it should be made outside of the candidate's place of work. Because many qualified candidates will be financially satisfied with their current positions, they are likely to place a high priority on the quality of the new project. Nevertheless, the minimum salary increase a candidate would expect to get in order to jump companies would be 15 percent, with smart negotiators initially asking for a 30 percent hike.

4. Universalism-Particularism

Closely related to Anglos' high sense of individualism is the belief that rules come first, loyalty to friends second. Anglos place great trust in the rule of law to get what they feel they deserve. Group-oriented Latins put relationships first, the rule book second. Subordinating impersonal rules to personal loyalties is called particularism. Its opposite is universalism, the belief that the same set of standards should be applied uniformly to everyone.

Latin American particularism can be traced to an age-old characteristic of human behavior in Spain. There, according to Spanish philosopher José Ortega y Gasset, the feeling of particularism found its origin within the individual himself, expressed in the notion that each man is his own political party.[16] It is a tendency that Cervantes immortalized in the epic work *Don Quijote de la Mancha,* and one that makes it admirably common for Latins to appreciate the normality of a moment in which a humble youth may recite his own poetry as he shines shoes at a bench on the plaza. Particularism permits outsiders to practice nonthreatening idiosyncracies but refuses to grant them social equality.

As the ability to move a profitable deal forward may hinge on gaining the approval of a high-level company or government official, U.S. executives in Latin America often see at close range how in-group members, such as friends or relatives, are treated more favorably by someone in authority. In a study on how culture-based differences affected ethical decisions, some 15,000 managers in 40 countries were surveyed. They were asked to respond to the following situation:

> You are riding in a car driven by a close friend. He hits a pedestrian. You know he was going at least 35 miles per hour in an area of the city where the maximum allowed speed is 20 miles per hour. There are no witnesses. His lawyer says that if you testify under oath that he was only driving 20 miles per hour, it may save him from serious consequences. What right has your friend to expect you to protect him?
>
> a. My friend has a definite right as a friend to expect me to testify to the lower figure.
>
> b. He has some right as a friend to expect me to testify to the lower figure.
>
> c. He has no right as a friend to expect me to testify to the lower figure.[17]

The results of this study are used as a proxy to classify cultures by the extent to which judgments and rules are influenced by personal loyalties (particularism) or impersonal law (universalism). The scale below shows the percentage of respondents from Latin America and the United States who responded to "b" or "c" (Yugoslavia and Norway are included to mark the low and high extremes of the scale).

Among U.S. managers, 78 percent rejected friendship (option "a"), whereas only 45 percent of Latin American managers would have placed rule by law before rule by personal loyalties. The contrast in results does not mean that Anglo managers are more trustworthy. Indeed, a Latin viewing the same results could conclude that Anglos cannot be trusted

RULE-ORIENTATION RANKING

Loyalty—Particularism		Law—Universalism	
12	45	78	90
Yugoslavia	Latin America	United States	Norway

because they would not be willing to help out a friend in need. The results show that the domain of legal rigor in Latin America is constrained by the radii of trust that define the affinity circles mentioned earlier. They also suggest that the favoritism enjoyed by in-group members can play a large role in determining who gains a competitive advantage in particularist cultures.

Here are some lessons that can be learned about doing business in a particularist culture:

1. As a source of competitive advantage, core competencies can count less than close customer relations.
2. Unless your situation is exceptional, avoid the Anglo penchant for going it alone. There is simply no way to overstate the value of locally well-connected, reliable associates who know the ropes.
3. The habit of universalist executives to depend on intricately written contracts to define the rules of a business relationship is at odds with the loosely written, short agreements and personal trust that particularist Latins use to bind an agreement. Latins may regard a lengthy, tightly written contract, especially one that includes penalty clauses, as an indicator that in-group trust is missing. Thus, they will feel little personal obligation to adhere to the terms of the agreement.

5. Communication

Listen to Latin America's silent language. Communication is a contact sport in Latin America. Hearty *abrazos* (embraces) between men; kissing on the cheek (not between men); standing closely together; pats on the back; tugs and squeezes on the arm; two-arm handshakes; energetically expressive arm, hand, and facial gestures; and dancing body movements are standard fare in the warm personal encounters practiced among Latin Americans.

But experienced travelers know that the physical gestures that are so common in Latin America are only one means of expression in the various forms of nonverbal communication practiced across the globe. Cross-cultural researchers distinguish between explicit (called low-context) and implicit (called high-context) styles of communication.[18] Explicit communication styles depend heavily on transmitting the meaning and content of messages through words. Although not as plainspoken as the Swiss, Anglo Americans say what they mean, and mean what they say, because

CONTEXT RANKING

Low—Explicit		High—Implicit	
1	4	9	11
Switzerland	United States	Latin America	Japan

they are low-context communicators and use spoken language to convey meaning. In high-context cultures, much of the message is carried by often subtle, nonverbal cues. This explains why, compared to low-context Anglos, high-context Latins rely on the silent language of subtle signals to convey their messages. Those signals are important cues for you to detect, and may include indicators such as the kind of clothing being worn, facial expressions, hand and arm gesticulations, posture and stance, eye contact, office size and trappings, lapel pins, educational titles and certificates, the use of silence, eating habits, and displays of family and social affiliations.

As low-context communicators, Anglos invest little time in preliminary social exchanges, preferring to advance rapidly to the business at hand. The art of the deal takes longer in the high-context culture of Latin America, as business cannot be conducted effectively until trust levels are established and the parties build personal bonds by getting to know one another.

High-context Latins use a deductive communication process that low-context Anglos, accustomed to building ideas inductively, find frustratingly bewildering. The inductive communicator moves from specific issues to the general framework, building the structure of the discourse piece-by-piece and premise-by-premise from the ground up until the edifice enclosing the deal's elements is complete. When an inductively precise Anglo engages a deductively open-ended Latin who is attempting to build the structure of the transaction from the roof downward, it is not surprising that the patience of both parties will be tested. As a result, the intended deal may never come together in the middle.

The Latin focuses his immediate attention on the overall relationship binding the parties together. He is asking himself: is the right chemistry present to build strong personal bonds between the individuals, and is there enough strategic fit between the companies to expect that the relationship will have a long-term potential? In contrast, the Anglo's concern is about closing today's transaction. The Anglo may believe in the abstract that the possibility exists to build a roof in the future that could be supported by strong personal and strategic ties. Yet, the Anglo also believes that it is premature and pointless to invest much time in talking about the design of the roof until the foundation, formed around the cornerstone of the first transaction, has been set firmly in place.

6. Time and Space

Why do Anglos and Latins often fail to connect as business associates? The answer may be that they inhabit different realms of space and time. Although many humorous anecdotes allude to that space-time separation, it is a real and serious cultural factor that has sabotaged countless deals.

It's about Time.   Anglos' and Latins' differing views about time have spawned much questionable humor and unverifiable anecdotes.[19] The Anglo's notion of time is linear, or monochronic. He has systematic checklists, sequential schedules, punctual meeting times, and hard deadlines. Latins have a polychronic or cyclical view of time, believing that, like the repetition of the natural seasons, there will always be another opportunity to do tomorrow what was put off today. The Latin's agenda is filled with multiple and conflicting activities, a jumbled program that preordains (and thus excuses) schedules that cannot be kept, meetings that are interrupted, and personal and business priorities that are constantly reshuffled. The higher her level of responsibility, the greater is the chance that a Latin executive will be subject to scheduling conflicts.

It is a mistake to think that the Anglo places a higher priority on time than does the Latin. It is more instructive to understand that each has a high regard for the value of time as a finite resource, but chooses to allocate it to different priorities. The Anglo belief that time is money decrees that no time should be wasted in getting down to business. In contrast, the Latin believes that the essence of a successful life is to learn to enjoy the passage of time. Applying this broad view to business, the Latin sees time as a means to judge whether a potential business colleague may be trusted and whether an enduring, warm personal relationship can be developed. Whereas time is the master of Anglos, it is the servant of Latins.

Anglos tend to be future oriented, a condition favored by the relative stability of their U.S. operating environment, and use the present to plan for future events. The volatility of the Latin American environment makes predicting the future a chancy venture. It inclines Latins toward a present orientation, responding to events when they happen, and solving problems with people and patience rather than with plans and procedures.

Although punctuality is somewhat more widely practiced now than in the past, particularly in private firms, it still remains an elusive concept. Calling, the morning of the day they are scheduled, to reconfirm appointments will help minimize no-shows or tardy-shows. If your appointment with a Latin government official is scheduled for 9 A.M., know that, although the designated hour is regarded more as a suggestion than a precise assignment, you should arrive on time. But do not be disappointed if you are placed in a waiting-room holding pattern where the others present know that the only difference between 9 A.M. and 11 A.M. is that the latter is two hours closer to lunch. Use your waiting time productively: strike up a conversation with another visitor or the receptionist. You may learn some useful information. If your linguistic skills preclude easy conversation, always bring a book or something to work on, so that your wait will not be misspent time. Of course, the consequences of a late appointment are that all of your subsequent appointments will get backed up. For this reason, experienced U.S. executives schedule more mealtime appointments per day during a Latin American business trip than when traveling in the United States, Europe, or Japan.

When you are finally received by your Latin colleague, avoid appearing irritated at having had to wait. No matter how exasperated you may feel, you must act genuinely pleased to see her. Be attentive to the social exchanges and extraneous discussions that almost inevitably precede the main business topic. The meandering conversational path that the Latin follows may be significant indicators of what issues she considers to be important.

You may find it consoling to learn that the issue of flexible time standards can cause as much disruption to Latins as it does to schedule-precise Anglos. For example, the wedding band of the wife of a Honduran executive is forever inscribed with a date that precedes the date of their betrothal by seven days. At a dinner party to celebrate the couple's anniversary, the wife was asked why there was a one-week mismatch between the true date and the inscribed date of the wedding. She offered a simple explanation: "Pablo and I wanted to be certain that the jeweler would have our ring ready in time for the ceremony." Consider another example: Having estimated that tardiness cost the country almost five percent of its annual GDP, an Ecuadorian civic group launched a national punctuality campaign. Given much fanfare in the media, the campaign's standing-room-only inaugural had to be delayed because of the tardy arrival of its principal backer—the president of the country.[20]

As a social guideline, know that if you are invited to a Latin's home for dinner at 8 P.M. (your invitation will likely read 20:00 hours because Latin time is based on the 24-hour clock), it would be a mistake to show up sharply at 8. Your host will be surprised and possibly upset, because he did not expect you before 8:30. At the arrival time specified in the invitation, he will probably be bathing or making last-minute preparations for the event.

Life in the United States is fast paced. We want to squeeze as much immediately measurable performance as possible out of every available moment. Latins live *al paso tropical* (at a tropical pace), placing a priority on the leisurely pace that makes enjoying personal relationships possible. Visiting U.S. executives who insist on pushing the clock are not likely to return home with the order. They must learn, as Latins have known for generations, that you cannot make a baby one month from now by getting nine women pregnant today.

My Space or Yours? Notions of personal space vary markedly between Anglos and Latins. It is the physical distance that a person feels comfortable in maintaining with a conversational partner. As individualists, Anglos enjoy their privacy, drawing circles of personal space around themselves and feeling comfortable talking to a person at a distance of about 24 inches. Latins are group oriented. They like to gather together, drawing tight circles around a companionable group, so that its members are compressed to within about 8 inches of one another. If the Anglo perceives that the separation between the conversationalists is too little, he may feel that the Latin is brash for having invaded his privacy. If not interacting within his 8-inch comfort zone, the Latin senses that the separation is too great. He may feel that he might as well be shouting across a valley, and that the Anglo is *anipático* (unsociable).

Given their different perceptions about what constitutes a proper personal space, Anglo and Latin conversationalists may follow a predictable dance movement. Their dance steps are not complicated: feeling threatened by the Latin's closeness, the Anglo steps away; feeling denied by the Anglo's retreat, the Latin moves to close the gap; the Anglo withdraws again; the Latin moves in; and the strange shuffle continues until one or both of them lose interest, patience, or stamina.

The contrasting ideas that Anglos and Latins have about personal space extend to their living spaces. Anglos like to spread out, have homes with individually expressive, attractive exteriors, and gaze upon picket-fenced lawns. In contrast, the ideal Latin house is built around an open patio with a carved-stone fountain and exuberant tropical foliage. Its high-arched walls, adorned with tasteful murals and tropical-wood accents, define the sanctuary of the foremost in-group—the family. But the other sides of those same walls are rude and unpainted ramparts, built right out to the street. Their barred windows, rugged doors, and glass-shard parapets are a perimeter defense against an uncertain world of passersby to whom, as out-group strangers, neither trust nor aesthetic debt is due.

7. Formality

Latin America's historic ties to European elitism and continued separation by class lead Latin Americans to stress social customs and business protocol. Their emphasis on hierarchy accents formality in personal interactions. It is an attitude that contrasts with that of more casual U.S. executives, who, having a weaker sense of social tradition, prefer to dispense with ceremony and place today's profit ahead of yesterday's custom.

Education and Titles. Formal education is more highly esteemed in Latin America than in the United States. Possessing a postsecondary degree confers respect, and is reflected in multiple forms of personal titles. If your Latin associate has earned a title through formal education, it is imperative that you refer to him by that title. The most common title is *Licenciado,* referring to a trained lawyer or to one who has completed a formal university program. Most business school graduates use this title. Abbreviated as *Lic.,* it is the safe title of choice to use when you are not certain what level of education your Latin associate has attained. *Ingeniero* is the second most frequent professional title you are likely to encounter, and refers to a graduate engineer. An *arquitecto* is a trained architect. Occupying the top of the hierarchy of educational titles is *Doctor,* a title that is sometimes appropriated by those who consider themselves well educated but who may not have earned the corresponding PhD.

Age. Whereas the energy and spontaneity of youth are valued in the United States, the wisdom and experience of age are venerated in Latin America. Therefore, it may not be a good idea to send your fast-track young manager to Latin America to pursue that hot new deal with a high-level officer of the Latin American firm. Senior Latin executives are used to being catered to by younger yes-men of mixed professional merit, in whom they seldom confide. Because of age-based stratification in Latin organizations, their senior executives ordinarily prefer to deal with other senior executives, and may be offended by younger envoys sent by a U.S. company.[21]

Meals and Manners. Perhaps more business transactions are nourished at restaurant tables than at conference tables. To the casual observer, the business meal in Latin America seems to have less to do with business and more to do with a convivial procession of dishes and drinks accompanied by lively conversation ranging from sports to current events, and art and music to ribald humor. The purpose of the meal's varied gastronomic and conversational fare is to get to know the person with whom one is dealing. It is easier for decorum-conscious Latins to gauge the social caliber of Anglo executives in a casual environment, where good food and ample drinks could make the latter drop their guard, than in a more inert office setting. It is in the less restrained ambiance of a restaurant that Latins can test whether prospective business associates are "their kind of people."

To help you pass the Latin's test of social pedigree, you should be aware of some mealtime customs. The most frequent business meals in Latin America are breakfast and lunch. Breakfast is gaining ground because it can be a healthier, less filling meal (appealing to Latins' recent greater concern with physical fitness) and does not break up the workday as much as lunch. Nevertheless, lunch still remains the premier Latin meal. Taking place between 2 P.M. and 5 P.M., lunch is a convivial affair, with liberal amounts of food and drink.[22]

You should avoid discussing any business topic at meals unless it is broached initially by your Latin colleague. If it is necessary to bring up a business issue, wait until dessert has been ordered. You should also avoid discussing host-country politics and problems, U.S. foreign policy, or religion. Safe topics are children, local cultural and historical features, sports, hobbies, and travel. When it is time for the bill, the person who made the invitation, usually the seller, pays.

Latins will observe your eating behavior and table manners as indicators of your breeding. Although eating the way your mother taught you will usually allow you to pass muster, some tips may help raise your final score:

- Keep your hands exposed above the table.
- Order your meal in a decisive manner; avoid prolonged searching of the menu. If in doubt, order the same plate that your Latin colleague orders. Avoid ordering anything that is messy or difficult to eat and that could distract from the easy flow of conversation.
- Dine with Old World decorum: no elbows on the table, no beer drunk from a bottle, no eating until all are served, no slurping or drinking from bowls, and talk only when your mouth is empty.

- Fork etiquette is a germane topic. Latins are curious about the Anglo's use of the fork at meals. Whereas the fork always remains in the left hand of right-handed Latins (and Europeans), it is passed back and forth between the Anglo's left and right hands. This peculiar shuffle begins with the fork in the Anglo's left hand as he holds the knife in his right hand to cut. Finishing the cut, the knife is laid to rest on the right side of the plate. Then the fork, with its impaled content, is shifted to the right hand. From that hand, food is introduced to the mouth. The odd five-stage cycle is completed as the fork is reintroduced to the left hand. To add to the Latin's wonderment about why there is any need for a fork to ever have to leave the left hand, the tines of the Anglo's fork, when introducing food to the mouth, are always pointed upwards, in a position opposite to the natural curvature of the palate. With practice, you may learn to adapt your fork management habits, an adjustment that will make you appear less strange to Latins and, incidentally, will make your dining more task-efficient.

Dress. Jackets and ties are appropriate for business in the cooler mountain and higher latitude locations in Latin America. In most of the humid tropics, the *guayabera* (pleated light-cotton shirt worn outside the pants) is the garment of choice among executives. Your sartorial score will suffer if you show up in shorts, even for informal social meetings. For those occasions, khakis or jeans and an open-collar sport shirt are appropriate.

Table 4.1 is a synopsis of how cultural differences shape management differences in the Americas. The risk of overgeneralizing is great when compressing a large body of information into a small table. Accordingly, the reader should be aware that Table 4.1 describes prevalent behaviors, excluding anomalies in which U.S. managers mirror behaviors common some 40 or more years ago and Latin American managers exhibit modern practices. Nevertheless, the table previews the nascent but unmistakable trend of Latin American firms to be evolving from a traditional to a modern management model.

LATIN AMERICAN BUSINESS CULTURE: PROFILE OF MARKETPLACE BEHAVIOR

Consumer Behavior: Then and Now

Although it seems paradoxical, only 30 years ago the market in Latin America for middle-class consumer goods was mostly limited to

Table 4.1

Contrasts in Management Practices between the United States and Latin America

Characteristic	Anglo American (Modern)[a]	Latin American (Traditional)[b]
Rationale for authority and income differences	Individual merit—a mailroom clerk can rise to become CEO	Family background and formal education credentials
Decision-making process	Structured participation, delegated to lowest competent level; information is systematically shared	Centralized, concentrated at top; impulsive, autocratic; information is compartmentalized
Decision makers	People who know the most	People who rank the highest
Attitude toward work, employer, competition	Live to work; loyalty to self; use information cooperatively to enhance own performance, earn promotion	Work to live; loyalty to *patrón*; hoard information to consolidate self in current position; avoid conflict
Responsibility	Employees are self-starters, don't expect company to look after them	Employees expect close supervision, paternalistic supervisors
Hiring criteria	Demonstrated performance	Family or personal ties to company
Purpose of hierarchy in organizations	To define problems, then delegate task authority to resolve them	To define holders of authority, then attempt problem-solving tasks
Position in hierarchy	Indicative of unequal abilities	Indicative of unequal roles
Organization chart	Reflects information flows needed for key operating functions	Reflects personal interests or power relationships of key family members

Table 4.1 (*continued*)

Characteristic	Anglo American (Modern)[a]	Latin American (Traditional)[b]
Delegation	Performance expectations are assigned with discretionary authority	Task functions are assigned with symbolic authority
Model boss	Expedient communicator	Benevolent dictator
Performance evaluation	Employee accepts accountability	Critical feedback resented
Task performance	Do whatever must be done to perform task, be willing to get hands dirty	Some tasks are too menial or undignified for one's position
Activity modality	Accomplishments and "doing"	Personal relationships and "being"
Planning process	Long term, proactive for predictable contingency scenarios; premise: future can be controlled; formal, deliberate	Short term; reactive to volatile environment; premise: destiny is preordained; unstructured, impulsive
Policy decisions	Formally stated	Not stated
Records	Data must be accurate	Accuracy subordinated to convenience
Logical perspective	Inductive, action oriented, factual	Deductive, analytical, conjectural
Time orientation	Present activity is the means to future accomplishment; time commitments are taken seriously	The future is subordinate to the past, the past is subordinate to the present; deadline dates are initial estimates

[a]Anglo American characteristics describe practices common to U.S. firms operating in the modern, high-productivity sector of their respective industries.
[b]Latin American characteristics describe practices common to Latin American firms operating under traditional (ISI) management norms.

upper-class buyers. A massive lower class, an exceptionally wealthy upper class, and scarce numbers in the middle defined the region as having the world's most unequal income distribution. Although glaring income inequalities still remain infamously intact, untold millions of Latin Americans have risen from poverty to join the consumer class in the years since the Lost Decade. As beneficiaries of the open-market policies of the 1990s and 2000s, a rising wave of middle-class consumers has swelled Latin America's marketplace. For example, between 2003 and 2009, more than 32 million Brazilians—in a nation of 198 million—joined the middle class and 20 million escaped poverty.[23] These new consumers sought to satisfy their pent-up demand for world-class goods and services. They were fed up with the inferior products imposed on them during the long era of protectionism. They had money and wanted to spend it on products that offered good value. By the 2010s, Latin Americans were savvy and demanding consumers. Marketers who understand how the new Latin Americans consume will profit as the latter's buying power expands in concert with the region's economic growth.

Globalization's effects are also expanding the role of women in Latin America's markets. As globalization creates new markets by lifting purchasing power, it is also undermining Latin America's stereotype of a *macho*-dominated society.[24] Indeed, one A. C. Nielsen study of households in Argentina, Brazil, Colombia, Chile, and Mexico[25] revealed that women were responsible for 85 percent of the purchases of consumer items, and were also becoming more selective: looking at product expiration dates, checking nutritional values, and avoiding preservatives. Another Nielsen analysis[26] reported that 44 million women entered the region's labor force during the 2000s, and that their "time-starved households—those balancing both work and home responsibilities—are looking for convenient products that save time and are easy to prepare." Hot products include flavored waters, treatments and conditioners, pet food, deodorants, mayonnaise, and soups. The same time pressures have boosted door-to-door sales, especially of health care and beauty products.

A small but growing fraction of the 10,000 baby boomers who reach retirement age every day in the United States constitute another enticing consumer segment in Latin America—one that may be particularly responsive to U.S. marketers. The market for senior (referred to as *tercera edad*—third age) services in Latin America was a long-shot business bet just 10 years ago. But today's forces of demography, geography, and economics have aligned to make Latin America an appealing buying proposition for the growing wave of U.S. retirees who are flowing south to buy retirement homes or move into active- or assisted-living communities. Sunny, senior-friendly locales in places like Mexico, Costa Rica, and Panama have special appeal to this affluent market.[27] Significantly, a similar market for Latin seniors is beginning to arise in or near the region's major urban centers as the forces of globalization alter social behavior within the Latin American family.

Life on the Bleeding Edge: Avoid Making Experience Something You Get Just after You Need It

Procter and Gamble spends a lot of money on marketing research and still launches duds in its pursuit to place first-to-market products. An example of the opposite approach is the one taken by Volkswagen in Brazil, the last place in the world where the company still makes the venerable VW van. Although considered a Woodstock-era anachronism in the United States, the classic van is the workhorse of choice for postal workers, contractors, ambulance drivers, convenience-store operators, and mobile food vendors in Brazil.[28] If your firm has neither a large marketing research budget nor a large marketing duds reserve, it should heed a lesson from nature: sometimes the early bird does get the worm. But observe the less exalted, but well-fed second mouse. It has learned important lessons about how to avoid first-mover risks in the quest to gain share in the perilous cheese market.

For the smaller company planning its new-to-market product launch, a moderate-cost value-tweaking of the first-mover's offering is a prudent course.[29] The key to profit is to find the right tune and learn to play it, not to get the band to play a new song. Then, when you and the market are in harmony, follow up with a speedier, higher investment product rollout. That second-mouse strategy could attain the same eventual market position and profitability as the early-bird approach, but at substantially less cost, risk, and embarrassment.

Less experienced U.S. firms, however, occasionally rush headlong into a new deal, assuming that the ways they do things at home is the world's best practice. Given how difficult it is to survive in the hard-hitting competitive environment of the United States, it can be easy to assume that your way is best. But acting on that assumption can land you between the jaws of a painful trap in Latin America.

On the one hand, you could be trapped because you are right. Let us suppose that the U.S. way is the best way. In that case, the danger of putting it into practice in Latin America is that your up-to-date offering may threaten to displace an antiquated local cash cow. If the cash cow is backed by politically or financially powerful players, they could force you out. Here is an example. A U.S. transportation firm in a Central American country was interested in brokering freight services between smallish shippers of winter vegetables and tramp steamers that charged a fraction of the international freight rate pegged by the large, scheduled conference carriers. The investment was so low and the profit potential so high that the proposed venture smelled like a trap. It was. Some discreet nosing around revealed that the local agencies of the large carriers were entirely able and ruthlessly willing to pull the political levers necessary to block the U.S. interloper from obtaining the business permits necessary to set up shop. The political potholes protecting the status quo knocked the wheels off this business venture even before it was rolling.

On the other hand, you can be trapped because you are wrong. In this, the more common experience, the would-be innovator discovers that there are good reasons for the way things are done locally. Look at this example. A U.S. manufacturer of construction equipment centered its export marketing campaign on the ability of its product to reduce labor costs—a promotional theme that it had used successfully in the United States and that competitors were not emphasizing at that time in Latin America. It was not surprising that the product bombed in a region saturated with dime-a-dozen, low-skill laborers of the type the equipment was intended to replace. But the story ends happily. After licking the wounds inflicted by its initial market failure, the manufacturer revised its value proposition. This time, the sales campaign emphasized the financing-cost savings available by reducing job times. Contractors were quick to respond to the savings made possible by shortening cash-to-cash cycles in a hyperinflationary financial environment where, if one was fortunate enough to find a lender, annual interest rates on construction loans exceeded 600 percent.

Moral: Being bold is not always the best strategy. Eagles may soar, but weasels don't get sucked into jet engines.

Understanding the New Latin American Consumer

As you travel in Latin America, you will see centuries-old cultural behaviors that are disappearing before your eyes. These changes determine who are the final consumers of your product, what they buy, how they buy, and how much they are willing to pay. But the pace of change is greatly uneven, and the rate at which it proceeds is a function of the degree to which markets are subject to the forces of globalization. Some of the effects of these tradition-slashing forces may be visualized best through the prism of marketing's venerable four Ps: product, price, place (distribution), and promotion.

Product

Regional Similarities. The Gap, Nike, Levis, McDonald's, and even Taco Bell are top-brand franchises in Latin America. How have these brands been able to command so much awareness and loyalty so far from home? It is plainly because the mystique of U.S. trends and fads spreads as rapidly to Latin America as it does to Cleveland or Kalamazoo. The United States transmits tastes and shapes product preferences among Latin America's consumers through movies, the Internet, tourism, and TV.

Make no mistake, you can still find vestiges of anti-U.S. political sentiment in Latin America. But even the anachronistic handful of park bench nationalistic fanatics are preaching their anti-imperialist doctrines behind Foster-Grant sunglasses, sporting stone-washed Levis, sipping Diet Coke to wash down slices of Domino's Pizza, and distributing Xeroxed propaganda flyers. Surely the culture of the Big Mac has outstripped the most ambitious of any imperialist conspiracies alleged to be hatched in the CIA or Pentagon. A 60-something journalist friend in Buenos Aires confided to me, with some bitterness, that "my generation venerated European culture. Paris, Rome, and London were the places of our intellectual dreams and were the standards against which we measured not only our aesthetic, fashion, and culinary inclinations, but also our buying habits when we went shopping. Nowadays, my grandchildren dream only about Hollywood, Miami, and New York."

Regional Differences. But product preferences oriented to the United States by no means signify that there are not great differences in tastes within Latin America. Consumers in warm Caribbean climates favor sweet-tasting orange soda, but temperate-zone Argentines prefer their orange soda to taste more like orange juice, as it does in Europe, from where Argentines still take many of their purchasing cues.[30] *Mole* (a spicy concoction—not the burrowing animal) sauce is a perennially popular cooking favorite in Mexico, but a slow seller anywhere else in Latin America. *Pupusas*, the national dish of El Salvador, are virtually unknown in any nonadjacent country. The *guayabera*, a pleated and comfortable cotton shirt that is the de rigueur business uniform in much of coastal Latin America, is considered appropriate only for dentists in sweltering San Salvador. Boxed cereals, consumed in Mexican cities as a breakfast food to be eaten with milk, are used more commonly as snacks in Central America. Hair-straightening products sell well in Santo Domingo but are not on the shelves in Santiago. Coffee, the most-consumed caffeinated beverage in Mexico, Central America, and northern South America, runs a distant second behind tea and tea-like *mate* in Argentina and Uruguay. Body armor, armored car conversions, and personal security products sell well in Colombia and Mexico but are in low demand in Chile, Costa Rica, Paraguay, and Uruguay. Industrial and construction equipment, priced to reflect the cost of complying with U.S. environmental and safety standards, sells more easily in Mexico than in Brazil. Although Latin America's high uncertainty-avoidance cultures tend to prize cleanliness,[31] cleaning products show wide intraregional differences in per capita usage. The average Ecuadorian, for example, buys only 50 percent as much powdered detergent as a Peruvian, but buys 265 percent as much hand soap as a Venezuelan, and 41 percent of the chlorinated bleach purchased by a Peruvian.[32] Incidentally, package color exerts a strong influence over what brand of detergent Ecuadorians buy: research has shown that Ecuadorian consumers think that yellow is too strong and can damage clothes, blue is too weak and gets nothing clean, but detergent in a yellow package with blue highlights is perceived as the best.[33]

The proliferation of product and packaging variations within Latin America, and between Latin America and the United States, underscores an important product-strategy question: should you export the same product to Latin America that you sell in the U.S. market, or should you adapt it to fit local conditions? As a general rule, industrial goods require less adaptation than consumer products. The former may have to be modified to comply with electrical, climatic, safety, environmental, labeling, or specification (metric vs. English standards) differences. Consumer goods are more culture bound, and the closer they are to the body (e.g., clothing, foods, and beverages), the greater the need for adapting them to local cultural preferences. If they could sell their standard U.S. products in Latin America, most exporters would do so to capture economies of scale, thus minimizing unit costs. But, as ignoring local preferences can mean having to surrender price and market share, the U.S. exporter's decision to standardize or adapt becomes a tradeoff between cost and revenue, and is specific to each product and each market.

Price

Geographic proximity, historical ties, and cultural similarities combine to give U.S. sellers a price advantage in Latin American markets. The lower expenses U.S. firms incur in advertising, credit, freight, inventory, pre- and post-sale services, insurance, and tariffs can give them a potent cost edge that European and Asian rivals find hard to beat. Although Asian—especially, Chinese—suppliers are beginning to erode U.S. market share, Latin American imports from the United States typically exceed those from any other origin. Its greater total market share does not mean the United States always leads in every product in every Latin market. Preference for U.S. products means that if your price, design, quality, warranty, and delivery are reasonable, the cost savings you may have in production, overhead, and logistics can potentially translate to larger market share and/or profit margins.

Exploiting that potential requires an understanding of today's more price-conscious Latin American markets. It would be natural to assume that price-based competition will become more prevalent as Latin markets become more open and local prices fall to align with international costs. The reality of what is happening in Latin America, however, parallels what occurred in U.S. and Western European markets: to maximize profit, price should not be set as a function of cost, but as a function of the consumer's perception of value. That awareness is shifting the game strategy of Latin consumer marketing away from price cutting and toward managing consumers' perception of value. By offering customers a bundle of product benefits tailored to meet their needs, a seller makes it more difficult for them to draw price comparisons between its brand and a competitor's.

The broad factors that influence consumer perception of value are no different in Latin America than in the United States. Only the details change. Strategies designed to strengthen the appeal of product performance, branding, design, packaging, advertising, and the like have universal appeal and can displace price as the top buying motive for value-oriented consumers. Good marketers know that, by shifting consumer focus from price to value, they can increase unit profit margins without having to suffer a proportionate drop in sales volume. This strategy seems to work in all Latin markets, including the least affluent. For example, I noted during a recent visit to Nicaragua, one of the region's most battered economies, that two packaged breakfast cereals were offered at widely disparate prices. Whereas the Central American brand was priced at twenty-three cents per ounce, the well-advertised Battle Creek brand was tagged at thirty-four cents per ounce. Interestingly, although the listed ingredients showed the products to be almost identical, the store manager told me that the high-ticket import was moving off the shelf at the same rate as the local inexpensive brand.

Selling at the bottom of the pyramid[34] has received more fanfare than specific operating directions, especially on pricing matters. Given the masses of Latin American consumers living at the poverty level, a desirable goal would be to convert their latent demand to profitable revenue. The Singer Sewing Company seemed to have struck the right pricing model to sell electric sewing machines to low-income buyers in Latin America's second-largest market. Singer knew that seamstresses and tailors across Mexico were stitching away on the same foot-powered machines used by their grandparents. Owning a new sewing machine was an impossible luxury that they could only dream about, because Mexico, like the rest of Latin America, was a cash-only market for millions of working-class consumers. To tap into that huge market, Singer offered a lease-purchase plan to circumvent the liquidity barrier faced by low-income customers. Thanks to strong personal pride and low transient rates, Mexican buyers went to great lengths to avoid defaulting on monthly lease payments, thus avoiding the shame that would have befallen them if their machines had been repossessed. That threat of social stigma kept repossession rates down to two percent. Knowing the income pattern and cultural behavior of a ripe market and devising a matching pricing strategy worked well for Singer. Mexican sales of the firm's sewing machines and white goods went up by 500 percent within five years of offering the leasing plan.[35]

Distribution

It is not surprising that the distribution system used to bring modern, world-class products to Latin consumers has undergone notable transformations. Only 20 years ago, the bulk of the region's retail sales were groceries and were purchased through neighborhood *tienditas* (small stores). As customers typically walk to these neighborhood stores and carry their purchases home, decisions regarding package size and handling ease are paramount in merchandising strategy. These crowded shops have such limited shelf space that point-of-purchase promotional materials often are hung from the ceiling to take advantage of the store's vertical dimension.

But the *tienditas'* market share declined as incomes rose in Latin America. Consumer spending began to shift from food items for household consumption to discretionary items for personal use.[36] Accordingly, the preferred retail formats for today's middle-class shoppers are malls, category-killer stores, supermarkets, and discount outlets. In countries like Brazil, Chile, and Mexico, where purchasing power has risen the most, organized chains control some three-fourths of the retail market.[37]

Nonetheless, the convenience of the ubiquitous *tienditas* still makes them frequent places to buy staples in residential neighborhoods of all incomes. And in *barrios* (neighborhoods) at the bottom of the pyramid, the *tienditas* are becoming the distribution centerpiece of food and beverage suppliers that are focused on selling to lower income consumers. Consider how Nestlé is moving in Mexico to capture the purchasing power of this massive market. The consumer goods giant decided to sidestep supermarkets and distribute its new powdered milk product exclusively through *tienditas*. Nestlé's decision was grounded in market research showing that "local shopkeepers exert outsize influence in tightly knit, low-income neighborhoods. 'It's the shopkeeper who can recommend or disavow a product.'"[38]

Promotion

Cultural differences between Anglos and Latins leave their print on advertising. In low-context cultures like the United States, advertising tends to have a high factual content. In high-context cultures like Latin America, the advertiser is more likely to use symbolic or emotional content to arouse the consumer's interest.[39] Advertising in low-structure-need cultures, like the United States, uses more humor. In high-structure-need Latin America, expert endorsers—like physicians in white coats or sports heroes—are used.[40] Mother-daughter[41] discussions are a widely used advertising scenario. But, whereas in low power-distance cultures, like the United States, the direction of advice is often from daughters to mothers, in high-power-distance Latin America, mothers more commonly advise daughters.

Although uncertainty avoidance may have played a role in delaying Latin Americans' usage of electronic communication, they are now participating in ever-increasing numbers in the e-commerce revolution. In 2009, there were about 175 million Internet users in Latin America. They represented an 883.7 percent increase over the number of users in 2000—two and one-half times the world's growth rate.[42]

CONCLUDING TIPS

As a U.S. executive doing business in Latin America, you are constantly exposed to new cultural behaviors. Your reaction to these unfamiliar ways can take either of two forms:

1. **Cultural dominance**. This view assumes that U.S. practices are superior and are the right way to do business. In the past, U.S. managers took this approach because there was no other model to challenge it. The arrival of strong European and Japanese firms and the advent of professionally managed Latin American organizations are challenging the primacy of the U.S. management model.

2. **Cultural synergy.** This perspective assumes there is the U.S. way, and there is the Latin American way. There is no right way. The view is predicated on a solid grasp of both management models and the cultural forces that underlie them. It foresees that the best elements of each culture will combine to create a new system of management that could transform Latin America into a world-class competitive force.

I have written about the competitive need to adjust U.S. viewpoints to the cultural perspective of Latin America. It would be folly to finish this chapter without issuing a warning: never go native. Although it is surely good business to adapt some of your surface behaviors to the Latin milieu, once you begin to relax core standards, you set both feet on the slippery slope of mediocrity. If allowed to continue, small infractions of principles gather momentum, soon becoming the operating equivalent of an industrial-grade migraine headache. If you lose sight of the finish line, it makes no difference what horse you saddle or how you ride. Do not compromise your ethical or performance standards. The only people who make money by bending over backward are acrobats.

Notes

1. Edward T. Hall, *Beyond Culture* (New York: Doubleday, 1981), 12.

2. John Herman McElroy, *American Beliefs* (Chicago: Ivan R. December, 1999).

3. Geert Hofstede, *Culture's Consequences: International Differences in Work Related Values* (Beverly Hills, CA: Sage Publications, 1980).

4. Geert Hofstede and Geert Jan Hofstede, *Cultures and Organizations: Software of the Mind* (New York: McGraw-Hill, 2005).

5. André Laurent, "The Cultural Diversity of Western Conceptions of Management," *International Studies of Management and Organization* 13, nos. 1–2 (1983): 75–96.

6. L. J. Bourgeois III and Manuel Boltvinik, "O.D. in Cross-Cultural Settings: Latin America," *California Management Review*, Spring 1981, 75–81.

7. B. M. Bass et al., *Assessment of International Managers: An International Comparison* (New York: Free Press, 1979).

8. Alejandra Clavería, "Emprendimiento: La Nueva Importación Latinoamericana," *América Economía*, August 5, 2009, http://www.americaeconomia .com/Noteprint.aspx?Note=315904 (accessed March 21, 2010).

9. Fons Trompenaar and Charles Hampden-Turner, *Riding the Waves of Culture: Understanding Cultural Diversity in Business* (New York: McGraw-Hill, 1998), 145–160.

10. Ned Crouch, *Mexicans and Americans: Cracking the Cultural Code* (Boston: Nicholas Brealey International, 2004), 137.

11. "Latin America Extends Search for Top MBA Talent," *International Business Times*, November 20, 2009, http://www. ibtimes.com/services/pop_print .htm?id=8320&tb=ct (accessed March 3, 2010).

12. Ellena Granell de Aldaz, "Cultura Gerencial y Organizacional en Venezuela," *Debates IESA: Gerencia y Cultura* 3, no. 2 (1997): 33–45.

13. Lawrence E. Harrison, *Who Prospers? How Cultural Values Shape Economic and Political Success* (New York: Free Press, 1992).

14. See, for example, Mark Stevenson, "Mexicans Have Mixed Feelings on Slim's Richest-man Status," *Arizona Daily Star*, March 12, 2010, A8 (Business).

15. Crouch, *Mexicans and Americans*, 99.

16. Jose Ortega y Gassett, *España Invertebrada*, 2nd ed. (Madrid: Espasa Calpe, 1922).

17. C. Hampden-Turner and F. Trompenaars, *Building Cross-Cultural Competence* (New Haven: Yale University Press, 2000), 16.

18. Edward T. Hall and Mildred Reed Hall, *Hidden Differences: Doing Business with the Japanese* (Garden City, NJ: Anchor Press/Doubleday, 1987).

19. An example of questionable humor is the Anglo view that "time flies like an arrow" vs. a putative Latin view that "fruit flies like a banana."

20. "The Price of Lateness," *The Economist*, November 20, 2003, 39, http:// www.economist.com/world/americas/displayStory.cfm?story_id=2238214 (accessed March 20, 2010).

21. The author once heard a Latin executive assess the competence of a visiting young U.S. manager as "unable to pour tequila out of a boot, even if directions were written on the heel."

22. The relaxed pace of the traditional Latin American lunch break is succumbing to the pressure of fast-paced Anglo habits. In tropical locations, the hot and humid climate was good reason for dedicating afternoons to leisurely pursuits, chief among which was the large afternoon meal preceding the *siesta*. To adjust work schedules to the demands of the climate, employees traditionally began their workday at 8:00 A.M., left for lunch at 1:00 P.M., and returned to complete their shifts during the cooler hours from 5:00 to 8:00 P.M. Because air conditioning makes afternoon work a comfortable experience, the traditional long lunch break is in the early stage of becoming an endangered species. In a growing number of Latin American business and government offices, 9–6 shifts with a one-hour lunch break have become the norm. In the process, leisurely *siestas* are being subordinated to speedy Big Macs.

23. Juan Forero, "Booming Economy, Government Programs Help Brazil Expand Its Middle Class." *Washington Post Foreign Service*, January 3, 2010, http://www.washingtonpost.com/wpdyn/content/article/2010/01/02/AR2010010 200619.html?referrer=emailarticle (accessed March 3, 2010).

24. Jesus Rios and Steve Crabtree, "Is South America Moving beyond Machismo?" Gallup, Inc., November 29, 2007, http://www.gallup.com/poll/102928/South-America-Moving-Beyond-Machismo (accessed March 3, 2010).

25. Vanessa Zeballos, "Comportamiento del Consumidor en America Latina," *Una Manera Diferente de Ver el Mundo* (blog), November 11, 2007, http://vanessa-zeballos-ccmk27.nireblog.com/post/2007/11/17 (accessed March 3, 2010).

26. "Latin American Women Increase Purchasing Power," *NielsenWire*, October 6, 2009, http://blog.nielsen.com/nielsenwire/global/latin-american-women-increase-purchasing-power/ (accessed March 23, 2010).

27. Charles Crespy, Thomas Becker, and Raul deGouvea, "Information Asymmetry in Foreign Direct Investment Decisions: A Microview," *International Journal of Global Business and Economics* 2, no. 1 (2009): 97–103.

28. Alan Clendenning, "A Long, Strange Trip for VW Van," *Sun-Sentinel* (Fort Lauderdale), September 11, 2003, 16–17.

29. Manuel Pereyra Terra, "Reflexiones Claves Para el Directivo de America Latina: Riesgo y Cultura," *Occasional Paper*, Universidad ORT Uruguay, 2009, 7.

30. Doreen Hemlock, "Familiarity Breeds Success," *Sun-Sentinel*, September 20, 1999, 16–17.

31. Marieke de Mooij, *Consumer Behavior and Culture: Consequences for Global Marketing and Advertising* (Thousand Oaks, CA: Sage, 2004), 154.

32. "Los Detergentes de Cinco Paises se Venden en el Mercado Ecuatoriano," *El Comercio* (Quito), January 22, 2004, B1.

33. "El Sector es Uno de Los Grandes en la Publicidad," *El Comercio* (Quito), January 22, 2004, B1.

34. C. K. Prahalad, *The Fortune at the Bottom of the Pyramid: Eradicating Poverty through Profits* (Upper Saddle River, NJ: Wharton School Publishing, 2005).

35. Candace Siegle, "Sewing It Up," *World Trade*, March 1994, 122, 124.

36. "Retail Industry in Latin America—IT Market Assessment," TechNavio, November 24, http://www.technavio.com/content/retail-industry-in-latin-america-it-market-assessment (accessed March 26, 2010).

37. Ibid.

38. Antonio Regalado, "McCann Offers Peek at Lives of Low-Income Latins," *Wall Street Journal*, December 8, 2008, B6.

39. Edward T. Hall and Mildred Reed Hall, *Understanding Cultural Differences* (Yarmouth, ME: Intercultural Press, 1990).

40. Hofstede and Hofstede, *Culture and Organizations*, 180.

41. de Mooij, *Consumer Behavior and Culture*, 153.

42. "Latin American Internet Usage Statistics," *Internet World Stats*, c. 2010, http://www.internetworldstats.com/stats10.htm (accessed March 4, 2010).

THE ART OF MAKING AND KEEPING THE DEAL

This final part takes you from concept to application. Chapters 3 and 4 in Part II set in place cornerstone concepts of history and culture that underpin why and how business is done differently in Latin America. In Part III, Chapters 5 and 6 build on those same historical and cultural foundations, applying their concepts and tools to the dual task of making productive business deals happen in Latin America and of preventing them from falling apart. Chapter 5 tells how to get your hands on the ball; how to run with it is the subject of Chapter 6.

Negotiating and Selling Tips

THE NEGOTIATING GAME

It is a fact: research confirms that the way we behave as bargainers has a potent effect on the outcomes of negotiations. Indeed, negotiation outcomes tend to be either much better or much worse than what hypothetical outcomes would have been if based purely on the economic merits of the deal under negotiation.[1] So, no matter how exceptional your company considers its offering package, it will not automatically get the result it believes it deserves. It will only get what you are able to negotiate for it. It follows that an investment in learning how to gain an edge at the negotiating table can pay off. Although literature dedicated to the art of bargaining could fill libraries, this chapter includes only those concepts that have concrete value and are directly applicable to Latin America.

Playing the Away Game

Do you trust your instincts? If you are playing on your home turf, you should. Your good instincts surely have played a major role in getting you where you are today. The longer you have been in business or practiced your profession in a given place, the more skilled you have become in sizing up the people, market, and business possibilities of that place. Your ability to make more right than wrong decisions is an indicator of your familiarity with your customary operating environment. It is the same reason why a ball team's home-field playing record is usually better than its away-from-home performance. Naturally, the tables are turned when it becomes the home team's turn to be the visiting team and it finds itself at a disadvantage on the opponent's home field. As a negotiator traveling to Latin America to play that away game, you have the disadvantage of competing on unfamiliar terrain that is sprinkled with economic and cultural land mines. You sometimes notice that the Latins are playing a different game with its own ground rules and that calls are made by referees whose eyes seem sometimes turned the wrong way.

But the record shows that, in spite of their visiting-player disadvantages, U.S. negotiators are not regularly blown away by unfamiliar hazards when they travel to Latin America. Indeed, they possess at least three potential advantages that can go far to compensate for having to play in the opponent's ballpark:

1. Being on your Latin associate's home turf makes it easy to acquire firsthand knowledge of his plant and office installations, his operating environment, and his reputation among local suppliers and customers. In Latin America it is often difficult, through any means other than a personal visit, to reliably verify the truth about a company's situation.

2. That same in-country proximity affords you an opportunity to size up other local firms you could deal with in case negotiations fall through with your primary target.

3. The third advantage is especially applicable if you represent a smaller U.S. company that lacks a large and imposing physical presence: the favorable impression you wish to convey as a prosperous, well-established potential business associate to appearance-sensitive Latins will not be compromised by having to reveal a lean and sparsely appointed home facility.

These situational advantages are trivial when compared to the advantage afforded by cultural literacy. For U.S. executives in Latin America, cultural literacy can be a business game-changer. It has only two conditions, and they are too plain to be misunderstood:

1. Understand the pivotal role played by cultural differences in negotiations.

2. Understand how to use these differences to control negotiation outcomes.

Used in tandem, these conditions create a bargaining-table chip that can substitute for cash. This chapter helps you to become culturally literate with only modest effort.

Getting to *Sí*: Styles, Strategies, and Stages

It is the single most elemental fact of business life: everything you want is controlled by someone else. And making yours what is theirs is the fundamental motive underlying business everywhere. But before any transaction takes place, decisions must be made about the terms of exchange. Some terms of exchange are straightforward and simple (e.g., the dark-alley ultimatum: your money or your life). Other exchanges are more complex and are preceded by more lengthy, but not necessarily more civil, negotiations.

If you have witnessed the high-pitched, back-and-forth haggling that takes place in Latin America's bustling *plazas de mercado* (open-air markets), you know that bargaining for the best deal can be a lively event. The ubiquity of spirited haggling in Latin America means that Latins are more experienced bargainers than Anglos. Does this mean that Anglos are doomed to finish in second place when trying to strike a deal with Latins? No. To the contrary, experience shows that U.S. executives regularly negotiate productive deals in Latin America. But those executives who score the most negotiating points are those who know how to hit home-run deals in negotiating's three sweet-spot power zones: Styles, Strategies, and Stages.

STYLES: HOW CULTURE AFFECTS NEGOTIATING STYLES IN LATIN AMERICA

Anthropologists know that distinctive personality patterns exist for people who share a common culture. Culture conditions the way individuals view the world about them, react to situations, and relate to other individuals. Differences in cultural behaviors dictate that productive international negotiating is not simply a matter of understanding what happens between negotiators at the bargaining table. Rather, the outcome you achieve depends on your ability to read and react to culturally driven behavior that controls what is happening inside the heads of Latin Americans and what shapes their unique negotiating styles.

Culture as a Bridge to Productive Business Deals

The success of any transaction hinges on management's ability to negotiate productively and extract a favorable *quid pro quo* for their company. When transactions span national borders, the relationship between negotiators as cultural strangers provides such rich soil for misunderstanding and suspicion that cultural gaffes are cited as the largest reason for U.S. companies' sales failures in international markets.[2] Thus, it is no mystery why experienced international executives assign high values to cultural factors in the negotiating equation. By doing the same, you become the "pro" between the *quid* and the *quo*; thus,

1. Avoid costly surprises and prepare for what Latins will do next by anticipating their culture-informed responses to your proposals.
2. Present yourself in the most favorable light by showing Latins that you deserve respect because you (a) appreciate their personal values and (b) behave in a predictable and trustworthy manner.

These are potent advantages for winning the negotiating game with all Latins, but they really ring bells when dealing with those Latins who behave traditionally. That is why you should know when and why you may encounter negotiating patterns in Latin America that adhere to traditional patterns.

All Latins Do Not Dance to the Same Beat

The unique personality traits associated with a given national culture do not attach to all of its members. Everyday experience tells us that all individuals raised in the same country do not behave identically. When we describe a personality pattern associated with a certain national culture, therefore, we are referring to a predisposition of people from that country to behave in a particular way.

Behavioral variation in Latin America is increasing at a brisk pace because of the region's rapid insertion into the global mainstream. You can estimate whether the cultural profile of a Latin American is likely to be traditional or modern by considering how that individual's experience has been conditioned by four rough correlates of globalization's advance: sector, age, locale, and education. Let's call these the four SALE indicators. They are pointers that can help you decide whether the Latin across the table from you is likely to depart from the traditional personality profile and to be aligned with U.S. styles of negotiating behavior:

- **Sector.** Belonging to the modern service, manufacturing, or non-traditional export sector, rather than a sector marked by undifferentiated products or sold primarily in the domestic market

- **Age.** Born after 1975 (i.e., having reached an impressionable age during or after the definitive economic and political reforms initiated during the late 1980s and early 1990s)
- **Locale.** Raised in a major urban center, rather than in a rural or provincial setting
- **Education.** Trained at the postsecondary level in management, engineering, information technology, or other business-relevant field

The march of globalization will likely cause Latin American and Anglo American negotiating styles to converge, transcending the divide between traditional and modern negotiating behavior. But the cadence of that march is irregular, and, for the immediate future, tradition will remain very much alive in Latin America. Thus, the negotiating practices described as Latin American will often be characteristic of traditional behaviors.

Seven Guideposts to Negotiating Success

Negotiations between buyers and sellers from different cultures are at the cutting edge of globalization. Although the field of cross-cultural negotiating is a magnet for commentary, much of it is of limited value, consisting of cultural stereotyping or self-serving anecdotes. The missing intelligence that U.S. executives could profitably apply to Latin America is a tightly organized body of practical information that describes in specific terms how negotiating styles in Latin America and the United States differ.

This section fills that void. By orienting the seven business culture guideposts described in Chapter 4 toward the specific task of negotiating, the process moves U.S.-Latin negotiating behavior from the other-world realm of mysterious art form to the real-world realm of predictable behavior and controllable outcomes.

1. Power Inequality (Hierarchy)

Ranking high on the hierarchy scale, Latins tend to concentrate decision making at the top. As the goal of the Latin executive is to hold on to power, delegating decision making makes little sense because it is tantamount to giving power away.[3] Consequently, all but the most routine matters are decided at the top. The top executive's distance from the negotiating process can cause his own whims and preconceptions to color his decisions. Because lower level Latin negotiators seldom attempt to second-guess their superiors, they will get approval before taking any action, even on trivial issues. The back-and-forth exchanges entailed in seeking approval delay negotiation proceedings and can exasperate U.S. negotiators who are new to the game.

There are two key ways in which knowing the gap in hierarchical attitudes between Anglo and Latin negotiators could boost your negotiating performance:

1. By knowing who is the Latin team's decision maker, you can tailor your approach to the top man. Understanding that middle-management members of the Latin team often have no authority to make key decisions can save you the lost time and motion that could drag negotiations out forever. They are at the table to play one or more roles: (a) to aggrandize the top man's status, (b) to get information and be prepared to implement any decision made by the top man, or (c) to provide the leader with technical expertise.

2. If the third reason, providing technical expertise, seems to explain why subalterns are present on the Latin team, it is especially advantageous to have them on your side. Efforts at interteam social integration can go far to open communication channels between the technical levels of both organizations. But cultural differences can sabotage these attempts. As the Latin technicians often are more socially polished and educated in the arts than are their U.S. counterparts, they may view the latter as technically competent but culturally narrow. Conversely, Anglo technicians may perceive the former as defensive on technical matters, autocratic in their behavior toward subordinates, and socially aloof.

TIPS to help you deal with a hierarchy-conscious Latin negotiator:

• Negotiate with the decision maker only. Avoid dealing with subordinates. They have neither the big-picture knowledge nor the authority to fashion the creative tradeoffs demanded by a win-win negotiating strategy.

• Latins hold sellers[4] and smaller companies in lower esteem than buyers and large companies. If your company is smaller and is selling, it is doubly important that it be represented by a high-ranking executive. The extra clout will help to offset its perceived lower status and to gain access to the Latin firm's decision maker.

- Latins' concern with status makes it important that the head of your team has a position title (e.g., Director or Vice President) and a professional title (e.g., Dr. or Engineer) at least equivalent to the Latin's team head. Whatever the circumstances, always make the Latin feel he is drinking upstream from the herd.

- Hierarchy breeds paralysis of the tongue. Subordinates will agree with the head of the Latin team because he is the boss, not necessarily because he is right. As this process contains the ingredients of a circular firing squad, you may be able to shield the head of the Latin team from a face-losing bullet, thus gaining valuable personal equity at little cost. Helping the buyer to save face always helps you to save the order.

- Show deference by an adept choice of gifts. Many Latin executives have a penchant for "me-wall" displays of paraphernalia attesting to their stature. Prize memorabilia include framed letters, pictures, or prestigious-looking certificates.

- Astute Latins are aware of a cultural tendency of egalitarian Anglos to champion the underdog. They can use that tendency to gain advantage, playing "the position of the weaker partner in negotiation, of the side that needs special consideration for being disadvantaged, even to flatter the stronger [U.S.] partner's capacity to provide extra help."[5]

2. Structure Need

High-structure-need Latins are risk averse, being more motivated to preserve what they already have rather than risk a loss. Lower structure-need Anglos are ready to take a risk if there is a prospect of high profit.

TIPS to help you understand and deal with a high-structure-need Latin negotiator:

- He will not "bet the farm" on a potentially high-return but moderately risky venture.

- He will avoid the risk of a short-term loss, even if taken to achieve a high long-term potential payoff.

- He is looking for quick-payback deals in limited-size local markets, so he will find high unit profit more appealing than high-volume sales.

- He will ask for pie-in-the-sky terms and boilerplate protection in written agreements, especially in clauses dealing with exclusivity, seller financing, shared expenses in market development (e.g., training, co-operative advertising, promotional giveaways), warranty returns, after-sale service, and technical support.

- He may be slow to settle his accounts payable[6] if you concede the open-account or consignment-sale terms he requests.

- If you refuse to invoice in local currency, he may attempt to hedge his exchange-rate risk by negotiating an adjustment in the dollar-denominated invoice amount he owes.

3. Social Orientation

The high propensity of Latins to be group oriented, rather than finding social identity within themselves as Anglos are prone to do, inclines Latins toward placing a high priority on cultivating long-term relations. As a result, U.S. negotiators who have formed a bond with Latins often discover that the relationship that has evolved is one of a close personal nature between two individuals, rather than a detached business nature between two companies. Therefore, if the U.S. negotiator is replaced, the personal relationship may have to be reestablished before negotiating can advance. The easy interchangeability of negotiators in the United States is less common in Latin America.

Social orientation also affects the choice of who sits at the bargaining table. Negotiators from group-oriented Latin cultures are often chosen for their family or social ties. These criteria contrast with proven competency as the basis for choosing team members in the United States.

TIPS to help you deal with a low-individualism (high-group-oriented) Latin negotiator:

- Without an introduction from an individual within a Latin's trusted circle, U.S. executives may not be taken seriously. Nonetheless, opportunities to penetrate in-group barriers abound, and extend even to telephone behavior. If you have a name to drop, do not hesitate to drop it early during a telephone contact. If you do not have a name to drop, get one. During initial telephone calls to the Latin firm, an alert U.S. caller will get, recall, and use the name of whoever answers in order to establish relational connections in later calls.

- Frame your negotiating proposition in terms that are important to a Latin's group culture. If the company is a family business, you should appeal to the family's pride, reputation, and traditional values.

- Always portray yourself as a long-term player. For example, greet your opposite by saying, "I am happy to be here with you today because, for many years, my company has wanted to work closely with another high-quality company to establish a long-term position in your market."

- Relative to individualist Anglos, group-oriented Latins are more interested in the interpersonal dimension of the negotiation and less focused on the cold, factual content of the deal. Therefore, a U.S.-style assertive sales or negotiating approach will not be warmly received by Latins, who seek to build long-term relationships based on trust between friendly partners. It is in your best interest to be low key and not appear constantly on the prowl for the last drop of short-term profit. If you refrain from shooting for the basket every time you have the ball, the Latins will view you as a cooperative player rather than a predator.

- In contrast to U.S. executives, who make decisions impersonally on the basis of cost-benefit factors, group-oriented Latin negotiators are very conscious of saving face. If you disagree with a Latin's position, be subtle about expressing any criticism. Giving face (by using titles, praising any success, or recognizing expertise) builds your negotiating advantage. But if you slam a door in a Latin's face, he will make it swing back to break your nose.

4. Universalism-Particularism (*Rule Orientation*)

Universalism underpins the Anglo sense of fairness and equal treatment. That mindset collides with Latin particularism, the attitude that a particular situation is outside the scope of any single rule. Latins refuse to be stamped with rank-and-file uniformity and dispute rules imposed by others, especially outsiders.

TIPS to help you deal with a particularist Latin negotiator:

- In addition to remembering and repeating names when you meet Latins, try to find some common ground in an effort to share and enjoy a mutual interest.

- Do not be surprised if Latins request highly personalized customer service attentions.

- Remember, where rule of law is subordinate to rule of men, the trust you establish with Latins will be worth more than their signature to ensure compliance with the contract.

- When proposing an offer or conceding a position, make it appear that you are extending a special favor or advantage not normally available to others.

- Expect at least subconscious resistance to the implied assumption that your systems, standards, and best practices are transferable to the Latin American operating environment. They may not get past the audition stage.

5. Communication

Communication differences lead many U.S. executives to view negotiations as short-term exercises in problem solving. They approach the current deal as a matter that should be conducted with as much expedience and as little ceremony as possible. When today's deal is done, they put it behind them and move on to tomorrow's deal, expecting the current deal to develop as foreseen in the written agreement. For the Latin, the written agreement is a token document, taking on value only when backed by a continuing personal relationship with the U.S. negotiator.

TIPS to help you deal with a high-context Latin negotiator:

- Do not expect Latins to be held hostage to the tyranny of practicality. For Latins, negotiating calls for a level of rhetoric and imagery suitable to the import of the occasion. They gain little joy from an unceremoniously initiated, coldly conducted, and abruptly finalized negotiation.

- Your congenial demeanor, education, and pedigree are among the signs Latins will note in assessing whether there exists enough interpersonal traction to move the business relationship into the future. Without the expectation of a continuing personal association, Latins will seldom be predisposed to make any significant negotiating concession.

- Dress to impress. High-context Latins tend to associate quality in dress with personal power. By projecting an image of authority and success, you increase your negotiating advantage.

6. Time and Space

Time. A timely translation rule: *mañana* only means "not today." For Anglos, time waits for no man. Once a moment has passed, it is lost forever. We concentrate on doing one thing at a time, following plans, and meeting deadlines. Polychronic Latins are adept at dividing their attention among multiple time demands. While negotiating with you, a Latin executive may also be conferring with his plant manager, signing a purchase order, instructing his driver to pick up a customer's blueprint, and scheduling a tennis game. His just-in-time agenda is not discourtesy. It is the way he is culturally programmed to respond to simultaneous demands. When those demands exceed the time available to satisfy them, he will reschedule his agenda of meetings and deadlines. Latins will understand that deferring an event to *mañana* merely means that it will not happen today. Only non-Latins believe that scheduling it for *mañana* means it will happen tomorrow.

TIPS to help you deal with a *polychronic* or *multifocused* Latin negotiator:

- Follow the mood, not the schedule.[7] To Anglos, time is scarce, so it must not be wasted on economically nonproductive pursuits. To the Latin, time is also scarce and should be used to enhance the quality of life. Adjust your pace to respond to another cultural rhythm.
- Lifestyle orientation predisposes Latins toward negotiating goals centered on personal relationships, whereas Anglos focus more on enhancing business performance and market power.
- Be tactful, but do not allow effusive rhetoric to trump factual reality at the negotiating table. The eloquence, emotion, and conviction with which a position is expressed are more important to some Latins than the facts that support that position.
- Be prepared to play the waiting game, especially if you are to meet with a government official. If so, you will join others being served strong coffee in a waiting room that varies in size according to the rank of the official. Even if you are kept at bay for hours, avoid showing any irritation when finally you do gain access to the official's office. For all you know, you may have been bumped ahead, not farther back, in the waiting line. While waiting, you can chat amiably with the other detainees, attend to a work folder or book, or jot down notes to include in your own book on doing business in Latin America. Above all, put your watch away.

Space. Arm's-length negotiating? Not here. Offices that seem like public meeting halls, embracing when meeting and leaving, and jostling in lines can exact a psychological toll on Anglo visitors to Latin America.

Although both Anglos and Latins know intuitively what is the right distance to keep between people, that distance is less for Latins than for Anglos. As guests in Latin America, Anglos should adapt to the host culture's custom, and be prepared to negotiate at hand's length.

TIPS to help you deal with a *close personal space*:

- When a Latin moves in to be physically close to you, do not back away. Over time, you will learn to act unfazed as the space between you disappears.
- For Anglo women, following the Latin custom of maintaining close personal space straddles a thin line between being socially congenial and sexually available. Female executives can maintain proximity without inviting intimacy by facing their bodies at least 60 degrees away from their conversational partner, placing most of their weight on the leg closest to him (to lean slightly away), and making only occasional, brief eye contact.

7. Formality

Mind your manners. As appearances are important indicators of social status in Latin America, U.S. negotiators should pay attention to the image they project. Dressing appropriately, staying in quality hotels, not chewing gum or slouching, and not being seen carrying their own luggage (or any item larger than a briefcase or laptop computer) may seem like unnecessary affectations in the United States, but they are important behavioral details in Latin America. For your first meeting, dress conservatively. Subsequently, you will probably follow the example set by your Latin associates. Formal business dress is expected in the large cities and more temperate mountain regions of Latin America. Even in some of the smaller provincial cities of tropical Latin America, the dress code for business meetings is formal, and negotiators are expected to appear in suits or sport coats with stylish ties. The *guayabera* is a most practical and welcome exception to the formal dress code. It is popularly accepted as a substitute for the coat and tie in much of Central America, Cuba, and the coastal areas of Brazil, the Dominican Republic, Ecuador, and Mexico.

TIPS to help you deal with *high-formality* Latin negotiators:

- Commensurate with the high position they may be perceived to hold by Latins, U.S. executives should learn to become comfortable when being deferred to, while at the same time respecting in a formal manner the personal dignity of lower level managers, secretaries, workers, and drivers. This is a delicate balancing act that informal and egalitarian Anglos sometimes find unnatural.[8]

- Do not gloss over or attempt to redirect Latins' comments about history, tradition, social position, or family past. To Anglos, they may appear as extraneous to the mainstream of the negotiation. But Latins use these social references to subtly communicate an important point or to judge the suitability of business partners.
- Business protocol requires you to always use formal titles, even in the heat of negotiating, and never address Latins by first name until invited to do so.
- Be especially deferential to the oldest Latin at the table. In addition to the respect that age commands in a formal culture, that senior member of the negotiating team should have your esteem because he is likely to be the key decision maker.

For a summary of these differences, see Table 5.1.

STRATEGIES: WIND-AT-YOUR-BACK NEGOTIATING

International negotiating is no longer reserved for Fortune 500 power brokers or silver-tongued diplomats. It is a staple of today's global marketplace and is simply a plan to get you where you want to go at the least cost. It divides conveniently into two clear-cut approaches. One is to confront your Latin negotiating opposite as a headwind that must be overcome. The other is to work in harmony with her, using her own desire to move forward as a tailwind assist to take both of you to where you want to go.

Win-Lose versus Win-Win

Negotiations everywhere perform two purposes: (1) they bring people together who have interests in common, and (2) they bring people together who have interests in conflict. Stated succinctly, "without common interests, there is nothing to negotiate for, and without conflict there is nothing to negotiate about."[9]

The instinct of competitive bargainers is to dominate. Viewing negotiation as an irreconcilable conflict, they use a take-no-prisoners approach, leaving few crumbs on the table for the other side to take home. This is a win-lose perspective and is at odds with the win-win approach of cooperative negotiators that focuses on satisfying each side's common interests.

Table 5.1

Summing Up Differences between U.S. and Latin American Negotiating Styles

Negotiation Variable	U.S. Tendency	Latin American Tendency
Basis of trust	Legal contract, then experience	Friendship, then legal contract
Role of personal involvement	Avoid involvement and conflict of interest	Personal involvement is major component of decision making
Negotiator selection criteria	Technical expertise, function in organization	Family or social ties, title in organization
Role of face-saving in making decisions	Slight, decisions are based on cost-benefit analysis	Great, preserving personal dignity is paramount
Decision-making process	Systematically organized	Spontaneous, impulsive
Negotiation agenda	Fast paced	Slow paced
Interpretation of *mañana*	Tomorrow	Not today
Extent, type of prenegotiation preparation	Medium-high, financial and technical analysis	Slight, limited to awareness of company or brand name
Focus of negotiating goal	Cost-benefit ratio	Best bargain
Negotiation perspective	Win-win	Win-lose
Time perspective for deal under negotiation	Medium term	Short term
Time perspective for business relationship	Medium term	Long term
Adherence to agenda and deadlines	Strict	Casual
View of opposite party	Neutral	Friend, social equal
Emotional sensitivity	Not highly valued	Highly valued

Table 5.1 (*continued*)

Negotiation Variable	U.S. Tendency	Latin American Tendency
Emotional display	Impersonal	Passionate
Loyalty to employer	Low	High (may be family)
Risk tolerance	Medium-high, if justified by profit	Low
Opening bid	Reasonable	Extreme
Type of arguments used to defend position	Concrete, rational	Vague, emotional
Power tactics	Real power, legal enforcement	Threat of withdrawal or stronger consequences
Taking a settlement position	Making a final offer	Reopening previously closed issues
Form of final agreement	Formal legal contract	Word of honor supplemented by brief legal agreement

Win-lose strategy is also called zero-sum, because if one party is to win a larger piece of the pie, the other must surrender a slice of equal size. It is a strategy influenced by the commodity traders who once dominated Latin America's international trade. It is also used by unskilled U.S. negotiators who fall into the trap of status games and power plays. In either case, zero-sum bargainers see price as the main chip on the table and, as in a poker game, see nothing to be gained from cooperation among players. Indeed, as players scheme to win the pot, it is in their best interests to use bluffing, deception, intimidation, and aggression against their adversaries. At some point in their lives, these types of predatory bargainers bought the lie that negotiating is something you do *to* others for your own benefit, rather than something you do *with* others for mutual benefit.

The headwind resistance common to win-lose approaches can be transformed into tailwind cooperation with win-win negotiating. Win-win strategies are also called positive-sum because their aim is to increase the size of the pie so that both sides get a fair slice. They rely on both parties cooperating honestly to discover, among the possible negotiable tradeoffs, what the real and nonconflicting interests are that could be combined to create an acceptable package for both. If the buyer's priority is quick delivery for immediate use on a project, and the seller's priority is to have a working unit in the market to use as a demonstrator, there is a basis for agreement that may not require much haggling on price. Skilled win-win negotiators distinguish between stated positions and true needs. They understand that by looking beyond positions and focusing on meeting the needs underlying those positions, each side can be a winner. To convince Latins to choose you over your competitors, get into the habit of uncovering their highest priority needs.

Given a cultural backdrop tolerant of bludgeoning into submission weak power holders or outsiders, hierarchy-conscious, group-oriented traditional Latins tend to approach negotiations from a win-lose perspective. If the Latin you are dealing with has these traditional values, and if you wish to achieve the outcome that a win-win strategy can produce, you must earn the trust that will give you in-group membership. It is toward the win-win model that experienced negotiators, nurtured in non-tradition-bound, high-trust, and egalitarian social environments such as the United States, tend to gravitate.[10,11] The new generation of Latin negotiators also know instinctively that "we" is stronger than "me" and that they can gather more mangoes when both sides shake the tree.

Alternatives to Price

Positive-sum negotiating gets win-win results because the parties make tradeoffs from among a wider range of possible concessions than price alone could provide. These tradeoffs give you a chance to win a high-value concession in exchange for one that costs you less than it is worth to the other side. The way in which you make concessions may be of greater consequence than their economic value. Sizeable concessions have been won at small cost in Latin America by U.S. negotiators who know how to make a small counterconcession look like a gold mine to the other party.

The counterconcessions that are least costly for you to make tend to be those that are not directly tied to revenue. Tradeoffs dealing with warranty, seller-arranged financing, minimum stocking requirements, packaging, exclusivity, advertising materials and samples, technical support, prospect lists, and the like can be nonprice bases for making relatively low-cost concessions in exchange for ones that directly boost revenue.

Smaller U.S. exporters commonly misperceive that they must negotiate on price because their size precludes them from having nonprice advantages of value to an international buyer. What they fail to grasp is that, for many Latin American buyers, dealing with a smaller U.S. firm can be desirable. For large U.S. firms, a smaller Latin American customer can be a nuisance account, one that represents the same overhead costs to service as a large buyer but does not have the latter's buying clout to merit giving it priority attention. Smaller U.S. firms, however, can give red-carpet treatment to that same Latin American customer because the latter's account can represent a large portion of the former's total sales. Smaller U.S. firms can accept small orders, adjust production runs, accommodate last-minute changes in shipping arrangements, and—important for Latin firms—be available for technical support or hand-holding whenever needed. By making responsiveness part of their value proposition, smaller U.S. companies can gain nonprice advantages that enable them to hold firm on price.

Weighing When to Use the Two Approaches

Even if the advantage is all yours and you could drive the other party to the wall, you should not do so. A "take it or leave it, it's not negotiable" approach may work once, but it is not a formula for long-term profit. By squeezing the last drop out of the deal for yourself, you motivate the other side to not perform as agreed. Your Latin counterpart will have little incentive to do more than comply with the absolute minimum terms of the contract. He may not even perform at all. If so, your ability to force performance or seek damages through legal recourse may be slim. Moreover, the Latin will not be anxious to do business with you again and will do whatever is within his power to smear your name in the local business community. The best alternative to poor negotiating is good negotiating—not *no* negotiating. Avoid sitting at the bargaining table with a catcher's mitt in both hands. If your game plan is to win over the long term, leave one hand free to throw something back. A sick sheep will follow anyone. Once it has recovered, though, it will look for a strong leader who values its long-term health.

Win-Win

When should you use a win-win negotiating strategy and when should you use a win-lose bargaining strategy? Win-win negotiating can deliver more profit over the long term. But it comes with a price. It will take more of your time to persuade and educate your Latin counterpart to play a role that is in sync with the free-flowing, honest positions that are the mark of win-win negotiators. Making the effort to get Latins on board for win-win negotiating can repay your time when any one of the following conditions are present:

- The foreseeable business at stake is long-term and sizeable.
- You require a high degree of commitment by the Latin to make that sizeable business potential a reality.
- It is important to the Latin to do business with you.
- The trust level between the parties is high, and the meeting mood is positive.
- The Latin's negotiating position is strong.
- You and your Latin associate find the search for tradeoff options to be not just good business, but an intellectually satisfying game, akin to the greater scope for creativity that chess offers over checkers.

Win-Lose

If the requisite conditions for cooperation are absent, having a productive win-win negotiating session is not a likely prospect. But, if you still want the deal to happen, do not resign yourself to folding your hand. A better option is to mount a win-lose strategy. Be aware in advance that the mood in the zero-sum negotiating game you are about to play will be one of competitive haggling with an adversary, rather than cooperative problem solving with a partner. You and your opponent have mutually exclusive goals, and those goals are probably directly related to price issues. The following suggestions will help you make the most out of a no-holds-barred bargaining battle with a tough, hard-nosed opponent.

TIPS to help you deal with a hardball Latin negotiator:

- If this is to be a one-time deal, there is little reason to be "Mr. Nice Guy." You can be intimidating and tough, especially if your opponent uses similarly confrontational tactics. The occasional pushy Latin you encounter may be taken by surprise and subdued by what he had presumed to be a Gringo pushover but soon saw was someone who unexpectedly slammed his fist on the table, cried, screamed, and threw papers into the air.

- Beware of the extreme "first pencil" quote. If you are buying, this will be an extravagant offer designed to test your reaction while simultaneously creating bargaining space for the buyer to raise his own bid and still make a good profit. If you are accustomed to negotiating rationally, you probably assume that the final price would be at the approximate midway point between the buyer's first bid and the seller's first asking price. If you are given a ridiculous initial price, react in one of three ways: (1) show shocked disbelief, then respond with an equally extreme offer in the opposite direction; (2) use silence, simply sitting, not saying a word; or (3) begin gathering your things together and stand up. Before walking out, however, make certain that you have considered the consequences of a scrubbed deal, and have backup options available. The sight of you heading for the door will always get your opponent's attention, but it may not always stimulate him to sweeten his offer.

- Hard-bargaining Latins want you to surrender, not settle with a compromise. They use the force of personality to intimidate and issue ultimatums. In this scenario, your worst enemies are confusion and lack of information. To take them out of their game, insist they use objective claims supported by fact.

- Always separate fact from faith. If your Latin opposite makes an unsubstantiated claim, do not accept it as truth until you can confirm it. If you need time to verify it, do not hesitate to delay the negotiation. If requesting a delay evokes anger, hysterics, or a guilt trip for impugning the Latin's honesty, your doubts are probably valid. Feel free to walk away.

- Information is your best ally. Guard it closely. As a buyer, do not disclose what you think is a fair price. A tough Latin opponent will not budge from that point. As a seller, never disclose your cost. Your opposite will pressure you to sell at that level. Similarly, use information to find chinks in the Latin's armor. Piece together bits of information to estimate the Latin's likely target and resistance points.

- Just before reaching final agreement, try to extract additional small concessions from your opposite. The excitement of being close to a finalized deal may drive an anxious negotiator to cave in on a demand if he believes that not conceding would kill the deal. Small nibbles can add up to a big bite.

- Beware the booby-trapped negotiating environment. Office temperatures that are too warm are not uncommon in midsize companies in the tropics. Steamy settings can impair your ability to think clearly. So too can endless small but potent servings of expresso. Although that tasty coffee is a common companion of discussions in Latin America, too many of those demitasse servings can jangle your nerves and distort your judgment. Also abundantly present in out-of-office negotiating sessions is alcohol. Avoid drinking until after the deal is completed, feigning a medical condition if necessary.

STAGES: UNDERSTANDING THE PATTERN OF NEGOTIATING IN LATIN AMERICA

Formal studies of how real negotiations take place confirm that the process conforms to a predictable pattern. As if following an unwritten law, the negotiation process divides itself into clear and predictable stages. As many as 80 percent of firms do not follow any systematic negotiating process, thus leaving "hundreds of millions of dollars . . . on the table."[12] The takeaway value of understanding the stages pattern is the edge it gives you in knowing what to anticipate from the other side at each stage. This understanding must be tempered with the knowledge that negotiating stages are not neatly sequential, and discussions do not necessarily follow a linear logic in Latin America. A new stage may begin while the earlier stage is still going strong, and issues raised in an earlier stage may still be present during a subsequent one.

Academic researchers differ on the number of negotiating stages, finding three, four, and five distinct stages.[13,14,15,16] But countless experiences of negotiating veterans of Latin America reveal yet another pattern. The six-stage pattern described next is the way that winning deals are made among smaller U.S. and Latin American firms. This pattern gives smaller U.S. firms a heads-up framework to plan and prepare their negotiating strategy and tactics. Its ability to see around corners helps firms define goals, estimate costs, allocate time, and assign staff responsibilities to their Latin America negotiations.

Stage 1: Preparation

A man surprised is half-beaten.

—Thomas Fuller

He who fails to prepare, prepares to fail.

—Thomas Becker

Time taken to prepare is an investment, not an expense. Researchers confirm that planning is never wasted, finding that negotiators who spent two or more times the average amount of time in planning doubled their success rate while reducing the time spent negotiating by more than two-thirds.[17] Planning dividends are especially large in Latin America, where you can routinely expect the unexpected to happen.

Do Your Homework

There is no substitute for good intelligence. Research the target firm and team. Know its competitive position, both locally and internationally. Learn the business and industry environment in which it operates. Know the advantages or problems that could result if it did business with you. Find out if it is known for being ethical.

Although the benefit of going into a negotiation with good information can be priceless, it does not have to be costly. Banks, chambers of commerce, industry associations, trade show contacts, commercial officers at U.S. embassies, country desk officers in the U.S. International Trade Administration, freight forwarders, and even Latin American MBA students at your local university can give you first-rate intelligence at little cost. Some weeks before departing the United States, make it part of your daily routine to read online the local Latin American newspapers to become familiar with the operating environment and issues that will be on the minds of the people with whom you will be talking.

Having taken care to be current on business-related issues, be certain you will not be blindsided by logistical concerns. When planning travel arrangements, make it a point to factor in enough time for settling in and recovering from jet lag. Your appointment schedule should be less compressed than if you were traveling for business in the United States. Having to cope with entire offices on *siesta* breaks, Friday afternoon absences, meeting delays and cancellations, and holiday conflicts is inevitable when doing business in Latin America.

The Power of Partnership

It is surprising how many seemingly routine business transactions begun by smaller U.S. firms in Latin America have evolved into close-knit partnerships with their Latin associates. For the smaller firm, especially, there is truth in the old adage that there is safety in numbers. Such firms know that 50 percent of a profitable business with a reliable partner is worth more than 100 percent of a failure. To make cash flow happen as soon, as much, and as long as possible, prepare for each negotiating situation as a potential long-term relationship, rather than as a one-time deal. It is no coincidence that superior negotiators comment twice as much about long-term issues than do negotiators of average performance.[18]

Vision without Action Is a Daydream, Action without Vision Is a Nightmare

Step back, take a wide-angle look at your game plan and their game plan. Weak negotiators make up their goals as they proceed. Being in control of negotiating outcomes requires you to specify your objectives. Picture your objectives as the end points of a scale of possible price outcomes. At one extreme is your firm's target, a price that is acceptably profitable and one that you could reasonably expect to bring home. At the opposite end is your company's resistance point, the minimum price your company would accept. Make a sworn oath to yourself that any offer that falls short of your resistance point constitutes a walk-away number.

Your next step is to estimate the same target and resistance points of your Latin opposite. By estimating what the other side expects to get out of the deal, you will have a clear idea in advance of where your goals are likely to overlap with the other side's and where they could be in conflict. Keeping those limits firmly in mind puts you in position to control an outcome that makes it possible for both parties to win. By having estimated in advance the true cost of the concessions you may be asked to make, and knowing the value of what you can expect to receive in exchange, you will be prepared to defend yourself against any surprise assault.

By superimposing one scale over the other, as shown in Figure 5.1, you possess a big-picture view of how negotiations are likely to proceed before they begin. That overview will also enable you to adjust your approach by sensing when the Latins are taking a hard position and when they are bluffing. To play this poker hand, you must have a clear idea of the value to the Latins of what you can afford to give away, as well as the value to you of what they may concede. Figure 5.1 shows how, by comparing the target and resistance points of buyer and seller, you can estimate whether an agreement can be reached and, if so, to what extent effective negotiating could improve your position.

Because the ranges of acceptable prices overlap in Figure 5.1a, there is room for a mutually satisfactory agreement to occur. You will know you are in an agreement zone if the response to your offer was a reasonable

Figure 5.1
Price Negotiation Range

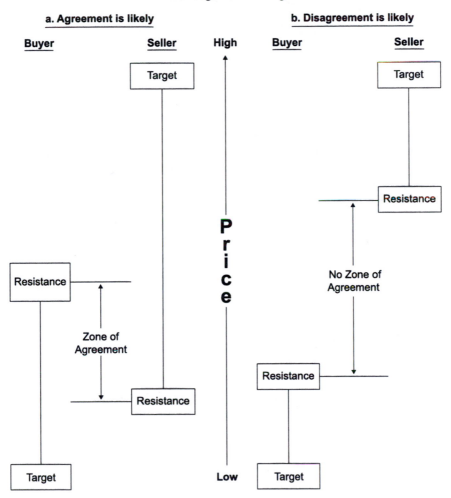

counteroffer. If so, with each successive counteroffer, you and your Latin opposite will be converging on a final settlement price. To help move this process along and encourage the buyer to make a sizeable order, you should consider giving a quantity discount or a cooperative advertising credit. In both cases, you will be helping your buyer develop the market, and the resulting unit savings in packing, documentation, freight, handling, warehousing, and insurance may significantly offset your revenue sacrifice.

Figure 5.1b poses a trying negotiating scenario. If the parties cannot move beyond price, the talks will fail because there is no zone where any price is acceptable to both parties. The talks can succeed only if nonprice factors can overcome the price impasse. To sell "beyond the wallet," nonprice benefits must be created that buyer or seller values enough to close the price gap. For example, if you are the seller, and the Latin buyer objects to your lowest (resistance) price, you could shift the buyer's focus from purchase cost to usage cost by responding, "Yes, you could buy a [competitor's brand] product for a little less. But if it does not arrive in Villahermosa on time, or if it fails on your offshore rig, it will cost your company many times the slight difference in price you would save."

Avoid being a slave to a finger in the wind. It pays to plan the play, and play the plan. Research shows that negotiators who invest more time in defining their negotiating limits and preparing their options are remarkably more successful than those who spend less time and have rigid objectives.[19] Moreover, successful negotiators tend to have five or more options prepared in advance, while less successful negotiators focus on only one main objective and are seldom prepared with a backup alternative.[20]

Latins who rely more on appearances and oratory than on solid preparation may have only one or two vaguely defined goals (most often price, credit terms, or exclusivity) in mind. Whether it be through expensive clothing, stylish grooming, an imposing office décor and furnishings, framed credentials and pictures, a large negotiating team, or "important" telephone-call interruptions, projecting an appearance of power is a poor substitute for an objective, well-conceived negotiation plan.

Organizing Basis of U.S. and Latin Negotiating Teams

Maintaining appearances can be the Achilles heel of image-conscious Latin negotiators. But obsessively individualist Anglos can fall into the I-can-go-it-alone trap, thinking that, after all, the Lone Ranger never had to check back with the home office, so why should they? Excessive self-confidence can place U.S. negotiators at a serious numerical disadvantage when the negotiating pace accelerates. There are good reasons to have at least two people with complementary skills on a negotiating team:

- Negotiating can be physically, intellectually, and emotionally exhausting. Your performance will improve if you have a colleague to handle distracting tasks like running spreadsheet scenarios, verifying information, editing a PowerPoint presentation, copying, e-mailing, or finding a 24-hour pharmacy to subdue the ill effects of last night's socializing.

- In the heat of fast-paced negotiations, you may find yourself pressed to make a decision, either when you have little time or at an inopportune moment. Having a workmate on board lets you buy time to reassess things by calling a break to confer.

- By sending only one representative, your company runs the risk that it will be seen by status-conscious Latins as attaching low priority to the negotiation.

U.S. negotiating team members are usually selected for their professional competence and less often for their interpersonal or language skills. Anglos may assume that technical criteria were also applied when the Latin team members were chosen. That assumption is becoming more valid today among publicly held Latin American corporations. But among traditional family businesses, you will often see examples of Latins chosen to represent their employer because of family or club ties, or their *ubicación* (span of informal influence) in their firm's unseen hierarchy. Although not always the sharpest technical knives in the drawer, their rhetorical and social skills are likely to be highly honed.

Latins may use an all-hands-on-deck team strategy. Their premise is that the sheer weight of their team size will put the (usually) smaller U.S. team at a psychological disadvantage. When facing legions of bodies across the table, you may find comfort in knowing that few of those bodies will affect decision outcomes. Most are empty suits, on stage only for show.

The U.S. penchant for participative management clashes with Latin traditions of one-person decision making. An early priority, therefore, is to spot the decision maker on the Latin team. The member holding the greatest personal authority will be the Latins' kingpin. It would be a mistake for a U.S. negotiator to assume that the Latin team's power center necessarily resides in the member displaying the highest position authority (i.e., the most impressive job title) or the highest expert authority (i.e., the most technical skill). You could lose time and stature by misdirecting your attention to someone who has no final authority to buy or sell, and by offending the power figure by not showing him (seldom her) the respect that he is owed. Sometimes the key decision maker is easily recognized by the presence of a deferential underling who screens calls, carries documents, or acts as a gopher for the main man. At other times, appearances may be deceiving, and the top man may be neither the one who seems to be orchestrating the meeting nor the one sporting the Rolex watch and the Giorgio Armani suit, but the rumpled-looking chap sitting on the sidelines who has not spoken at all. When dealing with family firms, elders having the same family name as the firm's are likely candidates for the top-dog role.

Be smart when organizing your team. If you decide to send a group, travel, lodging, and meal expenses argue to keep it small. Take care to match the status of your team leader with the Latin team leader. As it is common for the Latin team to be headed by a senior officer, make sure that an executive of equal or higher rank is at the helm of your team. Ideally, your team head will be both a technical ace and a relationship engineer.

Regardless of your team's size, each of its members should play a defined role (e.g., marketing, engineering, financial, legal) and be responsive to the team leader, whose purpose is to coordinate these roles and provide policy guidance. Prior to leaving home, the team should meet to discuss objectives, strategies, fallback plans, competitors, and responsibilities, and to be briefed on the economy and culture of the target country and firm. A good plan can be a powerful organizing tool. But, by itself, it gets nothing done. Only well-prepared people make plans happen.

Each member of your team should have an ample supply of business cards. These will be exchanged formally and frequently. Academic titles should be used to the fullest extent possible. In addition to your firm's Web site address and the usual contact instructions, do not forget to print your firm's regular telephone number in place of your 800 number (unless you have international 800 service).

Failing to prepare is preparing to fail. Achieving success in negotiating is like achieving success in sports: the quality of preparation is the single most important determinant of the outcome. Regardless of how urgent it seems to seal the deal, do not let yourself go into negotiations unprepared. Trying to fix at the negotiating table in San Luís the mess created by having failed to prepare in St. Louis is like trying to overhaul an aircraft engine while flying at 500 miles per hour at 30,000 feet.

Stage 2: Building Relationships

Trust Means Business in Latin America

Where the rule of law is weak, personal trust is the only secure foundation on which business transactions can rest. Personal affairs take precedence over business affairs in Latin America, and executives there accept no substitute for knowing the person with whom they are doing business.

It takes cultural literacy to build trust. Culturally literate U.S. executives know that earning Latins' trust is the competitive-advantage equivalent of night-vision goggles. Their goal is to relate so well that their Latin customers refuse to buy from anyone else. The shortest road to a buying decision is to be sincere with your Latin associates and to treat each of them as a unique and special person.

You never get a second chance to make a first impression. A Latin's process for deciding whether to trust you is emotional. It bypasses his intellect and is formed during the first moments after meeting you. As you project personal integrity, warmth, and concern, you are behaving at the emotional level required to overcome the Latin's trust barriers. Until you penetrate those trust barriers, any statement you make will have to pass through a fine-mesh screen before it is believed. Once trust barriers are pierced, you will enjoy the professional cooperation and personal warmth Latins extend to their *amigos de confianza* (trusted friends).

The personal touch pays. If cold-calling is a hit-or-miss approach to sales in the impersonal United States, it is always a miss in relationship-oriented Latin America. The balance of your personal-power account with a Latin is the sum of all the personal ties you have in common. A referral from a friend, an old classmate, or a colleague respected by your Latin opposite can be a good first deposit in your power account. And that referral need not be prearranged: if legitimately possible, say "My friend, Mr. X from ABC Company, thinks highly of your company." If no personal acquaintance is available to introduce you, references from your local chamber of commerce or your bank (preferably one that is a correspondent with a prominent bank in the Latin's country) can help move you toward *de confianza* (trustworthy) status.

In Latin America, industry associations and chambers of commerce (especially the local affiliate of the U.S. Chamber of Commerce) are substantial organizations with influential members. They serve members' needs to make business contacts, influence government policy, and exchange informal information on topics such as supplier performance, customer payment behavior, and the honesty of public officials. Membership in these organizations opens doors by making you more credible, and also supplies pivotal information you will need if you intend to do more than sporadic business in a country. Trying to compete without being a member of these networks will dilute your ability to achieve your firm's full business potential.

Obey the negotiating speed limit in Latin America. Old Latin America hands know that time and deals are lost by U.S. executives who are in a hurry to get down to the numbers and not waste time on small talk. Speeding to the business agenda is prevalent in the United States, where Vince Lombardi's advice on competing prevails: "Winning isn't everything. It's the only thing." But rushing through the relationship-building stage makes U.S. executives commit the negotiating equivalent of drawing so fast that they shoot themselves in the foot. Their linear logic compels them to view the negotiation process as a means to close a sale in the shortest time possible.

Latins, on the other hand, view negotiations as a first step to test if the two parties can relate as individuals. For Latins, the time taken to build personal rapport is essential because, in its absence, no advance can be made toward a productive agreement. That is the reason why, in Latin America, it is usually pleasure before business. It is also the reason why you must allow time in your travel schedule for warming-up exercises: local tours, ceremonies, social functions, and small-talk sessions are the cornerstones in building a foundation of personal trust. In general, the more important the deal, the more time that will be spent building relationships.

International business and negotiating are not for short-term players. The surest way to bring negotiations to a quick end is to agree to whatever proposal is in front of you. It gets you home sooner, but you will not bring much back with you. Investing the time to negotiate *al paso tropical* (at tropical speed) pays off in two ways. The first is the personal trust you convey by not appearing to be impatient to just sell a bill of goods before rushing off to the next deal. The other is to have time available for fact-finding.

Negotiating in a rush can blind you to crucial information. For example, if Latins seem to go off on a long, seemingly pointless conversational tangent, do not interrupt. They may be making an important point using deductive reasoning. You will know this is happening when they first describe the form they would like the relationship between the parties to assume in the future. Then they address the specific transaction being negotiated, couching it in the context of a longer term relationship. This is an approach to which many inductive-thinking Anglos are not accustomed. Listen carefully. As with a rehearsed cough at the beginning of a short speech, the prologue centers attention on oratory, allowing Latins to be creative and exercise their personal flair. The best information is likely to come at the very end. On one occasion, a U.S. executive was in the departure lounge of an airport with the head of the Latin firm with whom he had spent three days of leisurely recreation and wide-ranging conversation. During that period, there had been only rare references to business. Only after the boarding call was made and the executives were saying their final goodbyes did the Latin tell the Anglo that he looked forward to doing business with him. Returning to his office the next day, the U.S. executive found a faxed purchase order from the Latin's firm requesting, at list price, more units than he had expected to sell.

Two Different Teams from Too Different Cultures

The different criteria by which Anglo and Latin negotiators are selected can become an obstacle to building rapport between them. Because Anglo negotiators tend to be chosen for their professional skills and Latins for their social or family background, those contrasting criteria can interfere with developing relaxed personal relationships. U.S. team members may feel that the Latins are more concerned with appearances than technical substance. The Latins may view their U.S. opposites as parochial, limited in aesthetic awareness, and obsessively focused on narrow technical matters.

Compounding the social asymmetry between the U.S. and Latin negotiating teams can be cultural differences. Low-context members of the U.S. team may perceive their Latin counterparts as ambiguous, sneaky, or nondisclosing. For their part, high-context Latins may view Anglos as redundant, too obvious,[21] or *antipáticos* (unsociable). Small differences in communications context between Anglos and Latins can cause big misunderstandings. For example, it is normal for Anglos, while walking side by side with Latins, to converse by only occasionally turning their head toward the latter. As Latins customarily maintain eye contact while conversing, they may abruptly stop, turning to directly face their companion. If an Anglo fails to fall into this type of stop-and-go pattern, Latins may be uneasy about whether the Anglo was seriously interested in the topic.

To help bridge the sociocultural gap between U.S. and Latin negotiating teams, some U.S. companies have purposely included U.S. Hispanics as negotiators. Such attempts may be initiated by well-meaning Anglo managers who assume that U.S. Hispanics and Latin Americans will hit it off because they share a common language. The results of these initiatives are seldom neutral. In the best of cases, the U.S. Hispanics have been technically competent, well educated, well spoken in Spanish, and at ease in an urbane social setting. At the opposite end of the spectrum are many cases where, although the U.S. Hispanics were well qualified technically, their working-class origins placed them at a social and linguistic disadvantage with the upper-middle-class Latins with whom they interacted. U.S. executives who are culturally adaptable and make efforts to overcome the language barriers, even if their Spanish or Portuguese is weak, will be well received. "But there's far less acceptance . . . for a U.S. Latino who travels to Latin America for business with poor language skills and limited cultural understanding."[22]

The visible hand rule: U.S. visitors should be aware of the role assigned to hands in Latin American society. They are always seen on top of tables, never in pockets, and are used to reinforce spoken words with vigorous, expressive gestures. In addition, a hand may be used as a potent communicator of confidence and trust by laying it on the shoulder or grasping the upper side of the lower arm. The *simpático* Anglo should not draw away from such gestures when they are used to signal nonsexual personal regard.

Handshaking is always done when meeting and leaving. You should shake hands with everyone in the group, holding eye contact with that person before moving on to the next. Although their grip is gentler than the vice-grip used by Anglos, Latins frequently use both hands to emphasize personal warmth and shake hands considerably longer than the customary two to four seconds allocated to the ritual in the United States.

Feeding rules: Meals are considered more of a social ritual than a physiological imperative in Latin American business circles. The business lunch atmosphere may seem relaxed and casual, but it is governed by its own set of rules. The first rule relates to suitable conversational topics. Although the event is a business lunch, you should not bring up any business matters. If business becomes a topic, it should be initiated by the Latins. Preferred topics are sports (if you know the local soccer team statistics, you will be revered as a demigod), travel (especially to European destinations), ages and interests of your respective children, local historic and cultural attractions, literature and philosophy, and current events. Being aware of protocol, you will always address Latins by their professional titles, never using first names until invited to do so.

Finally, remember that lunches are the largest meal in Latin America, and they last at least two hours. Dinners and elaborate cocktail receptions are socially intensive fetes, often lasting well past midnight. Therefore, you will be facing large amounts of alcohol during business meal rituals. Even if the conversation does not touch on business, it is wise to control your alcoholic consumption if you wish to exhibit poise that evening and alertness the next day. If a bout with liquor is unavoidably in the wind, two suggestions can prevent you from being blown away: (1) never drink more than you can lift, and (2) ingest a half-cup of vegetable oil prior to meeting with the *compañeros*. It will coat your stomach walls, slowing the effect of the alcohol. (Do not despair if you overlooked the vegetable oil when packing: the salad oil served at your table will do nicely; just find an appropriately surreptitious moment to consume it without raising eyebrows).

Image management: Adding to trust barriers imposed by social distance is a long history of U.S. economic, military, and cultural dominance. Moreover, Latins see themselves stereotyped in U.S. TV and movies as unreliable, uneducated, lazy, or violent. Adding fuel to this smoldering resentment is a knee-jerk habit of some Anglos to view themselves as exemplars of progress in matters relating to business, economic development, technology, and democracy. Their self-perceived superiority compels some Anglos to prescribe rules of conduct for Latins. It requires a subtle sensitivity to say, "This approach worked for us when we had a similar problem," rather than "Your idea is all wrong. The right way is the way we do it in Cincinnatti." A warm showing of personal and professional respect defuses the potential for emotional face-offs. Smart U.S. executives know they are visitors in Latin America and display the social grace and modesty suitable to appreciative guests.

Stage 3: Information Exchange

This stage represents the beginning of formal business negotiations. It is customary for the senior member of each team to inaugurate the first session with a broad, upbeat statement about the purpose of the meeting (the U.S. speaker should not tell a joke at this ceremonially serious moment) and a commitment to proceed in good faith to accomplish that purpose.

Opening Moves

Following the initial general statements, your team should provide information on your firm's profile (e.g., sales, assets, number of employees, key customers), the personal and professional backgrounds of each member, its competitive position, and specific data regarding its product and quality control, distribution channels, pricing, and sales support. Unless you have good reason to believe otherwise, assume that the Latin team has no knowledge of that background information. This is the opportunity for the opposite side to gain a wide-angle view of your expectations and contributions, as well as your best offers and non-negotiable positions. As many Latins will have special needs for the nonphysical component of your offering, such as technical support, installation, training, financing, warranty, return policy, and the like, the presentation of your position should place the greatest emphasis on the competitive advantages of your total value package, not just your core product.

In all cases, but particularly when dealing across language frontiers, take pains to be certain that your points are understood. Slice your discussion into bite-size pieces, pausing to give Latins enough time to chew and digest each thought. Recapitulate often. Encourage the Latins to respond verbally or to rephrase your comments in their own words.

During this stage, you should ask questions to fill in information you missed collecting in the preparation stage. A bonus to asking questions is that the deductive mindset of Latins may predispose them to go beyond superficial or fragmentary answers, giving you big-picture insights into previously unseen patterns of market structure, economic policy, or competitor behavior.

Authority Limits

This stage also provides an opportunity to establish whether your Latin counterpart has authority to negotiate the final agreement. If not, you should learn what her negotiating limits are. You may learn, for example, that she has authority to approve purchases of up to $1 million. If your deal is likely to close at $2 million, and if her boss may be a tough dealmaker, do not despair. You now know that your negotiating goal is to structure two deals at $1 million each.

Easy Transition: Common Personal Interests to Common Business Interests

You created common personal bonds with the Latins earlier. Now is the time to capitalize on them by linking personal interests with business interests. Liberal use of the word *we* can be a simple means to engage the Latins in that process. Whereas using *I* and *you* calls attention to the space that separates you, reference to *we* points out the bridge that joins you. For example, if the Latin says, "I have too much capital tied up in slow-moving inventory," you say "That's an issue *we* need to solve. *Let's* see if *we* could apply to *our* situation here in Lima what worked in Phoenix." Your taking part ownership of the Latin's problem makes him feel that he is no longer alone and can rely on your help to find a solution.

That commitment to joint problem solving is the psychological bedrock upon which win-win negotiating strategies are built. Researchers find that negotiators who take more time to establish a collaborative feeling with their opposites are more successful than those who take less time, and who frequently become bogged down in confrontational disagreements.[23] By maintaining a collaborative mood, you minimize the potential for conflicts that may arise later.

U.S. negotiators tend to take firm stands and state positions frankly during the information exchange stage. Research shows that, by contrast, Latins often resort to evasive responses, indirect answers, a change in topic, or lengthy commentary of little substance when they feel uncomfortable with the way the negotiation is proceeding.[24] Backing off temporarily from the business at hand may help to reestablish a productive comfort level.

Active Listening versus Hearing

Because of cultural differences, Anglos may perceive Latins as suspicious and oblique. The reality is quite distinct. Latins are testing the waters for strategic comfort before diving into discussing particulars. They may see U.S. negotiators as being pushy and having too limited a view of the significance of this early contact between the companies.

Even when you disagree with the Latins, it will pay you to convince them that you understand their viewpoint. Ignorance of their limits (e.g., cost structure), language barriers, or emotion impedes clear communication. Therefore, when differences arise in how an issue is perceived, make those differences explicit, taking time to discuss them with the other side. To be aware of those differences, you must cultivate the habit of observing and listening, rather than merely seeing and hearing. One benefit of active listening is the added knowledge and rapport you can use to gain concessions later. Another benefit is that Latins will be more attentive when it is your turn to explain your position if they feel you made the effort to understand theirs. Developing a habit of taking notes will help you to be an active listener and will also encourage Latins to keep the discussion on track and make their points in a clear and focused manner.

Muscle-Building Exercises

It is important during the information exchange stage to get a clear fix on your relative negotiating power. Knowing how important it is to the Latins to do business with you will be useful later on. If you are selling, for example, find out early about your competition. Ask, "What other suppliers are you considering? Why?" If the responses do not seem plausible, they probably are not. If they do seem plausible, use them as cues to put the spotlight on the comparative strengths of your offering.

Another way to measure the strength of your negotiating power is to ask, "What is your target date for delivery?" The response to this question will give you an insight into the Latin's sense of urgency. If the buyer requires the product immediately, then you have gained the triple advantage of knowing that (1) you are not dealing with a shopper but a serious buyer, (2) price may not be the most critical factor in the Latin's buying decision, and (3) you should emphasize your ability to be time competitive in the persuasion stage.

Gathering useful information is only one advantage gained from asking questions. Asking questions is a powerful psychological tool. As the one who asks the questions, the negotiator is in a stronger position to control the negotiating process, thereby achieving better results.[25]

To further sharpen your negotiating edge, it will be advantageous if the Latins believe you have options. By implying you have other deals available, you gain the leverage to ask for concessions later. Any credible effort you make to reinforce that impression will help strengthen your position. The more subtle you are in conveying those other options, the more credible and *simpático* you will appear to relationship-sensitive Latins. One practiced U.S. executive improved his position during a negotiating session by "inadvertently" exposing the letterhead of the major competitor of his Latin opposite as he was removing work files from his briefcase. Without having to appear boorish by directly asserting he had contact with the competitor, he won strategic ground in the subsequent negotiations.

Image helps smaller U.S. companies punch above their weight. Many Latins view U.S. firms as having unlimited access to capital, managerial skills, technology, and markets. Playing plausibly to that image can enhance the negotiating clout available to a smaller U.S. firm that would be considered an industry lightweight back home.

Stage 4: Persuasion

By this stage, you have established the likely points of agreement and the points that still need to be resolved. Your goal is to persuade the Latins to resolve the points of conflict in a way that gives you what you need and also delivers what they need.

The most direct route to a successful outcome lies in making it easy for the Latins to make a decision in your favor. Helping them see that it serves their interests to agree to your proposal is the key to persuasion. The surest way to bring them into agreement is to make them think it was their idea. Latins are responsive to this tactic, falling comfortably into the cooperative dialog that underlies win-win negotiating. You can kindle a cooperative mood by making some low-cost concessions to encourage reciprocity. If you must refuse a concession request, a careful explanation of your reasons for having to do so will soften the blow. Your tone should be assertive, neither pleading nor aggressive, placing you in the middle ground between being soft and being tough.

Your middle-ground position is bolstered by presenting a strong, factually supported proposal. By comparing your product against that of competitors, you demonstrate why it is advantageous for the Latins to buy from you. But take care not to openly denigrate your competition. By impugning a competitor, you also point a finger at the prospective buyer for having chosen a rival as a supplier. The goal here is to ask the Latin questions that will make him expose your competitor's weaknesses. Your presentation of comparative benefits accomplishes three goals. First, you present yourself as a knowledgeable expert who must be taken seriously. Second, you show yourself as a source of technical support to a field representative. Third, you model an effective sales presentation that Latin resellers can use to sell to their own customers.

Always act to reinforce that cooperation-building middle-ground manner. If the Latin is buying and offers an unrealistically low price, avoid responding in a challenging manner: "That is unacceptable. We thought you were a serious buyer." Rather, answer in an even tone: "Our costs for that unit are much higher, and I know that headquarters will ask why I would even consider that price. Can you help me defend it? What market or cost factors support it?" Arguing creates a gulf. Questions create a bridge. Imply that the two of you are jointly determining a fair price based on objective, factual evidence. Use questions to invite fact-supported positions. But do not yield to the conditioned-buying response that compels some Latins raised in an open-air market environment to ask for a lower price, regardless of the amount initially quoted.

Neither should you be deterred by emotional arguments. Latins often rely more heavily on rhetoric and drama than on logic and fact when attempting to persuade.[26] Research shows, for example, that Brazilians use the word *no* nine times more frequently in negotiating discussions than do U.S. negotiators.[27] Although Anglos are culturally prone to treat emotional outbursts by Latins as antagonism or frustration, such conduct is common in cultures that emphasize passionate expression and energetic elocution to communicate. It is counterproductive to display resentment when responding to a Latin's emotionally intense behavior.

For similar reasons, it would be a mistake to believe that the frequent interruptions you may experience as you talk are a sign that the Latins are disregarding what you are saying. To the contrary, these interruptions may indicate that the Latins are interested in what you are saying.[28]

Nonetheless, the culturally ingrained emotional manner of some Latins can become a significant factor in the persuasion stage. The factual evidence you present to support your proposal may be ignored by the Latins. Their impatience with empirical data stems as much from a distrust of documentation as from considering it an obstacle to reaching an accord on general principles.[29] In such cases, it can be effective to remark, "Many of our customers asked the same questions initially. Now, they are our company's strongest ally." Then support your statement with testimonial letters or other evidence of satisfied customers.

It would be naive to assume that all your negotiations with Latins will be without pressures. If there are destined to be some hardball exchanges, the gloves are most likely to come off during the persuasion stage. When the mood turns confrontational, the exchanges may regress from win-win negotiating to win-lose haggling. If the process is to be turned away from fruitless shouting matches and redirected toward productive agreement, it is essential to understand the core reason for the change in negotiating climate. Experienced negotiators can turn a degenerating process around by discriminating whether the mood swing can be explained by real business-related differences or by interpersonal differences attributable to unfamiliar cultural behaviors. Do differences appear to be real (i.e., not fabricated to create a tactical advantage), and are they business related? If so, it is a signal to call for a time-out to reevaluate both parties' positions. Can other offers or counteroffers be made that could salvage the deal?

When resolving business-related differences, never lose sight of the role that politeness can play in bridging the cultural gap. The direct manner of many U.S. negotiators may appear rude, triggering animosity in Latins, who use diplomatic, indirect approaches to reconcile differences. To avoid friction, let Latins know you appreciate their point of view. Substituting *but* with *and* can be helpful. Because Latins have a trained ear for verbal camouflage, when they hear the word *but* they tend to discount whatever precedes it. Thus, rather than risk hard-earned rapport by saying, "You may think that price is important, *but* you're not taking into account . . .," say, "I understand your concern for price, *and* know that another important consideration for you is . . ."

If the fading spirit of cooperative problem solving is less a result of real business differences and more attributable to personalities, it is a sign that the trust you believed was well established earlier is now unraveling. The negotiation table is not the place to patch up the torn fabric of frayed relationships. More time and a change of scenery may be in order. Call for a break and schedule a round of golf or a social event after both parties have had a cooling-down period. Before doing so, reiterate your commitment to reaching a mutually beneficial agreement, and your belief in the good faith in which both sides are negotiating to achieve that goal. When you resume negotiations, avoid the temptation to make any significant "Monday morning concession." Instead, let the Latins make the first move to smooth ruffled feathers by conceding on a formerly rigid position.

Listening with Your Eyes

There is more to communicating than meets the ear. Many Anglos would be surprised to learn that face-to-face negotiations with Latins are conducted in three languages: speech, silence, and the body. Of the three, U.S. executives depend most on speech to transmit their messages explicitly. Being more implicit, Latins rely more on silence and body language to convey meaning. Overlooking those nonverbal messages can doom U.S. executives to the tactical equivalent of entering the bargaining arena blindfolded. By relying less on their mouth and ears, and more on their eyes, U.S. negotiators will move the ball farther into the Latins' end zone.

Silence. Experienced negotiators know that when the customer is talking, the sale is moving forward. But, there are frequent occasions in cross-cultural negotiations when silence prevails, and you should understand its significance and how to react to it.

The underlying reasons for Latins' silent response to a proposal vary. One reason is that polite Latins simply wish to maintain social harmony and use silence to avoid seeming rude by openly disagreeing with you. You must break the impasse in such cases, because you need to understand what lies beneath their opposition. To grasp their position, state your proposal in other terms. Then ask the Latins if they understand it, or which of its elements they would like you to further explain. This approach solves two problems: (1) it allows the Latins to avoid appearing rude by having to say no to you, and (2) it forces to the surface the information you need to identify and address the real sticking points.

Another motive stems from a tendency of Anglos to react awkwardly to silence, seeing it as an impasse that must be broken by a new proposal or concession. Hence, silence can become a tactical tool of culturally savvy Latins to make U.S. negotiators uneasy, pressuring them into taking a softer position or revealing sensitive information. Indeed, Latins may intuitively sense that "silence [is] deafening" to Anglos, whose low-context cultural orientation makes them feel a responsibility to keep the conversation in motion.[30] The Spanish saying "Uno es esclavo de lo que dice y rey de lo que calla" (one is slave to what he says and king of what he withholds) mirrors the culturally ingrained regard Latins have for the value of silence.

Whatever the Latins' motive for using silence, do not be shaken off-balance. Avoid making any loosely considered attempt to reengage the discussion. You not only risk giving the Latins a psychological advantage, but you may also reveal damaging information; it is easier to let the cat out of the bag than to put it back in. Instead of digging down deeper when you are in a hole created by your own culturally based responses, turn what you sense are manipulative intervals of silence to your own advantage. Excuse yourself to use the restroom, check your e-mail, or—if you believe the Latins are using silence as a power play and you know your position is strong—ask the secretary to call for a taxi to your hotel.

Body Language.   Your body language makes it difficult to hide your true feelings or to tell a lie. In Latin America's high-context communication culture, a mood, a change in posture, a tone, a gesture, a look, or a movement can convey more than words or silence can. It is estimated that as much as 93 percent of face-to-face communication is nonverbal.[31]

High-context Latins are masters of the art of body language. They constantly signal their meanings at a level that operates below the conscious threshold of many Anglos. Be attentive to your instincts; they are working full-time to transmit important messages to you, and they are probably right. Take the time, and have the patience to listen with your eyes, to what the Latins are saying nonverbally with their bodies. Be alert to nuances that silently signal whether you are going down the right or the wrong path. If something intuitively feels wrong, it probably is wrong. Fix any misunderstandings before they become a problem. But always act relaxed and in control while doing so. If you see the Latins getting tired, call for a break. When you resume, repeat points made earlier, especially if talks are being conducted in English. When communication is nonverbal, those who use only their ears to spot red flags are blind to hazards on the road ahead.

Anger

Anger is only one letter short of danger. As Latins react adversely to emotional outbursts by non-Latins, only serial underperforming Anglos regularly display it. When this happens, the least of their problems will be having to explain to the home office why they are returning with an unsigned agreement that the prospective buyer flung in their face. Having their company blacklisted forever in a Latin country by an offended and influential member of its business community is the real risk they take.

Executives experienced in Latin America know that when the negotiating atmosphere becomes emotionally charged, they have two options: they can either control their emotions or be controlled by them. So, before becoming unhinged when you feel exasperated, ask yourself, "Will this matter one year from now? One month? One week? Tomorrow?" And when you make a mistake, make amends immediately. It is easier to eat crow while it is still warm.

The cultural rules for dealing with incoming anger from Latins are not the same as the rules that control your outgoing anger. Latins are an emotionally spontaneous people who sometimes blow off steam. You can gain the upper hand when that happens by responding to their outburst with restraint. How to respond is a judgment call and depends on the legitimacy of their outrage and their need to make or save face. Four options are to (1) give the Latins plenty of airtime, allowing them to vent until they deplete their venom; (2) ignore their outburst, pretending that nothing untoward happened, and continue on a different discussion track; (3) invite their consideration, asking, "What would you do if you were in my position?"; and (4) cool heated emotions through humor.

The last option, humor, is a risky tactic to deflect anger. But it can also be the most effective because Latins have a deep-seated appreciation for wittiness. An incident that occurred not long ago serves as an example: It was well past midnight, and the U.S. and Latin teams, having been negotiating since midmorning, had moved the talks to a restaurant. The U.S. team wanted to include a dispute-resolution clause and suggested applying U.S. law in a U.S. state court. The leader of the Latin team, who I belatedly recognized as having had much too many drinks, asserted that I (as our team's interpreter and spokesman) had offended the dignity and honor of his nation's justice system. After lengthily berating Anglo arrogance and my own shameful complicity with U.S. economic and cultural imperialism, he paused long enough to pour himself another drink. In an even tone and with a straight face, I took advantage of the brief interlude, asking him: "You've been talking to my [assumedly Latin] wife, haven't you?" In an instant, he burst into an uproarious belly-laugh, the tension dissipated among all present, and he turned to give me an energetic *abrazo*. Without a word passing between us, we both knew that he had been testing my ability to relate as a human being, and not as a calculating machine, in the event a dispute should ever arise between the companies. We said our goodnights, agreeing to meet for lunch. When we met again at the same restaurant, he greeted me with an already signed memorandum of agreement. At that moment, I realized that a lighthearted response had allowed our team to pass his test.

Stage 5: Concessions and Agreement

Negotiation's fundamental truth is not complicated: agreement is reached when each side believes its own interests will be served. Engaging that simple fundamental truth, however, requires you to obey negotiation's equally uncomplicated fundamental law: once you have granted a concession, you cannot take it back. Therefore, always link your concession to the proviso that the other side make a counterconcession. Recalling that *if* is the middle word in the *life* of a successful negotiator, make your concessions conditional. Say, for example, "I will agree to 60-day payment terms *if* you will agree to order a full container." Knowing how to trade off a concession of low value for one of high value is the mark of a skilled negotiator. But, regardless of how satisfied you are with the concession you won, it is essential to make the other side feel satisfied. To make the Latins believe they have fared well, make them work hard for any concession you grant. Then compliment them on their prowess in helping to craft a fair deal for both parties, expressing that it was their sound suggestion rather than your intractable demand.

Time-conscious U.S. negotiators tend to be in a rush to make concessions, seemingly overlooking the fact that any position that can be conceded in the morning can also be conceded that afternoon. Or next month. Surrendering a position in small increments is an effective way to convince Latins that they worked to earn a concession. If you are given a $10 offer after making a high first-pencil quotation of $20, do not accept it at once, even if the $10 offer meets your target price. Counter at $15, and let the Latins draw you down to $12.50. Your stubborn descent down the price slope makes the Latins feel that they bought at a fair price at the same time that it allowed you to win a 25 percent premium above your target price. By retreating in small increments, it will appear to Latins that you would have refused to sell for less.

Whenever you make a concession, avoid creating the impression that it establishes a precedent for future negotiations. By magnifying the significance of any concession you make and setting a deadline to take advantage of it, you remain in control and fortify the perception that your offer is a one-time opportunity. Ordinarily, you will want to concede on nonprice issues before giving in on price. But, when you inevitably find yourself under pressure to acquiesce on price, avoid appearing desperate or yielding to urgencies, such as time demands. Never lower your price until you have answered these questions:

- How will this price affect profit?
- What is the value to you of any nonprofit advantage (e.g., market access, prestige, visibility) for getting this business?
- Can you add value rather than subtracting price?
- Will the customer invest the amount conceded to develop the market for your product?
- Review your bill of materials. Can you lower your cost?
- Will your buyer commit to a larger order?
- Will selling at a cut-rate price establish an irreversible and undesirable precedent?
- How important is it to the customer to do business with you?
- What is this client's potential to be an ongoing source of profitable business? Aggravation?
- What are the likely consequences if you do not lower your price?

If discounting your price appears unavoidable, consider doing it in the form of future markdowns via a cumulative discount. By crediting a portion of current invoice amounts to future purchases, you (a) create a price barrier that makes it difficult for competitors to lure away your Latin customer, (b) capture a larger share of your Latin customer's purchase total, and (c) postpone the cash-flow consequences of the discount.

Personal Pride, Saving Face, and Negotiating Etiquette

The agreement that is finally signed is the end product of a series of concessions. You can earn sizeable concessions by using cultural skills to leverage your negotiating power.

Many male Latins are acutely aware that their *macho* images are on the line and will be affected by how others perceive their negotiating results. U.S. negotiators will be careful not to let a concession appear as a weakness. Being respectful, coaxing egos, and doling out ample amounts of "ear candy" opens the door to future business opportunities. Implying in any way that you won or apologizing for your gains opens the door to the street.

The tendency of Latin males to avoid yielding turf is so ingrained that it is even reflected in their language. Whereas *compromise* is a routine assumption in the U.S. win-win negotiating mindset, the word connotes a different meaning in Spanish. A *compromiso* is an obligation and even implies a commitment made under duress, rather than a voluntary move toward conciliation. In the absence of a face-saving motive for doing so, Latins often resist making concessions. By understanding how to save face for Latins when they make concessions, you gain a potent advantage. Knowing how to deal with the issue of price is a key to that understanding.

Dealing with the Pricing Issue

Some U.S. executives see price as the negotiation centerpiece, an issue that should be addressed at the first possible moment. This is a mistake in Latin America. Playing the price card too soon can upset the negotiating process, clouding it with a win-lose bargaining mentality. As price is usually the most emotionally sensitive factor under negotiation, all nonprice issues should be discussed and agreed upon, at least in principle, before tackling the pricing issue.

Whenever you let price take center stage, the spotlight goes off the nonprice benefits that justify your price, and you risk relegating your product's star attractions to bit-part roles. Your aim is to negotiate the best possible price. You accomplish it by avoiding any discussion of price until you have had a chance to present your offering's merits. Price concessions made at an inopportune moment or under pressure can blow up deals. In the heat of the moment, what may have appeared to be a minor price concession can negate months or years of cost-cutting efforts and exact a serious toll on profits over the long run. If you have to compete on price, are in a low-margin industry, and are without a distinctive cost advantage, you will lose every time. You must show why your offering is worth the money, or offer a model without the bells and whistles of your higher cost product. If you are still deadlocked, be prepared to accept that this deal will not make business sense and that not going to the bargain basement with a price predator frees you to find more profitable customers.

Postponing the price issue is good negotiating strategy anywhere. It is an especially effective practice in Latin America, where it is considered socially boorish to rush business. Your Latin associate will not be shy about letting you know when it is time to discuss price. And, like all good negotiators, he will try to make you be the first to name a price. Being the first to name a price virtually ensures that you will commit one or the other of the two greatest errors a seller can make: (1) quoting a price that is too low, or (2) quoting a price that is too high. If you name a high price, it may be so far above what the buyer had in mind that he will walk away. If your price is too low, you will be stuck with having to accept less than the amount he was willing to pay. Moreover, a lower-than-anticipated price may arouse the buyer's suspicions: "Is there something wrong with this seller's product?"

Many experienced exporters quote an inflated initial price. Believing that when they ask for less, they get less, this technique gives them latitude to make price concessions later. This approach entails taking two gambles: (1) your credibility as a trustworthy, long-term business partner is at stake and (2) the focus of negotiating may become price oriented, thus weakening your ability to reawaken the buyer's interests in the desirable nonprice features of your offering package. If the game goes against you, you will have to be fast on your feet to avoid losing your wager.

Nonetheless, gambling on a high first-price quote may be worthwhile. Researchers support that practice, showing that more profitable outcomes tend to be achieved by beginning with extreme price positions.[32,33] One approach to asking for a high price (if you are the seller; a low price if you are the buyer), without risking the cooperative mood that you have created, is to quote a range of possible prices. You explain that the specific final price would be contingent on other variables such as product features, order size, payment terms, field support, or after-sale service. In this way, you can turn the focus of the negotiating discussion back to nonprice topics if you feel you need more time to demonstrate the value of the product's merits. Another escape mechanism is to use qualifiers such as "we estimate" or "approximately." These are signals that the price door could be open to negotiation.

Beware of invoice adjustments. Consider a not-uncommon concession-stage scenario: Over the course of several meetings with you, your Latinoland prospect has repeatedly complained about corrupt Latino officials. He has been particularly vehement about denouncing Latinoland's income-tax officials for extortionate practices. As you have been favorably impressed with the professionalism and integrity he has shown so far in dealing with customers, other suppliers, and employees, you tend to believe his claims and sympathize with his plight. Over a leisurely lunch, he asks you to alleviate his predicament by overinvoicing shipments to him, crediting the difference between the true price and the inflated invoice price to an accommodation account in his name in a Swiss bank. By overstating the invoice amount, your prospective representative's reported income would be understated by a like amount, and his liability to Latinoland fiscal authorities would be correspondingly reduced.

Be cautious about agreeing to this price-related concession. Like early signs of an ingrown toenail, it seems nonthreatening and can be easily prevented. But, if allowed to grow, it can become a painful experience. In addition to the possible legal penalties (see Chapter 3), the practice of adjusting invoices could complicate your relations with other company representatives, compromise your own accounting and tax-reporting practices, and undermine employee morale and organizational ethics.

Common Oversights

Agreements should always be written. It is common in Latin America to disregard unwritten agreements made out of passion or politeness. To ensure that written agreements are prepared correctly, you or a teammate should volunteer to take notes of what was agreed to verbally. As the one who takes notes, you gain the advantage of tinting the content of the formal agreement to match your own color scheme. But be certain that, in the rush to bring deals to a close, your agreement does not omit these common contingencies:

Exclusivity. If you are appointing a distributor, he will want reassurance that his investment in money, effort, time, and reputation to build a market for your product will pay off. Thus, it is natural for him to ask for exclusivity in representing you. That exclusivity can be defined by territory, market segment, function, or time, and is often subject to meeting a sales performance standard. Of those four types of exclusivity, you need to be especially cautious about conceding any of the first three: territory, market segment, or function. Latin America's national legal systems can impose harsh penalties for firing a distributor, making it impossible for your firm to ever again do business in a country. Only representation contracts specifying an expiration date have a chance in court, and even these have been successfully contested by fired distributors.

Choice of Agent. Distributor agreements can create painful severance liabilities. Thus, consider using an agent as your legal representative in Latinoland. Interposing an agent between your company and the distributor could make your exit problems less sticky should you later wish to change distributors.

Late Payment. The cost of credit is high in Latin America. Delaying payables allows buyers to stretch scarce working capital. Unless there is a strong business reason for doing so, do not become an accidental banker. Write stiff, enforceable late-payment penalties into your agreement.

Lawyers

Although lawyers can be a key tool in the process of structuring an agreement, they must be controlled. You can lose control of the negotiation if you let off-putting, fee-justifying attorneys muddy the waters you have been careful to keep friendly and clear.

Knowing When to Fold and When to Close

Because negotiating is often an emotionally intense exercise, negotiators can lose sight of the fact that the process they are going through is a means to an end, not the end itself. The end of negotiating is to reach an agreement that is better than the result you would have had without it.[34] Anything less is your no-deal resistance point. Be prepared to break off negotiations that do not exceed it. Your readiness to do so gives you a decisive psychological advantage. It enables you to present your proposal forcefully, signaling to your Latin opposite that the line you have drawn is both firm and fair and that you will not step over it.

The Fold. Most possible business relationships probably should not happen. In the heat of negotiating, it is easy to overlook that sales alone do not equate to business success. Sustainable profit and cash flow do. Trying to force an agreement to come that does not make business sense presages a deal that will fail. Skilled negotiators recognize when it is wise to walk away from formal talks and amiably agree to not agree. Ending negotiations without signing an agreement, but on *simpático* terms, lets you retain the personal rapport and trust balance you have on deposit and leaves the relationship account open to collaborate on a future project whenever the circumstances of either party change. By making a strategic withdrawal, you transform the certainty of imminent failure into the possibility of future success.

The Close. A different scenario unfolds if and when the gap separating the parties narrows. It is at this point that U.S. negotiators in Latin America can easily stumble. They may try to force a close prematurely, before the Latins are comfortable with personal relations and the deal's long-term business prospects. As timing is important, you should be alert for nearing-the-finish-line signals. They let you know when your Latin associate is getting close to putting the hook in his own lip:

- The gap between your positions is closing.
- Your arguments are being met with fewer and weaker counterarguments.
- Concessions are becoming smaller and taking longer.
- The Latin prospect makes references to final arrangements.
- The Latin is leaning forward at the conference table and is asking more information questions.
- The Latin asks you to identify who in your organization would handle his account and resolve any controversies that arise.
- You are introduced to some of the Latin company's key stakeholders (e.g., division vice presidents, account managers, other suppliers, directors, or major stockholders).
- The Latin mentions the possibility of traveling to the United States to visit your company's facilities.
- The Latin extends a social invitation, particularly one involving spouses.
- The Latin asks if you could help arrange U.S.-origin financing.
- Agreement is reached on a timetable defining dates on which key events (e.g., financing approval, delivery, training) will be performed.

After the final terms of the agreement have been hammered out and the formal contract is being prepared, do not have that document delivered for signing. This is not a FedEx moment. It is the occasion for a formal signing ceremony (yes, even if it means taking another trip back!), followed by a celebration. The investment required to congenially top off the formal negotiation stage will be repaid by the time and money you will save in the postcontract, follow-through stage.

Stage 6: Follow-Through

A deal is a deal.

—U.S. adage

A contract is only a pause in negotiations.

—Mexican adage

Successful negotiation is a cycle. It has no beginning or end. Although the formal stages of your negotiation ended with the signing ceremonies, the business stage of your Latin connection has just begun. Researchers infer that between 30 and 60 percent of international joint ventures fail after being formed.[35,36] The propensity for international accords to unravel underscores that this last stage controls whether the agreement you just signed is going to be a profitable, ongoing relationship or a found-and-lost opportunity. After the ink has dried on the contract, and the echoes of the celebration toasts have faded away, the Anglos and Latins who negotiated it may view their new agreement quite differently.

Low-context Anglos consider a signed agreement as the final act of the negotiation, a document defining the rights and responsibilities of the parties under all circumstances and sacrosanct under the force of law. That view contrasts with the view of high-context Latins, who find little joy in a cold, written contract. In fact, Latins regard the entire formal negotiating process not as a completed event, but rather as an initial means to test if there exists a basis for personal trust. The Latins view the contract more as a conditional intention. They are prepared to comply with the performance norms specified for as long as the bonds of personal trust are intact and for as long as acting in accordance with those norms produces the anticipated business result.

It is not surprising that, if the Latins had been driven to the wall or coerced into signing a dry-bone agreement during the negotiations, they will have little incentive to honor it. Indeed, even if the agreement was fair to both parties when it was signed, Latins may be motivated to walk away from it if conditions change. This does not mean that Latins act in bad faith when they sign contracts. Rather, it reflects the higher uncertainty that marks Latin American business environments. Political and economic circumstances regularly shift in Latin America, making the assumptions that underpinned an original agreement change over time. A purchase contract for construction equipment, for example, may have seemed a routine matter at the time it was signed. But if that contract specifies periodic fixed payments in dollars, and the peso later weakens against the dollar, Latin customers will suffer losses they had not anticipated. Under such conditions, Latins may expect the U.S. vendor to unlock them from their obligations, sharing in the loss imposed by an adverse exchange rate. Underlying that expectation is the Latins' assumption that the personal tie linking the two parties prevails over any contractual obligation, and that they will work together in good faith to absorb losses arising from an exchange rate fluctuation that neither could foresee.

If, under such circumstances, Anglos sue for breach of contract, they may be thwarted. As Table 3.1 (see Chapter 3) suggests, U.S. plaintiffs may find that relying on a Latin American legal system to enforce contract performance can be more lengthy and costly than they anticipated. Pursuing nonperformance penalties against a foreign defendant in a U.S. jurisdiction can be equally frustrating.[37] Anglos' dependence on formal documents rather than on informal personal ties can jeopardize a potentially productive business association. Indeed, such a reliance may set in motion the very forces of distrust that will provoke Latins to renege on the agreement, thus transforming what was originally a dream business relationship into a nightmare legal imbroglio.

Loyal Customers Are a Gift, Not a Given

Customer loyalty bypasses the terms of written agreements and is rooted in the circumstances existing when the agreement was signed: the business conditions, the intentions of the parties, and the personal relationship that prevailed. If any of these three circumstances change, so will the commitment to abide by the original terms of the agreement. But familiarity breeds content in Latin America, and having firm personal ties makes it relatively painless to amend an agreement when business conditions or intentions change. Consider some familiarity-building actions to keep your customer content and keep you at the top of his mind after you return home:

TIPS to keep new-buyer enthusiasm at a high level:

- Within 24 hours after returning home, send your associate a letter thanking him for his hospitality and time. The immediacy of your message will be appreciated. Also appreciated will be your commending some aspect of his personality or behavior. If you met a member of his family, comment on what a pleasure it was. Most important, mention that you look forward to a long professional and a warm personal relationship.

- Again, after returning home, send a gift that is compatible with your associate's interests. Include with the gift a note written in pen. Nothing expresses more individualized attention than ink on a personal thank-you note. Don't scrimp on this gift. It should be tasteful and have "me-wall appeal," something that he will be proud to display on his wall or desk. Its constant visibility will remind him of you when it is time to reorder or refer a business friend.

- Go the extra mile. Latins are not surprised when promises are treated as a momentary intention, not an enduring commitment. Thus, by promising small and delivering big, you build a level of credibility with your Latin associate that can make you a stand-out business partner.

- Establish a file of your Latin partner's key personal dates. Send cards or gifts on the occasion of his *onomástico* (personal saint's day) or birthday, his daughter's *quinceañera* (15th birthday, an important coming-out event), his wedding anniversary, and his country's independence day.

- Call often. Although e-mails and faxes may serve you well for matters of routine account management, nothing (short of a face-to-face visit) transmits personal regard as well as a friendly phone chat.

- Send your Latin associate a copy of your company Web site or newsletter, trade magazine, or local newspaper that reports on the new agreement and that mentions his name and his company's name prominently.

- Issue an invitation to visit your facilities in the United States. Remember to ask him to schedule an extra day or two for golf, fishing, or local sightseeing as your guest.

Notes

1. J. Z. Rubin and B. R. Brown, *The Social Psychology of Bargaining and Negotiation* (New York: Academic Press, 1975).

2. John Pfeiffer, "How Not to Lose the Trade Wars by Cultural Gaffes," *Smithsonian* 18, no. 10 (1988): 145–156.

3. Glen Caudill Dealy, *The Public Man: An Interpretation of Latin American and Other Catholic Countries* (Amherst: University of Massachusetts Press, 1977).

4. Nancy J. Adler, John L. Graham, and Theodore Schwartz Gehrke, "Business Negotiations in Canada, Mexico, and the United States," *Journal of Business Research* 15, no. 5 (1987).

5. Glen Fisher, *International Negotiation: A Cross-Cultural Perspective* (Yarmouth, ME: Intercultural Press, 1980), 41.

6. Geert Hofstede and Geert Van Hofstede, *Culture and Organizations: Software of the Mind* (New York: McGraw-Hill, 2005), 181.

7. Penny Carté and Chris Fox, *Bridging the Culture Gap* (London: Canning, 2005), 158.

8. Ned Crouch, *Mexicans and Americans: Cracking the Cultural Code* (Boston: Nicholas Brealey International, 2004), 143.

9. Robert T. Moran and William G. Stripp, *Dynamics of Successful International Business Negotiations* (Houston: Gulf Publishing, 1991), 84.

10. Barbara Perdue and John Summers, "Purchasing Agents' Use of Negotiation Strategies," *Journal of Marketing Research* 18 (1991): 175–189.

11. John L. Graham, Alma T. Mintu, and Waymond Rogers, "Explorations of Negotiating Behaviors in Ten Foreign Cultures Using a Model Developed in the United States," *Management Science* 40, no. 1 (1994): 72–95.

12. Stefan Stern, "Negotiate or Leave Money on the Table," *Financial Times* (London), January 26, 2010, 12.

13. John L. Graham, Alma T. Mintu, and Waymond Rogers, "Negotiators Abroad—Don't Shoot from the Hip," *Harvard Business Review* 61 (July-August 1983): 160–168.

14. Joanna M. Bantum and Leigh Stelzer, "Ethical Dilemmas in Transacting Business across Cultures," in *Global Business Management in the 1990s*, ed. Fariborz, Ghadar, et al. (New York: Beecham Publishing, 1990), 9–16.

15. Nancy J. Adler, John L. Graham, and Theodore Schwarz Gehrke, "Business Negotiations in Canada, Mexico, and the United States," *Journal of Business Research* 15, no. 5 (1987).

16. Helen Deresky, *Managing across Borders and Cultures* (Upper Saddle River, NJ: Prentice-Hall, 2000).

17. Robert Gulbro and Paul Herbig, "Negotiating Successfully in Cross-Cultural Situations," *Industrial Marketing Management* 25 (1996): 235–241.

18. L. W. McCarthy, "The Rule of Power and Principle in 'Getting to Yes'," *Negotiation Journal* 1 (July 1985): 59–66.

19. Gulbro and Herbig, "Negotiating Successfully."

20. Robert T. Moran, Philip R. Harris, and William G. Stipp, *Developing the Global Organization* (Houston: Gulf Publishing, 1993).

21. P. A. Anderson, "Explaining Differences in Non-Verbal Communication," in *Intercultural Communication: A Reader*, ed. L. A. Samovar and R. E. Porter (Belmont, CA: Wadsworth, 1988).

22. Doreen Hemlock, "Familiarity Breeds Success," *Sun-Sentinel*, September 20, 1999, 16–17.

23. Moran, Harris, and Stipp, *Developing the Global Organization.*

24. John Graham, "The Influence of Culture on the Process of Business Negotiations, an Exploratory Study," *Journal of International Business Studies* 16, no. 1 (1985): 81–96.

25. Graham, Mintu, and Rogers, "Negotiators Abroad—Don't Shoot from the Hip."

26. D. W. Hendon, R. A. Hendon, and P. Herbig, *Cross-Cultural Business Negotiations* (Westport, CT: Quorum Books, 1996).

27. J. L. Graham, "Brazilian, Japanese, and American Business Negotiations," *Journal of International Business Studies* 14, no. 1 (March 1983): 47–61.

28. Alfredo Behrens, *Culture and Management in the Americas* (Stanford, CA: Stanford University Press, 2009), 261.

29. Pierre Casse, *Training for the Multicultural Manager: A Practical and Cross-Cultural Approach to the Management of People* (Washington, DC: Society for Intercultural Education, Training, and Research, 1982).

30. Linda Beamer and Iris Varner, *Intercultural Communication in the Global Workplace*, 2nd ed. (New York: McGraw-Hill/Irwin, 2001), 183, 262.

31. R. L. Daft, *Organizational Theory and Design*, 3rd ed. (St. Paul, MN: West Publishing, 1989).

32. S. S. Komorita and A. R. Brenner, "Bargaining and Concession Making under Bilateral Monopoly," *Journal of Personality and Social Psychology* 9 (2000): 15–20.

33. L. R. Weingart, L. L. Thompson, M. H. Bazerman, and J. S. Carol, "Tactical Behaviors and Negotiation Outcomes," *International Journal of Conflict Management* 1 (1990): 7–31.

34. Roger Fisher and William Ury, *Getting to Yes* (Boston: Houghton-Mifflin, 1982), 2.

35. John H. Dunning, *Multinational Enterprise and the Global Economy* (New York: Addison-Wesley, 1995).

36. Michael J. Geringer, "Strategic Determinants of Partner Selection in International Joint Ventures," *Journal of International Business Studies* 22, no. 1 (1991): 41–62.

37. E. Buscaglia Jr., M. Dakolias, and W. Ratliff, *Judicial Reform in Latin America: A Framework for National Development* (Stanford, CA: Hoover Institution, 1995).

Chapter 6

How to Avoid Letting Your New Latin American Deal Go South

Chapter 5 described the key negotiating skills you will need to become a good horse trader in Latin America. But it is not enough to know how to trade horses. To stay in the money, you also must know how to care for and ride them. This chapter describes tactics to keep personal relationships healthy and business operations productive long after you have closed on your new Latin America business deal.

TAKING CARE OF RELATIONSHIPS

Hunters and Farmers: Would You Buy Again from You?

It cannot be overstated: profit is in the repurchase. To have customers come back to buy from you again and again, you cannot afford to be less than spotlessly trustworthy. Trust means business in Latin America. In today's Latin American markets, the strongest defense against competition is not to win the largest number of new customers, but to gain the loyalty of the most profitable customers.

Never underestimate the profitability of creating a customer for life. Managers who think that winning a new customer in the Latin American market is a one-time event, like shooting a lion on safari, should think again. And they should think differently the second time. Winning a good Latin customer is not like bagging a trophy animal. It is like planting a field. It will take longer and require more of your effort than shooting a lion, but if you steadily cultivate the field, it will yield continuing returns. Its yield will depend on your adeptness in managing the new personal relationships and the operating issues that arise when your Latin American venture has been transformed from a momentary negotiating exercise to a 24/7/52 business reality.

Communications Command

The most obvious difference between doing business in the United States and Latin America is language. Despite the prominence of the language difference, many business visitors to Latin America do not exploit its potential. That is a mistake. Your ability to communicate in Spanish or Portuguese lets you compete against others on a basis other than your product offering. Being able to converse in the language of your Latin associate is always a competitive advantage. But the advantage of being proficient in Spanish or Portuguese is especially applicable if either your firm or the Latin firm is not a multinational giant. Smaller companies everywhere, but especially in the United States, tend to lack the multilingual managers commonly found on the payrolls of the Fortune 500.

As business takes you to Latin America more frequently during the postnegotiation phase, you will expand your circle of contacts. As that circle grows, you will find yourself well positioned to acquire more business if you speak Spanish or Portuguese. If there is a language barrier, you can expect not only to miss new opportunities but also to spend costly time trying to untangle the effects of old opportunities gone wrong because of avoidable misunderstandings.

Language Tips for the Wise . . . and Language Traps for the Unwary

Many U.S. executives fail to appreciate the implications of not speaking at least a few Spanish or Portuguese phrases. They assume that as English is the language of international business, their Latin associates should already have learned to speak it. Their assumption that communication should be exclusively in English conveys an attitude of indifference toward the language and culture of their hosts. Moreover, it forces U.S. executives to rely on the linguistic competence and goodwill of their Latin associates, or to mix primarily with other expatriates. As a result, their English-only radius of contacts limits them to connect with Latins at a superficial level, consigning them to the personal-interaction equivalent of making love with gloves on.

Make Spanish or Portuguese Easy. If one could swallow an instant-speech pill and immediately be able to converse in Spanish or Portuguese, language chokepoints would no longer restrain the ability of countless U.S. executives to achieve their full business potential in Latin America. But, although science has not yet developed an easy cure for monolingualism, learning the rudiments of Spanish or Portuguese does not have to be a sweating-palm experience. It is a benevolent act of inter-American commerce that Spanish and Portuguese are among the easiest foreign languages for English speakers to learn.

Being able to hear the rhythm of the language and to learn and pronounce correctly 200 to 300 words will give you a surprising ability to communicate within your expanding community of Latin contacts. By learning as few as three words a day, within three months you will be comfortable interacting with a growing circle of Latins. Your core vocabulary will enable you to learn on your own. Your solo excursion into Spanish or Portuguese conversational space will trace much the same route you used to learn English, not by following a phrase book or dictionary, but through context, probing, and interaction with others. As you explore the new language, you will earn real admiration and respect from Latins for your effort, and you will become familiar with the local scene from a new perspective. Your new language ability will open doors on new worlds of business and social possibilities, and you will discover that you are no longer a tourist. As you step outside of the safety of living on cultural autopilot, you will also discover that doing business in Latin America is no longer a job. It has become a lifestyle.

As the instant-language pill is not yet an available option, how else can you put your second-language ability on fast-forward? For most busy executives, enrolling in a traditional university language course is not a time-efficient solution. Better alternatives are available through commercial language schools, CDs or DVDs, and the Internet. Of these alternatives, commercial language schools may be the most expensive, but they could prove to be the most cost-effective if you purchase their services through a contract that guarantees you will reach a defined performance level by a given date. Although the quality of CD products and Internet sites varies widely, these formats offer the flexibility of being able to study during otherwise idle periods. If your location and schedule permit, the best option could be tutoring by a Latin American student at your local university. Besides learning the language from a native speaker, this alternative exposes you to a uniquely qualified source of information on the culture, current events, key personalities, and, perhaps, the business practices and personalities of interest in your target market.

Make English Easy. Until your Spanish or Portuguese skills are advanced, you may find it impractical to rely on the services of professional interpreters for every conversation. That means your discussions will likely be conducted in English, and the Latins will have to bear the brunt of making communication happen. Unless the Latin who plays the role of interpreter is highly proficient in English, misunderstandings are inevitable in a language that permits one to park in a driveway but drive on a parkway, to send trucks by ship but ship by truck, to watch a house burn down as it burns up, or to take the same level of risk, regardless of whether your chances are fat or slim.

If interpreting English language can be difficult, interpreting English jargon can be impossible. To ease the task of Latins who serve as interpreters, avoid using language that:

1. Requires understanding U.S. sports jargon, like:

   slam dunk

   huddle time

   get on the ball

   step up to the plate

   play for all the marbles

2. Requires understanding homonyms, like:

   if he would get the lead out, he could lead

   he was not close enough to close the door

   the present is the best time to present the present

   the prospector deserted his dessert in the desert

Such examples suggest why Latins would prefer to strike a deal with Germans or Japanese whose English is limited but understandable, rather than with code-talking Anglos.

It is helpful to cite examples to clarify the concepts you are explaining. When doing so, avoid the temptation to be witty. The cultural and linguistic context of humor complicates communication. Moreover, Latins are not always amused by what some Anglos consider good humor, especially that invoking biological functions. Active listening helps ensure that the message you are sending is the same message they are receiving. So when discussing key points, frequently ask Latins to repeat in their own words what they understood you to mean.

One final precaution will help avoid misunderstandings: express all technical standards in metric units. The United States is the last outpost among the world's advanced nations to defend English-system measures.

As a result, U.S. executives often fail to appreciate that those standards are unknown or are considered archaic in Latin America. All references to physical (linear, area, volume) and temperature measures should be converted to metric units in your spoken and written correspondence, advertising, product labeling, and literature. Imagine how thwarted you would feel if the tables were turned and, as a prospective buyer for a fleet of delivery vehicles, you were given the following standards:

Vehicle fuel consumption of 8.6 kilometers per liter at 80 kilometers per hour with tire inflation of 2.82 kilos per centimeter² @ 25°C (= 20 miles/gallon at 50 mph with tire inflation of 40 lb/in² @ 77°F)

Failing to make some of your personal communications in Spanish or Portuguese is a social misdemeanor. But failing to make all of product-performance communications in metric units can put you on business death row.

Be Cautious about Second Languages.   Interpreters are like toll collectors. They charge to make a bridge between two parties who are separated by a language gap. U.S. and Latin businessmen with second-language pretensions can fall into the trap of thinking that they will avoid repeated toll charges if each builds one-half of the bridge. This misguided belief leads each to attempt to communicate in the language of the other. The usual result is two half-bridges that will never meet because they were built with faulty designs, with inferior materials, or at mistaken locations. The inevitable communication dead ends underscore the fact that whoever relies on half a bridge either is going nowhere or is heading for a fall.

The prestige value conferred by a second-language ability can create status obstacles that make it difficult for Anglos and Latins to interact smoothly. The education and lifestyle of Latin executives often make them more able to communicate in English than Anglos can in Spanish or Portuguese. Hence, Latins frequently prevail in playing the role of interpreter, and talks are held in English. With less frequency, U.S. executives will take the lead, attempting to conduct conversations in Spanish or Portuguese. In either case, the assumption implied by the executive who takes on the role of interpreter is that "My second language is better than your second language." The potential for that implied claim to offend is real, and is often at odds with the claimant's true second-language ability. If U.S. or Latin executives attempt to use a language beyond their ability, it will come as no surprise when frustration, misunderstandings, and perceived condescension combine to undermine the optimism, cooperation, and rapport that marked the celebration of the negotiation agreement. When things go wrong, it will be easy for each party to blame the other, recall-ing, "I clearly told him that. . . ."

Avoid Losing Your Brand Equity in Translation.   Assume you have made the right preparations to achieve success in your new Latin Ameri-can venture. But it is the market that has the last word in saying whether success is around the corner. Beware of second-rate translations that can make that last word sound like sales crashing. The words used in your marketing materials should be linguistically and culturally appropriate. They are the face of your company, and they communicate its respect for your customers' culture. Assigning a high-profile translation to an em-ployee simply because he or she has a Hispanic surname can throw sand in the gears of your new venture. Consider, for example, the revenue-robbing effect of the following product-launch misfires:

- Ford Motor Co. marketed a subcompact car in Mexico as the *Com-eta*, a direct translation of the Comet model name that its Mercury brand was selling successfully in the United States. Aimed at afflu-ent urban housewives as an economical vehicle to do errands and carry kids back and forth, the launch failed to meet sales targets in the key Mexico City market. Research revealed the culprit responsi-ble for the sales failure: *cometa* is slang in Mexico City for the flashy, brightly sequined nighttime streetwalkers with whom few high-society aspirants wished to be associated.

- To fulfill a large export order to Mexico, General Electric's Locomo-tive Division needed to translate its operating manual into Spanish. GE attempted to cut costs by contracting the job to a Chilean firm at three cents per word, instead of the 25 cents per word it customarily paid for translations in the United States. The anticipated savings proved to be a false economy when it was discovered that the Chilean translator had little familiarity with the technical terminology used for operating and maintaining locomotives. As a result, the job had to be redone at a much higher cost than GE would have had to pay the "ex-pensive" U.S. company to get the locomotive translation moving on the "write" track the first time.

- The soft drink *Fresca* was withdrawn from several Latin American markets after slow sales prompted management to engage research-ers to identify the problem. The researchers informed management that the name labeled on the bottle with the suggestively elongated neck was slang for lesbian.

- Now-defunct Braniff Airlines suffered a translation gaffe when it tried to promote luxury passenger service on its South American routes. Having reupholstered its first-class seats in leather, the carrier promoted its upgraded seats with a Spanish translation of the "Fly in leather" slogan that had been successful in the United States. While competitors and customers enjoyed a good laugh, the Braniff executives were embarrassed to learn that their translated slogan meant "Fly in the nude."

- A publicity campaign mounted in Mexico by U.S. dairy farmers turned sour when its translated slogan failed to produce an upturn in market demand. Its catchphrase, "Got milk?" connoted an unintended meaning when translated to Spanish. Mexicans interpreted the question to mean "Are you lactating?"

- Attempting to promote its product in Latin America, a U.S. swimsuit manufacturer's ad claimed that a beachgoer could spend all day wearing its product in the sun and the fabric would not fade. The advertising expense was largely wasted on Latins, who prefer not to spend much time outside of the shade because the hot tropical sun is uncomfortable.

- An advertising campaign for pens failed to write many orders in Latin America. Intending to convey that users of the leak-proof product would not be embarrassed by clothing stains, the ad translation instead assured that, while using it, customers could avoid pen-induced pregnancies.

Don't Call Him Phil

Picture this scene: You and your Chilean agent are representing your firm at a trade show in Santiago. You are momentarily alone while your agent has returned to his office on an urgent matter. An affable visitor stops at your booth and shows a lively interest in your product. Explaining that he has a previously scheduled appointment to attend, he leaves a business card and promises to return in 30 minutes to discuss making a trial order. Examining his card, you note that your Chilean prospect is the *director general* of a prominent firm that your agent has mentioned as a high-priority sales target. You also note from the card that the new prospect's name is printed as Ing. Felipe Santos Estrada.

Question: when he returns, how do you address him? Three rules govern this common situation. The first rule is to use the correct professional title. Latins venerate education and work hard to earn the privilege of acquiring professional titles through academic study. In this case, the appropriate title is *Ingeniero*, indicating that the prospect has completed a university program in engineering.

The second rule of address is uncomplicated: avoid calling Latins by their first (given) name until invited to do so. Using a Latin's first name without prior permission is considered a rude intrusion upon his personal dignity. If you are operating in a tropical climate, social conventions tend to be more relaxed, and chances are that you will soon be invited to refer to your new Latin acquaintance by his first name. Where the climate is cooler in mountainous or higher latitude locations, so is the social atmosphere. In Santiago, Buenos Aires, and Quito, you may find it will take longer before your Latin counterpart invites you to call him Felipe.

The final rule is sometimes confusing: when two surnames (last names) are used, you should only use the first when addressing Spanish speakers. In the present case, the engineer's paternal surname is Santos, his mother's maiden name is Estrada. It is no mystery that, as a male-dominated society, Spanish speakers expect only their father's surname to be used when being addressed directly. The mother's family surname is included in third-person references to identify the Latin's lineage, thus distinguishing him from others bearing the same patronymic. Curiously, the order of surnames is reversed in Portuguese-speaking societies. If the visitor to your booth were Brazilian, you would address him as Estrada, using the second surname.

In the time it took you to absorb the preceding information, the Latin prospect has returned to your booth. Your opening line is scripted according to the accepted formula: smiling broadly and warmly grasping his hand, you greet him saying, "Buenas tardes, Ingeniero Santos (Ing. Estrada, if Brazilian), what a privilege to see you again!"

TAKING CARE OF BUSINESS

Know the Customers and Competitors of Your Customer

There is no such thing as an average Latin American market. Each country and each region is unique. Still, some rules are common to all markets. As Latin American markets become more open and competitive, three rules will guide the practices of business winners:

1. Know thy customer
2. Know thy customer's customer
3. Know thy competitor

You Have to Eat Your Own Dogfood

There is no substitute for understanding the way your customers view your product. And, if your customers are resellers, your competitive edge will be at its sharpest when you know the reasons that drive their customers to buy your product, instead of choosing a competitor's brand. There is no better way to understand marketing's frontline than to spend time in the marketplace. The time you spend in the trenches will pay dividends. Making direct contact with consumers, wandering through retail aisles, or accompanying your distributor's salespeople on their rounds brings you closest to where the market battle is being won or lost.

Equally important are the gains you can make by transferring hard-won marketing and management lessons you learned in the United States to your Latin American representative. As the modernizing effects of globalization spread through Latin America, it is common for Latin marketers to suffer some of the same headaches your company experienced and solved in the United States, perhaps during the Asian onslaught of the 1970s and 1980s. Your expertise can make your representative view you more as a unique source of business solutions and less as a replaceable vendor who is only as good as his last deal. As your value to him as a mentor grows, his loyalty as a customer will grow, as will his order volume. In the process, your representative becomes an ally that is committed to work hard to promote your product in his market.

Much of your U.S. marketing experience is transferable to Latin America. But assuming that all of it applies can be fatal. It could be a mistake to infer that, because a few customers in Latinoland have bought your product, others will respond in a similar fashion to the same buying propositions that you promote to your U.S. customers. To assume that, in all but the most obvious ways, the Latinoland market behaves like your U.S. market will nullify much of the value of your considerable potential to guide your new representative by passing on the benefit of your U.S. business experience.

Know Customers or No Customers

The best way to assess your Latinoland representative's market in a way that will help you to help him grow his share of it, is to live it the same way he does, at the street level, the sales call, and the desk level of market analysis. Only by understanding who the buyers are and their purchasing habits will you be able to separate fact from assumption. Listening to the Latinoland market will enable you to understand what is different about its buying propositions and what is similar. Wise executives know what they do not know. Wise learning prevents them from offering X when Latin buyers want Y.

As you accumulate experience in the region, you will find sharp differences in buying motives from one country to the other. That low energy-usage product that sold so well in Ecuador, for example, may flop in Argentina. Why the difference? Electrical energy costs in Ecuador are almost five times the kilowatt-per-hour rate in Argentina.[1] Whereas you could count on lower operating costs as a strong motive for buyers to choose your brand in Guayaquil, you will have to find a different feature to move the product in Buenos Aires.

If your representative handles consumer goods, you may learn that the merchandise orders she fills vary widely depending on her customer's location. She knows that the tastes of buyers in mountainous locations (*serranos*) tend to be conservative, whereas buyers living on the coast (*costeños*) lean toward bright colors, light and informal clothing, loud-volume audio speakers, and spicy flavors. You may learn that, in traditional sectors of *macho* Latin America, most buying decisions are still dominated by the male leader of the household. Perhaps you will also find out that the best way to reach either the *serrano* or the *costeño* consumer is through advertising by means of hand-delivered flyers (*volantes*) and by local radio and TV spots, rather than by newspapers ads. Whereas *volantes* and radio spots are relatively inexpensive and can be tailored to reach a local market, most newspapers are directed toward a national audience, and most of the readers exposed to their costly ads are not viable prospects for geographically limited offerings. Although experience with coupons as a promotional tool was disappointing a few years ago,[2] casual observation suggests it may now be gaining some traction. In the meantime, smart retailers have scored sales by linking a customer's purchase to a chance to participate in a raffle or contest, thus taking advantage of Latins' zest for gambling. By being close to the market, you may also learn that consumer credit is a potent sales tool. Without the ability to buy on credit, the most attractive market segment for consumer goods in Latin America—the middle-class household—could slip away from your representative's reach. Credit enables the rapidly expanding middle class to access the much larger purchasing power that is based on buyers' future income, rather than on their current cash flow.

Trade Show Know-How

A trade show can be a cost-effective way for you to size up potential buyers and competition at the same that you help your representative to roll out the product in your new Latinoland market. But cost-effective does not mean free. After adding up the salaries, transportation costs, and lodging of the expert employees you brought to answer customer questions; free gifts or samples; direct mail promotion; and booth materials, it will not be surprising to learn that the charge for exhibit space amounts to no more than 10 to 15 percent of your total participation cost.[3] Latin American trade shows differ from the U.S. variety in some important respects. Assuming the show's calendar and industry theme are right for you, your plans to exhibit should consider some salient points:

- Customary booth visits in the United States are short-lived information-gathering affairs. Latin visitors tend to stay longer, spending more time on social preliminaries. To encourage productive visits, your booth (*estante*) should provide hospitality. As a good host, you should have coffee, soda beverages, and light snacks available inside, near the back of your booth, to offer to serious visitors.

- Remember that selling does not happen only in your booth. Use every tool available to mine the wealth of prospects present at any trade show: have socially skilled colleagues work the show floor; at least two weeks in advance of the show, invite prospects to breakfast meetings; meet and cultivate prospects at the show's luncheons, cocktail parties, and educational programs; and be certain that everyone on your team is able to give a one- to two-minute "elevator speech" about what your company does and why it does it best.

- Your promotional material and product literature should be available in Spanish or Portuguese. Use sales-objection white papers as talking points. A stack of inexpensive single-sheet, text-only materials should be available at the front of the booth, within easy reach of students and casual passersby who, although voracious devourers of printed materials, are rarely interested in buying. Such visitors can tie you up in endless, seldom-productive conversation.

- Tastefully display some copies of your expensive, four-color glossy translated materials on a visible angled surface out of easy reach toward the back or side of the booth. As you give these to serious visitors, replenish them from boxes located out of view, behind the booth's curtain. By appearing to have only limited copies left, you can avoid sacrificing premium literature to the tire-kicking crowd.

- Have some imprinted gifts on hand for distribution to serious visitors. Perennially popular items are baseball caps, T-shirts, pens, insulated beer-can sleeves, and key holders. Keep them removed from the sight of the crowds in the aisle.

- Your and your representative's ample supply of high-quality business cards should be printed in Spanish or Portuguese. An impressive card stock often used in Latin America is a thin, slightly translucent, parchment-like plastic paper.

- Take turns staffing the booth with your representative. In that manner, each of you can take a break without running the risk that an important prospect will be received by less prepared staff.

- During busy periods, staffing a booth can be demanding. To be able to follow up on leads, do not wait until after the show to wade through an ocean of business cards, trying to recall who was interested in what. Instead, immediately after talking to a visitor, and before greeting the next visitor, use preformatted software or a pocket recorder to rapidly summarize the key points of the conversation you just had. By reviewing your notes during more leisurely moments at the show or at the end of each day, you will be in a better position to take the right follow-up actions before a prospect's interest cools.

- Make sure that exhibition workers are on your side. Offering to buy lunch or tipping will reduce damage, pilfering, and delays.

- If you are displaying large or heavy products, such as machinery or construction equipment, consider selling them at a discount after the show has finished. Not only will you have put demonstration products in the local market, but the freight, insurance, and handling costs you will avoid by not having to ship them back may amount to less than the price discount you will grant the onsite buyer.

Do's and Taboos of Signing Up and Motivating Representatives in Latin America

Finding a Representative Who Will Work for You

Too many epitaphs have been written about the demise of what was conceived as a lively Latin business project, either because the wrong representative was signed up or because the right representative was signed up in the wrong way. The representative you appoint becomes both the legal face and the market image of your firm's new venture in Latinoland. That dual role affects your firm's chances of surviving long enough to achieve its potential in any Latin American venture. Yet, despite exposing themselves to serious legal and business threats, some U.S. firms approach the decision to appoint a country representative as if they are throwing the dice rather than making a strategic choice. They would be better served by having no representative than by gambling on one who could ruin them forever in a potentially important market.

A key step in that process of strategic choice is to decide which legal form your representative will assume. Representatives come in two basic varieties: distributors and agents. Distributors own the goods they have bought from your firm. They employ a sales force and advertise to promote the sale of those goods; maintain stocks of replacement parts; perform installation, repair, and maintenance; honor warranties; and handle returns. An agent, on the other hand, serves as the legal representative of your company; she may engage in some promotional efforts but usually lacks the detailed knowledge, capital, and organizational capability to market your firm's product effectively. Despite having less clout as a marketing force, some smaller firms new to the Latin American market prefer to use agents as representatives because, relative to distributors, agents generally:

- Are easier to acquire
- Make it easier to avoid costly legal penalties if they have to be fired
- Are subject to control over how the product is presented and priced
- Charge lower commissions or fees
- Provide a legal and physical beachhead from which to conduct low-risk reconnaissance patrols before launching a frontal attack on the market
- Can pull strings at high levels within the government to smooth regulatory wrinkles and get approvals
- Can be your best means to approach or attract a powerful distributor

For legal reasons, some U.S. companies have found it beneficial to set up a two-tier representative system in Latin America. This approach entails contracting with an agent who is legally responsible for all in-country company operations. If distributors are subsequently appointed by that agent, their legal relationship with, and possible claims against, the company are buffered by the agent. A downside to two-tier distributor appointments is that distributors may not feel very secure. As a consequence, they may be reluctant to carry large inventories, dedicate salespeople to your line, or invest in a service capability. For that reason, two-tier appointments are often made for a probationary period to test if a candidate is right.

Beware of Smooth Talkers. Latin America has its full share of local-born and expatriate influence peddlers who are looking for up-front money or an exclusive representation contract in exchange for a promise to move your firm's product. These parasites tend to surface and attach themselves to you at trade shows, in hotel lobbies and bars, and as airline seat partners. Although they may be quick to show how high they can jump, it is what they do when they come down that counts. Just as a good first act cannot save a bad play, neither can the glib initial claims of self-proclaimed local marketing wizards save you from high-loss market failures. The same good business judgment you use in the United States will prevent you from choosing one of the goats in a flock of sheep.

Another safeguard to observe on the road toward finding a suitable representative for your firm's product is to be cautious about following the advice of some Latin American consulting firms. Staffed by experts with academic credentials, these offices can be more oriented to intellectualizing at a relaxed pace over economic analysis issues than to grinding out concrete solutions to urgent business problems. Colin Powell described them well when he commented: "Experts often possess more data than judgment. Elites can become so inbred that they produce hemophiliacs who bleed to death as soon as they are nicked by the real world."[4] There is no substitute for a distributor who is reliable, well positioned in the market, and committed to serving you.

How to find Señor Right? Choosing a representative can be the most important decision a newcomer to a Latin American market can make. Yet, many otherwise prudent U.S. executives will bet their firm's future in a Latinoland market on the first good story they hear. When opportunists come out of the blue and are allowed to describe their awe-inspiring feats, without comparison or verification, they can tend to look like golden opportunities. To avoid losing their wagers on a potentially lucrative market opportunity by naming Señor Wrong as their representative in Latinoland, U.S. executives should place their bets on quality information to find a representative who is right for their firm.

Fortunately, quality information is available. Sources like Dun & Bradstreet publish trade directories listing data on Latin American representatives classified by country and by product. In most countries, the local affiliate of the U.S. International Chamber of Commerce is an excellent source for information on potential representatives. The U.S. Department of Commerce (USDOC) provides an array of cost-effective services to help U.S. exporters find suitable representatives. By signing up for USDOC's International Company Profiles (ICP) service, for example, your company can take advantage of the expertise of commercial specialists working for the U.S. embassy located in your target market. Within 30 to 45 days, you will receive a custom-tailored ICP giving you up-to-date information on potential representatives, including bank and trade references, principals, key officers, managers, product lines, number of employees, financial data, sales volume, reputation, and market outlook.[5]

A good representative is one who has good customers and good product lines. Do your due diligence: Visit top retailers or users of your type of product. Ask them what their service expectations are from a supplier, and from what vendor(s) they prefer to buy. As Latins tend to be forthright about their opinions of other Latins, chances are you will soon begin to hear the same names being repeated for the same reasons. Those reasons should form the core of your marketing strategy, and the roll call of buyers' preferred suppliers should form your candidate pool of high-potential representatives.[6]

When you approach those prime candidates about becoming your representative, do not be discouraged if they are somewhat cool and have little time to talk. Top-performing representatives are busy selling product to customers. They are probably distributors who stock products and have clean, efficient facilities that also offer good installation, maintenance, and repair services. They have their hands full handling the quality lines they currently represent. If, among those lines, a direct competitor is represented, be prepared to explain why your firm and brand would be a better supplier.

The one- and two-man shops that will be eager to come on board with you, but that you may want to avoid, are probably commission agents with no investment in inventory and no product service capability. These "line collectors" will be easily available to talk to because they spend most of their time selling promises upstream to sew up exclusive representation contracts. Then, having cast scores of mostly low-brand-name-recognition product lines in the water, their game is to simply wait for the phone to announce a bite and reel in a commission from you for every downstream customer who falls into their boat. In general, you should be wary of representatives that do not have large local accounts or local subsidiaries of multinational firms as active customers.

Hand-in-Hand or Arm's-Length?

The special roles played by personal trust, geographic distance, and the transfer of experience argue strongly for smaller U.S. exporters to maintain closer representative relationships in Latin America than in the United States. Those closer relationships are of two separate but mutually reinforcing interactions: mentoring and partnering.

In your role as a mentor, your new representative expects that you will transfer as much product and marketing expertise as possible to help him perform competitively. It follows that you will provide him and/or his technical and sales employees with training and materials on topics such as product standards and function, competitive profiling, selling propositions and sales-objection responses, advertising, repair, installation, maintenance, and ordering procedures. As a visiting Anglo, your presence on sales calls could help persuade Latin prospects that your firm is committed to the market. When on such sales calls, you may be pleasantly surprised to notice that closing rates in Latin America are higher than you are accustomed to in the United States.

You also may be in a position to coach your representative on management practices that will help him stay competitive as he copes with the more exacting performance requirements of a globalized operating environment. As discussed in Chapters 3 and 4, many of Latin America's family-owned, smaller businesses are still using management practices more suitable to yesterday's protected markets than to today's open markets. The most egregious of those obsolete practices is to micromanage non-family employees. If you see signs that your representative is taking on water because of outdated autocratic management methods, your tactful questioning and gentle coaching may prevent his (and your) business from sinking under the wave of modern management practices that is sweeping across Latin America. To help him keep his head above water, try to bring him around to seeing that the people who make up his organization *are* his organization.

If, on the other hand, your representative seems the type who routinely peruses the *Harvard Business Review*, attends management seminars, and is regularly ringing up new customer accounts, you may wish to borrow *his* management techniques. At the least, you should tie him down as a long-term partner.

Should you take on a partner? As a rule, the smaller the U.S. firm, the less advisable it is to attempt to go it alone in Latin America. Too many Lone Rangers have learned too late that having a piece of something always beats owning all of nothing. Others have learned that the modest beachhead they built yesterday with strong Latin American allies has become today's fortress of profitability. These allies are likely to be strong because, like you, they can be diplomats or street fighters in the market. But unlike you, they know the local streets.

In theory, you and your representative cast your lots together because each saw the other as the best player available to play on his team. Again in theory, these cross-locking dependencies made each of you a member of the same team, sharing the same goal of winning. In practice, however, too many supplier-representative relationships fail to score because they are playing a two-team game against one-team competitors. Rather than keeping their eyes on the playing field, they are distracted by discord over pricing, credit terms, market development costs, cooperative advertising, and product returns. These matters can become real problems when the arm's-length relationship that exists between supplier and representative makes the issues appear to be zero-sum outcomes: whatever one side gains, the other side loses.

Having an equity foot in each other's camp minimizes unproductive disagreements because the game strategy shifts from minimizing individual loss to maximizing mutual gain. Through means like gross-profit-sharing accords or cross-ownership of shares, each side has a stake in advancing the other's financial performance. Latin firms can find it appealing to diversify by having an interest in a U.S. company. Such arrangements can provide forward-motion traction to a supplier-representative relationship formerly stalled by friction.

Getting Paid: The Three *In's* of International Payments

Can Utopia for Latin America traders be described in few words? For U.S. exporters who used to face payment risks on their shipments to Latin America, an ideal state was having their settlement "*In*sured, *In* Gold, and *In* Zurich."[7] Although those payment terms were seldom realistic in times past, modern markets and tax treaties now make them the stuff of fantasy. Nevertheless, today's exporters to Latin America can rely on receiving secure payment through updated versions of the protection once wishfully sought through the three *In's*.

It is a dilemma that has plagued international trade since early exporters watched the sails of outbound merchant vessels slowly disappear with their goods over the Mediterranean horizon 3,000 years ago: buyers want product in hand before releasing payment; sellers want payment in hand before releasing product. Reconciling the conflicting positions of buyers and sellers involves practiced ways of interposing third parties between buyers and sellers.

During the quarter century following World War II, Latin America was a relaxed hunting ground for U.S. exporters. It was a period when there were few competitive local producers and only a modest presence of European and Asian rivals. Sales were in dollars, payments were up-front or by letters of credit, and the ability to sell was determined by nominally competitive levels of price, quality, and delivery. For the last 30 years, those happy seller's market conditions have been eroding. In today's rapidly modernizing Latin American markets, more demanding buyers have added a critical fourth factor to the traditional price-quality-delivery buying formula: the seller's willingness and ability to grant credit and to either invoice in pesos (or other local currency) or share in the risk of fluctuating exchange rates.

If, to remain competitive, U.S. exporters extend increasingly longer terms of direct credit, their cash flow will become increasingly tight. By extending direct credit, exporters assume the usually misguided role of acting as bankers for their customers, exposing themselves to nonpayment risk. For many smaller exporters, a default by a single customer could stretch their liquidity to the breaking point. As it is easier to avoid bad debts than to collect them, use reliable sources to verify customers' creditworthiness:

- International departments of regional and national U.S. banks can find out about your customer's credit standing through their own subsidiaries or correspondent relationships in Latin America.

- The U.S. International Trade Administration can provide credit information through many services, such as *International Company Profiles.*

- Fee-based business intelligence services such as Dun and Bradstreet, Standard & Poor's, Moody's, and Fitch Ratings provide foreign credit reports.

- If your carrier refuses to accept freight collect (on delivery), your Latin buyer may be a known credit risk.

At the other payment extreme, Latin buyers may pay CIA (cash in advance) or by letter of credit (if confirmed and irrevocable, a letter of credit gives the seller comfort, knowing she will be paid if she provides the required documentation). In either case, buyers face the costs of having working capital tied up and/or of incurring interest charges and processing fees. These are costs to buyers that, to remain competitive, U.S. exporters may have to offset through rebates or price concessions.

Just as credit terms exact a cost in cash flow and fees that must be absorbed by the U.S. exporter or the Latin importer, so too do the costs arising from fluctuations in the peso-dollar exchange rate. As in the case of credit cost, the policy chosen to cover exchange rate risk can weaken or strengthen a U.S. exporter's competitive position. If the U.S. exporter invoices in dollars, the Latin buyer will suffer loss if the local currency depreciates. Latin buyers are naturally hesitant to pay invoices denominated in dollars when they are reselling in pesos. Directly or indirectly, they will look to the U.S. exporter to help absorb the exchange risk either by paying for the cost of hedging or by conceding on price or credit terms. Alternatively, if the U.S. exporter accepts payment in pesos, he will suffer a revenue shortfall if that currency declines in dollar value between the invoice date and the collection date.

There are at least two means available for sellers to Latin America to be competitive on both credit terms and exchange risk. One is to use export factoring. This tool, which has been common in Europe for some time and is now beginning to be used in Latin America, enables U.S. exporters to sell in pesos on open account terms without having to assume credit and exchange risks. Not only does it enable buyers to save on letter of credit and documentary collection fees, but it also frees up their working capital, making more credit available to them for additional purchases. The U.S. exporter sells some or all of its accounts receivable at a discount in exchange for immediate cash in hand. Factoring fees are not trivial: they can range from two to seven percent a month, and they are paid as long as the receivable is outstanding.[8] A variation on the basic factoring model is termed "advance factoring" and is similar to the "red clause" used in letter-of-credit financing. It allows the exporter to receive in advance up to 90 percent of the order amount, thus providing the means to pay for the materials and labor needed to prepare the export order.

Another solution is export credit insurance (ECI). ECI insures exporters against nonpayment and exchange risks. It may be purchased through the U.S. Ex-Im Bank or private services such as Atradius, Coface, and Euler Hermes.[9] The cost of premiums on ECI is typically less than fees charged for a letter of credit.[10]

Getting It There: The Limitations of Good Intentions as Road Paving

Just as you should not test the depth of a river with both feet, neither should you trust shipping your goods without being certain that you will be standing on firm footing. The primary factors affecting secure and timely delivery of your product to Latin America are cargo insurance and logistics. Subsequently, communications, customs, and intellectual property rights come into play as factors that also affect your firm's ability to manage the physical movement of its product in the local market. The following sections deal with important practical considerations relevant to shipping your goods to Latin American markets.

Cargo Insurance

As banks will not lend money against uninsured goods in transit, protecting your goods against shipping risk is basic to both your risk management and your trade-financing strategies. Cargo coverage protects your maritime or air shipment (airfreight is covered under an all-risk attachment to the marine policy form) from its departure point to its final destination. Ocean cargo coverage ends at the port of arrival. If your shipment then is to be transported over land to reach its final destination, it will require inland marine insurance.

Know Your Coverage. It is imperative that the terms of your sales contract match the terms of your insurance coverage. A CIF (invoice cost, insurance, and freight) contract, for example, requires the seller to arrange and pay for the transport of goods from its U.S. warehouse to the buyer's Latin American warehouse. The seller is also responsible for arranging and paying the premium for warehouse-to-warehouse insurance. In contrast, an FOB (free on board) sales contract only obligates the seller to arrange and pay for the transportation and insurance required to move the goods to the port and be loaded onto the ship. As the goods pass over the vessel's rail, the responsibility for their protection passes to the buyer. Clearly, any misunderstanding of the sales and policy assignment terms between buyer and seller could lead to the shipment being either overinsured (by virtue of both the buyer and the seller each paying an insurance premium) or being completely unprotected. Take time to learn the standard international commercial terms (INCOTERMS). Not having to explain how your uninsured merchandise became an FOT (fell off truck) shipment will repay your effort.

Know Your Risk. Parts of Latin America are considered especially susceptible to loss by risk underwriters. Consider the direct and indirect cost effects of a sampling of recent incidents occurring in Mexico:

In 2009, cargo theft in Mexico cost businesses between $650 million and $750 million . . . some local gangs have committed up to 200 [truck] attacks per month . . . [and train robberies] average 4.5 per day.[11] Free-lance crime gangs . . . are armed not only with guns but heavy machinery to unload industrial materials . . . [and] can hijack a truck making a pit stop, empty out the cargo and dump the driver on an abandoned road.[12] [Trucking companies' precautions can include] GPS monitors, "panic" buttons that drivers can activate in the event of a hijack attempt, [and] dispatchers view[ing] computer screens in the U.S. . . . can shut down a truck's motor remotely. [Although] no trailer leaves . . . unless it's in a caravan of no fewer than ten trucks, . . . criminal gangs have spotters and . . . swarm trucks with gunmen deployed in pickup trucks or SUVs.[13]

The proliferation of cargo theft in places like Brazil, Colombia, and Mexico is forcing carriers to send armed escorts, reduce load sizes, intermingle high-value goods with low-value shipments, use double packaging (an unmarked outer package for protective purposes en route and a display package for customer destination), and stack at-rest containers end to end. But despite taking such precautions, losses are mounting, and when shippers are able to find a willing insurance carrier, the premium cost is high.[14]

Physical security is only one component of protection against cargo theft. The most costly injuries may not be inflicted from sharklike attacks mounted by predators on the outside, but by your own employees in the United States or by those of your representative in Latin America. Tight administrative security is essential to guard against "inventory nibbling" by insiders. Putting a logistics auditing system in place is the first step to let employees know that the company knows where its inventory is going. But establishing a paper trail is only a first step. Although the obvious solution lies in rooting out dishonest employees, an example shows this is not always easy:

A routine audit [of a Mexican manufacturing plant] uncovered more than $1 million waste of raw materials. Within three weeks of this report coming to light, two senior plant employees who had initiated an internal investigation—the HR manager and the Quality Control supervisor—were murdered.[15]

This and other examples have contributed to the alarming rise in Mexico's level of employee fraud: an increase of 51 percent in 2009.[16]

Honest employees will be sympathetic to antitheft actions if they are made to understand that such actions are necessary to maintain the firm's and the employee's financial well-being and friendly working environment. Inviting in a security expert to conduct the investigation can be a good measure. This objective outside presence can minimize what could otherwise be an emotionally upsetting experience of questioning long-standing and often high-level employees with whom one has developed a personal as well as a professional relationship. Finally, if it becomes necessary to fire an employee for theft, do not underestimate the need to support your action with an airtight case. Most Latin American labor codes give strong benefit of doubt to employees let go for indiscretions, imposing severance penalties if cause cannot be irrefutably established.

Protecting against cargo theft that takes place only in Latin America is not the only theft precaution that U.S. shippers to Latin America should take. Conservative FBI estimates place cargo theft at $8 billion to $12 billion per year in the United States. South Florida, the largest jumping-off point for southbound U.S. merchandise,[17] is among the most notorious locations for stolen Latin American shipments. As a direct result, policy premiums for cargo moving through south Florida doubled over a five-year period, and policy deductibles of $20,000 are common for easily salable goods such as cellular telephones, computer parts, and electronics.[18]

Experienced exporters have learned that it is better to have insurance and not need it than to need it and not have it. Hearing the news that your shipping container was last seen disappearing down a jungle trail leading to an armed insurgent camp is always an unpleasant lesson in risk management. However, if the value of its contents has been covered by an all-risk policy, you also will have learned that the premium was a small price to pay for being able to sleep soundly that night and have a job the next day.

Supply-Chain Management

Logistics costs are not insignificant. They range between 10 and 30 percent of the typical landed cost of international orders,[19–21] and they average about 15 percent in Latin America.[22] Consider that, if your company operates on a five percent profit margin and logistics costs are 15 percent of sales, reducing logistics costs by one-third can double profitability. Moreover, the act of physically filling Latin American customer orders can produce outsized operating headaches, creating dissatisfied customers and sucking up countless hours of management time. It can be an educational exercise by which unhappy shippers learn hard lessons from easy math. Here is an example: If your company successfully executes fulfillment activities at the 90 percent level, the good news is that its chances of satisfactorily performing any single 1 of 10 scheduled events is 9 in 10. The bad news is that the same law of probability decrees that the odds of getting all 10 independent events right is only slightly better than one in three. There is worse news: If you are relying upon a Latin company to provide logistics services, and that company's single-event execution success rate is only 80 percent, the chances of it coordinating all 10 events correctly falls to less than 1 in 10. Under those conditions, you rarely get what you expect, only what you inspect: make it a point to conduct field checks to ensure your product is reaching the point of sale. It will not sell if it is not on the shelf.

Be Smart about Customer Service Levels.   In times past, low customer service levels were not a critical business concern in Latin America's production-oriented economies. The goal was to minimize logistics cost. System flaws were routine. Globalization raised the bar on the willingness of Latin Americans to tolerate second-rate customer fulfillment. As an ever-more fundamental determinant of competitiveness and profitability in Latin America, the logistics function is swiftly shifting from a goal of minimizing costs to one of maximizing value. A 2009 study reported that 90 percent of shippers to Latin America believe that logistics represents a strategic, competitive advantage for their companies.[23] U.S. firms that can adapt, and can help their Latin American partners adapt, to a changing logistics world will win strong competitive positions in the region's markets. Many old-line competitors will miss the boat simply because tradition restricts them to seeing only the easily measurable cost of logistics, blinding them to the larger value-added potential to profit through greater customer satisfaction and loyalty. Such firms are Latin America's dinosaurs, menaced by extinction and unaware that globalization and modern logistics have shifted value toward the consumer, making downstream marketing more profitable than product manufacturing.[24]

But maintaining high customer service levels is not a cost-free option. Because speedy delivery and flexible order response can be pricey promises to fulfill, it can be a costly mistake to provide them to your Latin customers who do not need or value them. For that reason, you should clearly establish what constitutes an acceptable service level to your customer. If your policy is to deliver in five days to a customer who is willing to receive merchandise in 30 days, the higher cost you incur could prevent you from being more competitive on price or other features your customer values more highly.

However, if five-day or sooner delivery is required to be time competitive, airfreight is the likely alternative for most Latin American destinations. The direct transportation cost of Latin American airfreight may average some 20 times higher than ocean freight. In lightly industrialized, mainly agricultural areas, it may be even higher because the lack of backhaul freight means that southbound shippers are charged rates that pay for empty return flights to the United States.[25] Still, airfreight may be the only option for some Latin American destinations accessible from ports that may not be visited by your carrier's vessel for weeks or months. Moreover, airfreight often involves savings that result in a lower door-to-door expense than you might imagine, especially for high-density (weight-to-volume) and high-value (price-to-weight) merchandise. In addition to making the product immediately available for use or resale, tangible cost savings can help to offset the higher transportation cost of air shipment: less inventory dwell time; reduced insurance premiums for theft, pilferage, and damage; lower protective packaging cost; lower shipping minimums; and less internal transportation costs at destination. In addition, if you have airfreight destined for multiple consignees in a single country, it could be more economical to consolidate those small-package deliveries. By sending them as a bulk-palletized shipment to a central in-country distribution point, you may save by paying for airfreight charged on a per-pound instead of a per-package basis.

Keep Your Cash-to-Cash Cycle Short. In addition to matching service levels to customers' expectations, a central goal of your logistics strategy should be to shorten your cash-to-cash cycle. By reducing dwell-time cost (the cost of keeping a productive asset, say, inventory or delivery vehicles, idle), you gain the ability to remove cash from operations without lowering either productivity or customer service levels. At a 15 percent annual cost of working capital, for example, a shipper will save about $164 for every day saved in transit time for a container carrying goods worth $400,000. In Latin America's high capital-cost environment, free cash spin gives you one more competitive lever to pull. A cost-saving tool used by Toyota Motor Sales U.S.A. to reduce inventory dwell-time was to schedule its Mexican shipments weekly or daily, rather than monthly. The increased delivery frequencies lowered inventory levels by 8 percent.[26]

Sales forecasting is another tool that has a powerful potential to minimize dwell-time. It is also a tool that historically has not been well developed in Latin America. However, it is coming into its own today as modern information and communications technology bring the region closer to being able to implement inventory postponement strategies. The goal of postponement is to avoid ordering inventory until the sale is made, thus minimizing the possibility of building up a supply of dead stock when large changes in local buying patterns occur. Given the order-to-delivery reality of the region's slow-paced transportation and customs processing environment, this is not always easy. For example, the delay at destination to deliver an order to a Latin customer's facility could exceed by six times the time required for the U.S. shipper to have its carrier pick up and fly the shipment to the customer's airport. Still, a response-based production and inventory-ordering posture is realistically attainable if based on forecast sales rather than on booked orders. By planning collaboratively, U.S. shippers and Latin distributors can reduce inventory overstocking and redundancy, raising the certainty that whatever will be produced or ordered will be sold. As if living a procrastinator's dream, U.S. sellers and Latin buyers can share the rewards of increased cash flow by not doing today what they can postpone until tomorrow.

Know the Limits of Internal Transportation. The bad news: the obituary for the death of distance has not yet been written for Latin America. The good news: the transportation problems that abound in Latin America provide ample chances for you to raise your firm's profit flag over the region by finding creative ways to solve them. The challenge is not trivial. Internal air service is expensive and unpredictable. Nonstandardized track gauges and/or lackluster management make rail a dismal prospect almost everywhere except in limited areas of Argentina, Brazil, and Mexico. Few of the region's major markets either are directly accessible by boat or are served by ports that have modern and efficient container-handling capabilities.

By default, the backbone of Latin America's transportation system is truck-borne freight and bus-borne passenger traffic. It is an ailing backbone, however, sorely in need of attention to relieve the aches and pains it has accumulated over the years. Although land routes between major population centers almost everywhere in Latin America vary between adequate and excellent, access to smaller rural markets is often restricted by mountain roads that are temporarily blocked by rock slides or that remain choked with snow for much of the year. Secondary highways become regularly impassable when they are flooded for weeks at a time or bridges wash out. Even in major cities that enjoy good highway access, local delivery is impeded by frenzied traffic conditions resulting from a rapidly exploding population squeezed into the chaotic confines of narrow streets left over from the colonial era.

One may believe that the same colonial-era legacy explains the region's elderly truck fleet. But the difference in average age of trucks in the United States and in Latin America is really explained by the relative cost of labor and capital in the two locations. Putting a new truck on the road is a capital-intensive decision that is taken more often in the United States, where capital is comparatively cheap. Continuing to maintain and repair an old truck is a labor-intensive option that is routinely taken in Latin America, where labor is less expensive than capital. The ingenuity displayed by Latin mechanics to keep their aging relics rolling is unmatched by their counterparts in the United States. Many Latin American fleet managers truly deserve the title of curator.

Consider a Third-Party Logistics (3PL) Future. For many smaller businesses, managing logistics can be a complex, expensive, and high opportunity-cost headache. By outsourcing logistics management to reliable 3PL providers, these firms can convert a fixed cost into a variable cost and, in the process, free themselves to concentrate on their core competencies. Table 6.1 shows a wide range of logistics functions and the proportion of surveyed shippers to Latin America that outsourced those functions in 2009.[27]

Acting as consolidators, 3PLs are specialists in solving supply-chain headaches that can arise when delivering your product directly to local retailers, wholesalers, or storage terminals. By teaming up with a logistics partner that maintains a local management presence and physical infrastructure, you can offer customers a competitive advantage that laggard firms will be hard-pressed to match. Although a new wave of logistics outsourcing has entered the region, much of the old wave of mediocre in-house logistics performance still remains. As with all historic turning points, those companies that are slow to ride the incoming wave of modern practices run the risk of being swept out of the market by the outgoing wave of obsolete ways.

Table 6.1

Percentage of Shippers to Latin America That Outsourced Logistics Services

Logistics Services for Latin America	Percentage Outsourced
International transportation	88
Domestic transportation	80
Customs brokerage	74
Forwarding	66
Warehousing	52
Product labeling, packaging, assembly, kitting	34
Freight bill auditing and payment	28
Reverse logistics (defective, repair, return)	26
Information technology	26
Cross-docking	20
Supply-chain consultancy	20
Fleet management	15
Order entry, processing, and fulfillment	15
Customer service	14

Communication

Prior to the advent of cell phones, decades of neglect had produced decrepit telecommunications systems in Latin America. The existence of hopelessly obsolete and overloaded landline-based telephone systems spurred a leapfrog growth into wireless telephone technology. Competition, spawned by deregulation and privatization, is driving local telephone rates down and service quality up in Latin America. However, international rates are still high enough to represent a material cost of doing business with the region. For example, a recent call to a prospective buyer in Mexico City from an exporter in Dallas cost 69 cents per minute. If the same minute had been spent talking to a prospect in Tokyo, it would have cost nine cents, or four cents to a potential buyer in Quebec.

Dealing with Customs

The cultural customs discussed in Chapter 4 can be strange and frustrating. But they pale in comparison to another type of customs: that web of arcane regulations and often venal officials that make up Latin America's government agencies that control the entry of your merchandise into the region's markets.

Should the machine be lubricated? "I have an expensive doctor's appointment and can only work two hours today. I don't know if I'll be able to fit your shipment into my processing schedule." Variations on this theme are not uncommon from Latin American customs officials. They are thinly veiled invitations for you to speed up the official processing mechanism by providing lubrication to its otherwise immovable parts. It is said that, in a world populated by Latin American customs authorities, even a camel can pass through the eye of a needle—if it is well greased.

Although they are the target of ongoing reform efforts in countries like Mexico, Brazil, and Costa Rica, grease payments are still an unavoidable regular cost of doing business in much of Latin America. Whatever your ethical attitude toward a shakedown request by a customs official, you may find some comfort in knowing that routine facilitating payments are ordinarily permitted by the U.S. Foreign Corrupt Practices Act of 1977. The more relevant concern is that the increased operating pressures spawned by Latin America's more competitive business environment make it difficult to avoid complying with payoff demands. The cost of avoiding payoffs by outwaiting the *mañana* pace of customs processing is the failure to remain competitive because of not having product available for instant delivery to a new wave of time-sensitive customers.

The good news is that Latin American customs organizations are adopting some of the rapidly evolving improvements in logistics technology. One major result of this welcome trend is that electronic processing of customs paperwork is becoming common practice in the region. The bad news is that the speed of moving goods through the system, although improved, is still slow. This is because the fast-paced pull of modern processing is tethered to a short leash of tradition. The system's chokepoint is the dogged determination of many of Latin America's customs agencies to stay linked to the familiar and lucrative practices of the past by parallel-processing the mountainous accumulations of documents by hand. When a customs official pauses before lowering his right hand to impress your document with the mandatory hand stamp, the delay provides him an occasion to extend his left hand, palm up, in your direction.

Ambiguous and complex product standards, classification codes, and duty schedules give customs a wide range of discretion in interpreting under what conditions your product will be admitted for import to your target market. Local product standards may impede or even lock out your product's admittance. Examples: Venezuela has imposed some 300 product standards that are applied more rigorously to imported goods than to goods produced domestically. Colombia is enforcing country-of-origin certification requirements that rely on a largely unfeasible Colombian-certified testing process. Brazil has revived formerly disregarded measures to ensure that imports meet domestic standards of safety and quality. Argentina has changed the criteria for approval of electrical products, requiring imports to pass the certification process of a national standards body.

Latin America's varied structure of tariffs can also be frustrating. For example, the MERCOSUR customs union (Argentina, Brazil, Paraguay, and Uruguay) maintains a level of external duties that is some three times higher than that of the OECD (Organization for Economic Cooperation and Development), a group of the world's most developed economies.[28]

To mitigate the effects of exasperatingly slow clearance procedures, you may wish to hold contingency inventories ex-customs and close to the customer. Although holding dead inventory is never a costless option, it could yet be a cost-effective business strategy, especially if your firm is faced with profit-eroding contractual consequences of time penalties imposed upon late delivery or installation. Even if time penalties are not a factor, a warehouse presence sends a visible and reassuring signal to customers that your firm is committed to the market for the long term. Another option to reduce the pain of customs bottlenecks is to break down shipments by priority. If and when it is possible, send time-critical components early, to be followed later by less vital shipments.[29]

The ATA Carnet

ATA carnets are issued by customs authorities and act for goods like passports act for people. ATA is an acronym formed from the French and English words *admission temporaraire*/temporary admission. Although most imports enter a country permanently, some merchandise enters only temporarily. You can avoid having to pay duty if you are carrying demonstrator samples, promotional materials, trade-show gear, or any item that will leave the country when you do without a carnet. Customs may delay your entry or charge you unnecessary duty on items that should be duty exempt.

Is Your Product Ready for Prime Time? Intellectual Property Rights

Fake goods are not cheap. Indeed, piracy and counterfeiting of branded consumer goods cost companies as much as $250 billion in 2007[30] and were rife in Latin America.[31] Popular targets are computer software programs, music, videos, clothing, and luxury items such as watches and liquors. "Brand borrowing" has become so much of a concern to legitimate producers that Levi Strauss de Mexico bought ads in major Mexican dailies to thank the attorney general's office for seizing several hundred thousand of its labels that had been counterfeited.[32] A casual stroll through street markets in Buenos Aires, Rio de Janeiro, Lima, Caracas, Bogotá, Guatemala City, or Guadalajara will expose you to hawkers harassing you to buy merchandise brazenly branded as Microsoft Windows 7 for $5, Chivas Regal scotch for $8, Gucci purses for $24, Viagra for $1, Hermes scarves for $3, Tommy Hilfiger shirts for $6, or Rolex watches for $30.

The infringement on or loss of your company's key copyrights, trademarks, or patents could cripple its new Latin American venture. The commercial codes of many countries of the region either have inadequate laws to protect intellectual property or fail to enforce what statutes are on the books. The loss of intellectual property is inevitably costly in terms of time, money, market reputation, and lost momentum. Numerous, and especially smaller, U.S. firms have learned the hard way that not taking steps at the earliest moment to protect their intellectual property can push the fast-reverse button on the costly, time-consuming preparations they had taken to create a profitable business. Unlike in the United States, where first usage can establish the right to use a trademark, in most of Latin America protection belongs to the first company to register a trademark. Happily in the Andean Community (Bolivia, Colombia, Ecuador, and Peru), a cancellation of a trademark may be requested if it has not been used for three years.[33]

SUMMING UP

Only within the last quarter century has Latin America begun to throw off its historical burden of self-contained economics, self-serving politicians, and self-important bureaucrats. This is a Revolution with a capital

R because the forces it is unleashing are fundamentally altering economic, political, and social institutions throughout the Americas. As a half-billion Latin consumers enter the global economic mainstream, the region's markets are undergoing deep change, and winners and losers are being created daily. To be on the winning side and in a position to exploit its opportunities, Latin American companies are anxious to find U.S. allies as trade or joint-venture partners. As so many of those opportunities are responsive to competencies that are superbly present in smaller businesses, the ongoing economic shifts in Latin America pose uncommon profit potential for those smaller U.S. firms committed to developing their possibilities.

This book has been written to prepare you for those possibilities by explaining the requirements for doing business in the new Latin America. It is my hope that it will be your faithful guide as you capitalize on what may be one of the greatest profit opportunities for smaller U.S. businesses in the 2010s.

Notes

1. "Cinco Ejes Para Atenuar el Costo en la Baja de Tarifas," *El Comercio* (Quito), February 2, 2004, B5.

2. "World Business Roundup: The Americas," *Export Today*, May, 1998, 8–9.

3. Sherrie Zhan, "Trade Shows Mean Big Business," *World Trade*, September 1999, 86.

4. Oren Harari, "Behind Open Doors," *Modern Maturity* 2002: 40–50.

5. *Export Programs Guide* (Washington. DC: U.S. International Trade Administration, U.S. Department of Commerce, 2009), 18.

6. Thomas H. Becker, "Taboos and How-To's about Earning an Honest Peso," *Management Review* 1991: 17–21.

7. The author acknowledges Professor Michael Czinkota (of Georgetown University) for his succinctly expressed wisdom.

8. Mark Battersby, "Tame the Ebb and Flow," *Small Business Computing* February 2001: 25.

9. Clay Risen, "Trade Credit Insurance: You Want It, but Can You Get It?" *World Trade*, February 2010, 18–22.

10. *Trade Finance Guide* (Washington, DC: International Trade Administration, U.S. Department of Commerce, April 2008), 18.

11. Sivia Chávez and Guillermo Tello, "*Los Bandidos* Ride Again," *Kroll Tendencias*, no. 90, March 2010, http://www.latinbusinesschronicle.com/app/article.aspx?id=4060 (accessed April 15, 2010).

12. Mica Rosenberg, "Mexican Trains, Trucks Hijacked in New Crime Wave," *Reuters*, May 28, 2009, http://www.reuters.com/articlePrint?articleId=USN2644 884820090528 (accessed March 10, 2010).

13. Joel Millman, "Doing Business in the Time of Mexican Drug Chaos," *Wall Street Journal*, May 27, 2009, A15.

14. Peter Weber of Mexican insurance broker Protección Dinámica, quoted in Robert C. Meder, "Insuring Goods Internationally," *World Trade*, 2000, 44, 46.

15. David Robillard, "Tackling Compliance with Conviction," *Kroll Tendencias*, no. 87, October 2009, http://www.tendencias.infoamericas.com/search1/new/article4.html (accessed March 10, 2009).

16. "Global Economic Crime Survey 2009," PricewaterhouseCoopers, November 2009, http://www.latinbusinesschronicle.com/app/article.aspx?id=4060 (accessed April 15, 2010).

17. Diane Ritchey, "Harboring Need for Dollars, Tech," *Security*, December 2009, 84.

18. Peter Zalewski, "Cargo Theft," *The Herald*, 2002, 12–14.

19. Richard T. Hise, "The Implications of Time-Based Competition on International Logistics Strategies," *Business Horizons* 1995: 39–45.

20. "A Moving Story," *The Economist*, December 7, 2002, 65–66.

21. "Logistics Benchmarks," Apparel Search Logistics, c. 2009, http://www.apparelsearch.com/logistics_benchmarks.htm (accessed March 15, 2010).

22. "Panama Has the Lowest Logistics Cost in Latin America," Latin America Logistics Center, April 2, 2009, http://en.centralamericadata.com/en/topics/go/Latin+America+Logistics+Center (accessed March 12, 2010).

23. John Langley Jr. and U. S. Capgemini, LLC, *The State of Logistics Outsourcing: 2009 Third-Party Logistics* (Surrey, England: Capmegini Consulting, Georgia Institute of Technology, Oracle, and Panalpina, 2009), 7.

24. Richard Wise and Peter Baumgartner, "The New Profit Imperative in Manufacturing," *Harvard Business Review* September/October 1999: 133–151.

25. Shura Bary, "Delivering the Goods . . . ," *World Trade*, September 2001, 42–44.

26. Anthony Coia, "Keeping Mexico on the Road," *World Trade*, 2002, 24–26.

27. Langley and Capgemini, *The State of Logistics Outsourcing*.

28. Edgar Gómez Leiva and Carlos Ruiz Díaz, "The Common External Tariff of MERCOSUR: Is It a Tool to Stimulate the Competitiveness of Its Members?" Working Paper, Inter-American Development Bank, April 15, 2009, 10, www.iadb.org/intal/intalcdi/PE/2009/03770.pdf (accessed March 12, 2010).

29. Gail Dutton, "What Are You Going to Do?" *World Trade*, January 2002, 34–36.

30. "Magnitude of Counterfeiting and Piracy of Tangible Products: An Update," Organization for Economic Cooperation and Development, November 2009, 1.

31. Ronald Fink, "Battling the Property Pirates," *CFO* January 2004: 51–53.

32. Mary Sutter, "Mexico Piracy a Concern for Manufacturers," *Journal of Commerce* May 26, 1998.

33. "Ecuador: Right to Use of a Trademark and Registration," 2002, http://www.mondaq.com/article.asp?articleid=18985&email, *Bustamante & Bustamante* (accessed December 19, 2002).

Index

About the Author

THOMAS H. BECKER has served in 16 Latin American countries as a U.S. Foreign Service Officer, corporate executive, U.S. Agency for International Development Chief of Party, business adviser, and university professor. Dr. Becker holds degrees in International Business and Latin American Studies, has published some 100 articles in English and Spanish, and is former President of the Business Association of Latin American Studies. He may be contacted at DiscoverTheAmericas@yahoo.com.

CPSIA information can be obtained
at www.ICGtesting.com
Printed in the USA
LVOW10*0228220717

542217LV00022B/662/P

9 780313 383816